SIDEMAN

Stories About THE Band

ALSO BY PAUL TANNER, Ph.D.

Every Night Was New Year's Eve
On the Road with Glenn Miller

Conversations with a Musician:
Glenn Miller Trombonist Speaks...

SIDEMAN

Stories About THE Band

PAUL TANNER, Ph.D.

COSMO SPACE CO., LTD.

SIDEMAN Stories About THE Band

Published by
Hideomi Aoki
Cosmo Space Co., Ltd.
2-4-9 Nishi-Azabu
Minato-ku Tokyo 106-0031
Japan

U.S. contact:
Cosmo Space of America, Co., Ltd.
8800 Venice Blvd., PH401
Los Angeles, CA 90034

Cover and book design by John R. Webster and Francesca A. Droll, Abacus Graphics, Oceanside, CA.

First Edition
10 9 8 7 6 5 4 3 2 1

ISBN 0-9700167-0-0
Printed in the United States of America

TO JAN
my beautiful wife
whose loving devotion
has made me one lucky guy

CONTENTS

PART 2 INTERVIEWS

PART 3 STORIES

GLENN MILLER

Introduction

This book takes a bit of explaining. First of all, I realize that forgetfulness is a fact of life as one gets older. I became aware as I read some of these episodes that I may eventually lose some of the details. This would be a shame. It is almost an obligation to pass along authentic stories about such an organization as Glenn Miller and his Orchestra, especially coming from a person who was actually there. It seems to me that the logical thing to do is to put happenings and attitudes as I saw them into a book for others to enjoy.

The book is divided into three parts. Part One is a series of presentations that I have given concerning the Glenn Miller Orchestra and other luminaries in popular music in the Swing Era. I have tried to vary my talks considerably because I am often confronted with the same audience. They want to learn about these personalities and situations, and they want to be entertained. I surely hope I accomplish these results.

Part Two is a collection of interviews; I am interviewed often. Sometimes the interviewer goes straight from the telephone to a live radio program. On occasion, I receive a tape of the program. When this happens, I can transcribe the tape and pass it on to readers. I have tried to be straight-forward in these situations, and have written exactly what was said. I can see that this causes a problem which I sincerely hope you will excuse. I overuse such conversational terms as "you know," "yeah," "like," and so forth. I was merely talking off the top of my head.

I have intentionally left space for music to be played by the interviewer.

When the interview is first jotted down in the questioner's note book, then later, is carefully edited for a newspaper or magazine, the result is quite different. So Part Two consists of both types of interviews.

I always give time to audiences to ask questions. However, any of you who have exposed yourselves to such an activity have experienced the question: "Just One Question, Please." You will be asked the "One More Question" so many times.

Part Three is a series of short essays that don't fit in with either of the other parts. I hope you learn from some of them and enjoy them all.

About the photography–I have searched through all the books that I can find that concern Glenn Miller, and I have not been able to find any of the pictures that you see in this book. Serious collectors could have some of these I am certain, but what I searched through were published books, including my own. So I have tried to give you photos with which you were not familiar. Even with all the portrait type photographs of Glenn Miller himself, these don't seem to be in any books.

Designer's Note Regarding the Photos

The majority of the images reproduced in this book were scanned on a Crosfield drum scanner. A few of these images were scanned on a flatbed Umax Powerlook III scanner. All of the images were then expertly optimized for the best reproduction quality possible using Adobe Photoshop 4.

Adjustments were made to the highlight, midtone, quarter tone, and shadow densities for each image. Imperfections were carefully retouched and subtle dodging, burning, and sharpening applied as needed. In some cases, multiple layers were used so that adjustments could be made to different parts of the same image. The layers were then blended back together using air-bushed masks. Special attention was given to subjects' faces.

Nothing was removed from any of the images that may have any historical significance. In fact, many details were retouched or enhanced to improve visibility and readability. We hope you enjoy the results.

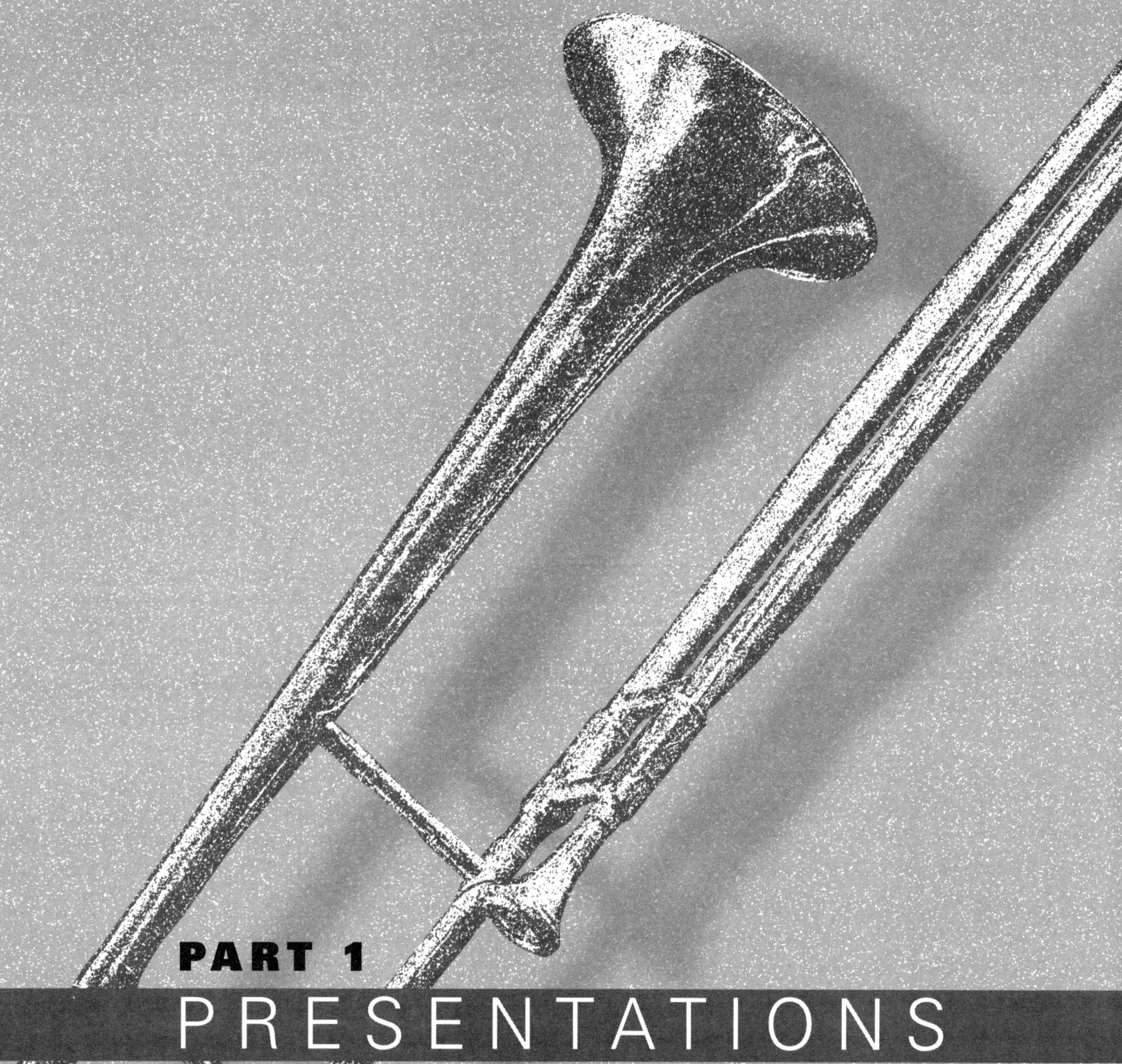

PART 1
PRESENTATIONS

The Magic of the Inimitable Miller Sound 1

Editor's note–This is the first of a series of presentations that I gave on cruises for my good friend and cruise entrepreneur, Gil Oftedal, president of the Fan-To-Sea Cruise Club. It was also the first presentation I gave for the Glenn Miller Festivals in Clarinda, Iowa, where I used plenty of blackboard space plus a piano and a tape machine.

The first issue is, of course, how to make the saxes with the lead clarinet sound the best. After all, this is the identifying signature sound of the Miller Band. Many other leaders and arrangers have tried and fallen short. Here is the essential approach that made the difference.

Reading from top to bottom in a chord played by the sax section, a clarinet would be playing the lead on top. Beneath him are two alto saxes and then two tenor saxes. The bottom tenor sax plays the same line as the lead clarinet except it sounds an octave lower. Miller had the two tenor saxes playing a half tone apart as often as the chords would allow. This was a disastrous looking voicing as far as other arrangers were concerned; these two tenor saxes were in a comparatively lower pitch only a half a tone apart. But Miller looked for opportunities for these clashes, they are actually beautiful sounds when executed well.

Of course, you must have the players. The tone that Wil Schwartz had on the clarinet was often compared to a sax tone because it was big and firm–but Benny Goodman had a big tone, so did Artie Shaw.

I have told Larry O'Brien and also the Jazz Ambassadors that Glenn's sax section with lead clarinet was quite loud. I think it helped bring out the dissonances. Both of these groups, even with their excellence, have a tendency to play delicately. Glenn's section could, and at times did; but at other times, they could just about blow the brass off the stand.

But remember the tenor saxes. You need two very good players to play a true half step from each other. Otherwise, they will do one of two things: they will either try to come together or they will try to get farther apart.[1]

1 *excerpt from* **"Sunrise Serenade"**

One more very easy thing with the saxes, Glenn used it often–the thirds on the clarinets and tenor saxes. It's easy to write and sounds nice. Two clarinets are an interval of a third apart and two tenor saxes are playing the exact lines only it sounds an octave lower.

Glenn, being an excellent arranger, thought like an arranger even when he composed. A good standard approach for an arranger is to let the melody stand still while the harmony moves.

"String of Pearls" ❷

Let's take a look at "String of Pearls." I was once at a concert where the leader gave the credit entirely to Jerry Gray. Nothing really wrong with that, and Jerry was talented, but Glenn sat down at the piano and showed Jerry how to write what he called "a string of pearls," then let him go from there.[2]

Glenn had been studying and his teacher, Dr. Joseph Schillinger, called this exercise (and that's what it was, an exercise) by that name. I remember Glenn saying how happy his teacher would be because Glenn named the piece by that title.

Once again, the arranger trick was to keep the melody on the same note while you move the harmony.

So here's how "A String of Pearls" was done–and how Jerry's tune, by way of Glenn, was conceived. They used the blues chord progression for solos–but then Bobby Hackett improvised a memorable gem for a solo–and there was a hit!

Now to carry that further, let's go to the theme, actually another exercise. Be aware of how the melody can be a bit static while the harmony moves–and it gives you a charmingly musical thought. Also that technique makes the melody more memorable. The verse to "Night and Day" does this.

It's fun to take risks while playing but it does nothing for precision work. If the ending of a tune sounded risky for the lead trumpet, Glenn would ask the lead player, McMickle about it. If Mickey said it was chancy, Glenn changed it, and yet Mickey was probably as consistent as anybody.

the last part of ❸ **"In the Mood"**

Listen to the ending to "In the Mood;" three trumpets in harmony work up to the climax while Mickey rests. Then he comes in on the high ending; today, the same fellow does all the work.[3]

On one tune, the movie record of "Chattanooga Choo-Choo," I think, Glenn even had Wil Schwartz on the clarinet play a loud high note on the clarinet, a high F concert I believe, on the ending. Everybody thought it was a trumpet, giving McMickle credit for a really solid high G.

One more thing–the Boo Bop plunger figures in the brass. This type of figure "un"complicates filling in the holes. When the brass is not in a high register, this type of fill-in makes good sense.

Another item about fill-ins: when a melody moved, Glenn usually had the fill-ins either lay out or stand still. When the melody stands still, or between phrases, that is the time to use a fill-in. Too many fills seem to clutter things.[4]

4 "Moonlight Serenade"

Glenn Miller had some special arranging thoughts that made his music different technically. He took a pleasant little phrase and made a charming million-dollar thought out of it.

A WALK AROUND MANHATTAN

1. **Hotel Pennsylvania**
2. **New Yorker Hotel**
3. **Paramount Theatre**
4. **Astor Hotel**
5. **Lincoln Hotel**
6. **Strand Theater**
7. **Capitol Theater**
8. **Roseland Ballroom**
9. **Cotton Club**
10. **Clubs on 52nd Street**
11. **Savoy Ballroom & Harlem Clubs**
12. **Nick's & Greenwich Village Clubs**
13. **Waldorf Astoria**

W. 145TH
E. 142ND
HARLEM
LENOX AVE.
W. 120TH
RIVERSIDE DR
MADISON AVE.
CENTRAL PARK
N

HARLEM
CENTRAL PARK
EAST SIDE
TIMES SQUARE
GREENWICH VILLAGE
N

CENTRAL PARK
PARK AVE.
W. 52ND
EIGHTH AVE.
TIMES SQUARE
W. 42ND
MADISON AVE.
BROADWAY
W. 33RD
SEVENTH AVE.
N

SEVENTH AVE.
WASHINGTON PARK
GREENWICH VILLAGE
HOUSTON ST.
N
W. BROADWAY
FOURTH AVE.

A Walk Around Manhattan 2

This particular presentation is naturally of most interest to those from New York City or those who have visited there often.

This will be sort of a "walk around," mainly Times Square, but with references to Harlem and Greenwich Village.

Let's start down at 33rd Street and Seventh Avenue–at the Cafe Rouge at the Hotel Pennsylvania. We would be playing there with the Glenn Miller Band—here's a sample—[1]

1 **"Pennsylvania 6-5000"**

Just one block over was the New Yorker Hotel with it's Terrace Room. There we'd find Jimmy Dorsey, his alto sax, his band, Bob Eberly, and Helen O'Connell would be singing—[2]

2 **"Tangerine"**

Right straight up Seventh Avenue to where it meets Broadway at Times Square–at the Paramount Theatre could be the Benny Goodman Band—[3]

3 **"Sing Sing Sing"**

Right across the street from the stage door was the Astor Hotel. Up on the roof would be Tommy Dorsey, his trombone, and his Orchestra; and backed up by the band, Jack Leonard is singing—[4]

4 **"Marie"**

Then back one block again to Eighth Avenue was the Blue Room of the Lincoln Hotel. The resident bands there seemed to be Charlie Barnet and Artie Shaw.[5 & 6]

5 **"Cherokee"**

6 **"Frenesi"**

Walking right up Broadway, we'd immediately come to the Strand Theater to be thrilled by Louis Armstrong.[7]

7 **"When It's Sleepy Time Down South"**

Then next we'd come to the Capitol Theater and listen a bit to Les Brown's Band of Renown.[8]

8 **"Leap Frog"**

Across the street from these theaters was the Roseland Ballroom, one of the homes of the Fletcher Henderson Band.[9]

9 **"Christopher Columbus"**

Of course, right in the middle of all this action, in the middle of Times Square, was the Cotton Club. The big attraction there was Duke Ellington.[10]

10 **"Take the 'A' Train"**

All the clubs right there on 52nd Street were almost door to door with talented jazz individuals. For example, The Famous Door had the Three T's featuring Jack Teagarden.[11]

11 **"I Gotta Right To Sing the Blues"**

"Shaw 'Nuff" 12

Some clubs featured the latest directions in jazz, like Charlie Parker and Dizzy Gillespie.[12]

"Fine and Mellow" 13

If you were lucky, you'd get to hear Billie Holiday at one of these clubs.[13]

"A-Tisket A-Tasket" 14

If you decided to take the 'A' train up to 140th Street and Lenox Avenue in New York's Harlem, you went to the Savoy Ballroom. There you would find three bands: Chick Webb, a semi-name band like Erskine Hawkins, and the Savoy Sultans, the house band. If you played a night there, you did not want to follow the Savoy Sultans on the bandstand, they just out-swung everybody. Chick Webb with his Ella Fitzgerald sounded like this:[14]

"Willow Weep For Me" 15

And all those clubs in Harlem where you could listen to Art Tatum—[15]

"I Ain't Got Nobody" 16

Or maybe Fats Waller—[16]

"I Wish I Could Shimmy Like My Sister Kate" 17

If you went the other direction from Times Square, you'd end up in Greenwich Village. Here you would get the very new and the older styles. There were clubs that had the *avant garde* of the day. Then there were clubs that just featured Chicago Style Dixieland, such as Nick's or Eddie Condon's. You could hear people like Muggsy Spanier—[17]

"Auld Lang Syne" 18

And I didn't even mention the swank hotels on the East Side like the Waldorf Astoria, the Lexington, and the Grill Room at the Roosevelt where you would hear Guy Lombardo play—[18]

The Biggest Attractions of the Big Bands **3**

When I have given this presentation, I have included two or three slides of each band leader and of course a tape of a famous selection that each has featured. This gives quite an advantage to those who can both see the picture and hear the music, so please add your imagination to my written word.

You notice that I have avoided the use of the word "best," that's just too subjective. I'd be called on as to why I haven't included Clyde McCoy, or like recently, when fans of Shep Fields got on my case. So I have included in this very exclusive list of twenty-one only those who were either the best drawing cards *during the Swing Era* or the most important in some other way.

I am *very* sorry if I haven't included your favorite, I've left out a couple of mine too. *And* I have set these up alphabetically (except that I put Glenn Miller on the end, for personal reasons I suppose). I'll try to tell you a little about each band.

LOUIS ARMSTRONG "Savoy Blues"

There once was an Armstrong named Lou,
He opened the world's door when he blew,
He thrills us today,
It'll never decay,
Off Louie's licks, we all sure drew.

Armstrong was better known in small groups, but he did front a big band lead by Luis Russell. I am happy to start out with a real jazz classic.

CHARLIE BARNET "Cherokee"

Charlie Barnet had a really great band,
He could swing you right off the bandstand.
His saxophone had drives,
He sure had lots of wives,
Of course, Charlie always had a drink in his hand.

Charlie Barnet was wealthy, and it is true that he had a half a dozen wives. He was a truly driving sax player. He wanted the band to sound like Ellington as often as possible.

COUNT BASIE "I Can't Stop Loving You"

Bill Basie was eventually named the Count.
Nobody made more swing than he could mount.
His piano was sparse,
But that was no farce,
He let you hear what was good so you wouldn't discount.

A picture of the Benny Moten organization shows the band that Basie sort of ended up with. His was probably the most swinging of all bands. The band is now fronted by Frank Foster.

LES BROWN "Leap Frog" (by Joe Garland) and "Sentimental Journey" sung by Doris Day

A gentleman band leader named Les Brown
Has a band called "The Band of Renown."
The singer Doris Day
Helped make Les some hay,
On which Les was never one to frown.

Les is a good guy, still going strong.

LARRY CLINTON "Dipsy Doodle"

Larry Clinton's arranging was his thing,
Although he never really grasped the gold ring.
His Dipsy and Doodle
Were certainly not futile,
And he fortunately hired Bea Wain to sing.

He was a pretty good arranger, an avid baseball fan, and lucky to have Bea Wain singing for him.

BOB CROSBY "Palestreena"

Crosby is a famous name that we all know,
And Bob added even more to the show.
With his dixieland fame,
He entered the game,
With his band who could really, really blow.

He made big band dixieland famous. He was a nice guy who became a band leader in front of fellows originally in Ben Pollack's Band.

JIMMY DORSEY "Tangerine"

The older of the two Dorseys was called Jim,
Battling with Brother Tommy never did deter him.
He played woodwinds with ease,
And always wanted to please.
The vocals by Helen and Bob never let things get dim.

He featured Bob Eberly and Helen O'Connell. The band is now fronted by Jim Miller.

TOMMY DORSEY "I'll Never Smile Again"

Tommy was the younger of the two,
And a more talented guy you never knew.
But for sweetness alone,
He relied on trombone,
And with Frankie, his fame even grew.

Like his brother, he also had good singers (Sinatra). The band is now fronted by Buddy Morrow.

DUKE ELLINGTON "Take the 'A' Train"

Royalty came in with Duke and Count.
Ellington showed us hills to mount.
Try as we would,
No one ever could,
Accomplish the moods we heard him recount.

Fronted by Mercer Ellington. Always a great inspiration to all musicians.

GLEN GRAY/CASA LOMA "Smoke Rings"

The Casa Loma Band was led by Glen Gray.
It was once called "Orange Blossoms," that didn't make hay.
With a change of the name,
They went on to fame,
And is still one of the favorites today.

Another pretty fair trombone player, Billy Rausch, so little he had to stand on a chair to play the theme. Gray's name was Spike Knoblaugh. It was a cooperative band at first.

BENNY GOODMAN "Let's Dance"

He was known as the "King of Swing," and rightfully so.
His clarinet playing was tops, this we all know.
Benny Goodman was great,
Unsurpassed to this date,
With his clarinet and swing band who could blow.

Benny Goodman became the clarinet image of the world. Bob Wilber is now traveling the world doing a tribute to Benny Goodman.

WOODY HERMAN "Four Brothers"

Woody was a favorite of many to the end.
With stars in his band, they started a trend.
He began with the blues,
Then new guys would infuse
A progressive style of jazz we commend.

He really proved how well fine jazz improvisers could work together. The band is now fronted by Frank Tiberi. It was once cooperative.

HARRY JAMES "You Made Me Love You"

You remember a famous James named Harry,
The one Betty Grable decided to marry.
But I'm sure he was born,
To blow on his horn,
It made him famous from here to Tucumcari.

He also loved baseball, and of course he loved Betty Grable. The band is now fronted by Art Depew.

SAMMY KAYE "Kaye's Melody"

There was a famous band led by Sammy Kaye,
He was a favorite of many so they say.
There was occasionally a moan,
That came from the trombone,
Alas, his style, be that as it may.

Band now fronted by Roger Thorpe.

STAN KENTON "Capitol Punishment"

Stan Kenton's style was considered to be new.
He played more concerts than music to dance to.
Dancers protested,
So the band attested,
"Why don't you dance something we can play to?"

Stan was a friend, didn't bother eating much which eventually bothered him. Miller introduced him at the Rendezvous Ballroom in Balboa, California. He told me that he had put in his will that there was never to be a "ghost" band of him, but they still do things like tributes.

KAY KYSER "Thinking of You"

You could surely recognize Kyser by his style,
By his shows which made you smile.
What he called his college,
That of "Musical Knowledge,"
You realized he was a business man all the while.

More of a show than a dance band, very successful financially. I was sorry about his statement saying, "You can make a musician out of a gentleman, but you can't make a gentleman out of a musician."

GUY LOMBARDO "Auld Lang Syne"

"The sweetest music this side of heaven" by Guy.
Was important to fans, also to banks, I sigh.
You'd be in fear,
To start a new year,
Without the Lombardo O.K. from on high.

This was a band making enough money they could fly to one-nighters, lots of money and lots of fans. Now led by Al Pierson.

FREDDIE MARTIN "Tonight We Love"

Then there was this Martin called Freddie,
He stood with his sax at the ready.
The band didn't jump,
But he got over that hump,
"I'll make Tchaikovsky my friend," so said he.

It's amazing how many jazz players wanted to directly emulate Martin's tone on tenor sax, starting with Coltrane, that's what he said. This was known as a hotel band, a real "hotel type" band. Merv Griffin played piano and sang in the band. Martin was even more indebted than the rest of us to Tchaikovsky (the theme song, "Tonight We love"). He also used lots of Grieg.

VAUGHN MONROE "Racing with the Moon"

It was said Vaughn had a muscle bound voice.
The polls showed he was lots of people's choice.
The ladies went goo,
The band was good too,
That was enough for bookers to rejoice.

He was a band boy who became a very successful leader. And a nice likeable fellow.

ARTIE SHAW "Begin the Beguine"

There once was an Artie named Shaw,
An excellent player, a fine band, as we saw.
In PR he fell short,
Wedding bells were his forte,
To go further might get me in trouble with the law.

For those who wondered, "Begin the Beguine" was written by Cole Porter. Shaw was, and is, I guess, an ego type, and with plenty of wives, but really a first class clarinet player and always with a real good band, which is now fronted by another very good clarinet player, Dick Johnson.

GLENN MILLER "In the Mood" and "Moonlight Serenade"

Should I make up a limerick about Miller?
Would it be no more than a mere filler?
All the polls that he won,
I guess he was number one.
All I can say is the job was surely a thriller.

Glenn Miller's Musical Changes 4

Some personnel changes altered things a bit. For example, the difference in styles of trumpet players–Johnny Austin to Clyde Hurley, Johnny Best, Mickey McMickle; both Billy May and Bobby Hackett added new colors. But because Glenn actually had a lack of personnel changes, the band kept improving, both individually and as an ensemble.

Most people don't even realize that the band did change. After it started to become well-known, any changes in personnel were actually written up in the trade magazines and papers. When trumpet player Johnny Austin and drummer Bob Spangler left the band in late 1938, I was afraid we'd break up or at least not be able to play some of our arrangements. I had no idea Glenn would get McMickle, Hurley, Best, May, Hackett, etc.

Let's go back to one of the most famous numbers–"In the Mood." Would you believe that some critics criticized Glenn for making a lot of money from Joe Garland's work? Actually, the arrangement didn't really "come off" until Glenn added his own creativity. But keep in mind that Garland, and now his estate, gets the composer royalties–and rightly so. BUT–did Garland really compose it? Let me play a couple of very early tapes for you. The first one is called "Tar Paper Stomp" played by Wingy Manone, he called the group Barbecue Joe and His Hot Dogs, this was 1930.[1]

1 **"Tar Paper Stomp"**

Does that sound familiar? Well, let's play a 1932 record of Don Redman, this was called "Hot and Anxious."[2]

2 **"Hot and Anxious"**

Then as late as 1939, we recorded "In the Mood."[3]

3 **"In the Mood"**

One more tape excerpt; you are a success when your hit is recorded by a flock of chickens. This is the Henhouse Five Plus Too (spelled TOO).[4]

4 *chickens'* **"In the Mood"**

Now let's turn for a few moments to "Tuxedo Junction." Would the piece have made more money for Erskine Hawkins if Glenn had not recorded it? I'm sure the *real* composer, Hawkins' piano player, Julian Dash, was happy with the eventual outcome. Hawkins was an Armstrong based trumpet player. In fact, in his solo, he does a direct quote from Armstrong's solo on "Struttin' With Some Barbecue"–nothing wrong with that! His record was made July 18, 1939, the problem was that it just didn't sell worth a darn.[5]

5 *Hawkins'* **"Tuxedo Junction"**

Miller's **"Tuxedo Junction"** 6

Glenn heard the tune and decided to do it himself, so he recorded it February 5, 1940. Glenn picked what he felt was a more attractive tempo. He added the trombones with their plungers. He also put the two musical thoughts (sax unison and the trumpet solo) together. Glenn's record went way over the million mark. Ours was slower than Hawkins. The arrangement was by Jerry Gray.[6]

Krupa's **"Tuxedo Junction"** 7

Then a month later, March of 1940, Gene Krupa did what is known as a "cover record." A cover record is when a record company hears a record by another company that seems to be doing well, then they will quickly get out a record of their own to cash in on a piece of that action. Now, on this version, the tempo seems slow, but there are some very nice moments on his record–the guitar fills are very charming and the trumpets play half of Hawkins' improvised solo harmonized for four trumpets. There was but one problem–it didn't sell, not by comparison. Maybe it wasn't rhythmic enough, but how can you say that about a band led by Gene Krupa?[7]

So what was the difference? Did Glenn pick a better tempo? Did putting an emphasis on the trombones with their plungers make Glenn's record do so much better in sales? Only the trombone players would decide that! Did Krupa and Columbia records undertake too big a challenge to take away some of Glenn's market? Hawkins and Miller both worked for Victor records. Maybe Miller knew how to plug his records, and by 1940, did he not have the where-with-all–radio? But "Tuxedo" is still a biggie.

Now let's go back to our first record date–September of 1938–"My Reverie" (by Debussy), "King Porter Stomp" (by Jelly Roll Morton) and "By the Waters of the Minnetonka" (which sort of sounds like "Indian Love Call").

"By the Waters of the Minnetonka" 8

Let's talk about "By the Waters of the Minnetonka." Miller was brave–a relatively new band, hoping for a record contract, and still he ventured into a two-sided record–a real rarity in those days. And who was featured on it–Tex Beneke on clarinet. Glenn liked it I guess; however, that was Tex's first and last clarinet solo–I don't suppose he even has a clarinet now. I imagine Glenn figured Tex would make it move along, even though (and gratefully) he kept it in the low register. Incidentally, it was Glenn's arrangement.[8]

In December of 1938, we went into the Paradise Restaurant in New York City, about 49th and Broadway. We got fired, didn't play the show very well I was told. Glenn didn't mind, he was overjoyed later when they wanted to hire him back and couldn't afford him.

"Pagan Love Song" 9

We were a smaller group then–3 trumpets, 3 trombones, saxes and 3 rhythm. But I promise you, we young kids did what we could to sort of dig in and make it move. It wasn't full but it did move.[9]

I'll play something in a couple of minutes that really sounds big by comparison even though the main difference was another trumpet and another trombone.

Now let's skip over to "String of Pearls" for a change. In October of 1941, Glenn backed Hal McIntyre and helped him get started with his own band. Hal had played lead sax with Glenn since 1937, and at first even played some lead clarinet and jazz clarinet solos. This was drastic–lead sax in the section Glenn was featuring. Glenn felt that Tex had a great swing feel, so he talked Tex into playing Hal's vacated chair. TEX HATED IT !

I remember the record date when we did "String of Pearls." Tex was on lead alto, then he alternated two-bar alto sax solos with Ernie Caceres. Glenn had hired a really fine tenor sax player named Babe Russin to fill Tex's tenor chair. So Babe and Al Klink alternated on the tenor solos on this tune. Well, Tex would have no part of playing alto sax; so with an immediate two weeks notice, Glenn had to let Babe go so Tex would go back over on tenor. In came Skip Martin for lead alto (he had been playing baritone sax with Benny Goodman I believe).[10]

⑩ **"String of Pearls"**

Now about the singers: Marion Hutton was in and out a little–pregnancy will do that I'm told. She was followed by Dorothy Claire, Kay Starr, Paula Kelly, and in the movies, Pat Friday. All had different sounds.

But let me play a couple Ray Eberle excerpts to show you how his voice lowered. The first one goes so high we couldn't believe it, he sounded like Tony Bennet or Kenny Sargent from the Casa Loma Band or Jack Fulton from the Paul Whiteman Band.[11]

⑪ **"The Nearness of You"**

Now the next excerpt is from a movie soundtrack. Ray is singing "At Last" with Pat Friday. Notice how his voice has lowered.[12]

⑫ **"At Last"**

Then came Skip Nelson, listen to his sound which may not be so much lower, but it is indeed huskier.[13]

⑬ **"That Old Black Magic"**

Now a little change in how people heard "Moonlight Serenade," our theme song. It was recorded in April of 1939. The brass is soft, but they have an intriguing sound by using metal cup mutes. Hardly anybody else playing this arrangement ever picked up on the fact that the brass is playing softly with a good swing feel, not stiff at all like most imitators. Of course, everybody just listens to the saxes here.[14]

⑭ **"Moonlight Serenade"**

Now an excerpt from a movie soundtrack to show you how Hollywood doctored it a bit, mainly with the harp and a slower tempo.[15]

⑮ *movie soundtrack* **"Moonlight Serenade"**

Now some critics used to say that the band played very pretty music, but that it didn't swing very well. So, let me play for you a couple of excerpts out of many that I think moved along really well.

"When Johnny Comes Marching Home" 16

"Caribbean Clipper" 17

Try to remember the earlier excerpt of the late 1939 band and see how much more powerful the band became.[16 & 17]

Now this next tape is "Swing Low Sweet Chariot," and it is from a live radio show. If Glenn needed a little more music (watching the clock), he knew he could repeat this one strain, he knew how long it took, how long it would take to finish the arrangement, add applause, and play the theme. So, he would have that one strain repeated until it got to a certain spot on his stop watch.

So, if Glenn holds up one finger, it means to take the first ending of that particular strain that we are playing (to repeat it). If he holds up a fist, it means to take the second ending which will take us out of the arrangement. Of course, if you are in the middle of an arrangement, he could hold up two fingers, meaning to take the second ending and go on.

In this case, it was either first ending–repeat it, or the fist–to take the second ending and go on out.

So, Glenn keeps putting up one finger, and we kept repeating (involving the saxes and rhythm).

Now it was really swinging, Glenn added another direction right there on the live radio program. He not only held up one finger, but also pointed to Chummy MacGreagor on piano–meaning for him to start improvising at the same time. At one spot, at the end of the second time through of just the saxes and Chummy, if you listen closely, you'll hear Glenn holler way off the mike, "That's pretty, Mac."

Finally, at the right time, Glenn holds up a fist, and at that time, he also points to the bass player. He is to play a gliss to bring the rest of us in. (On "In the Mood," the signal came from a cow bell by the drummer). So, we barreled on in and finished the arrangement.

"Swing Low Sweet Chariot" 18

Signals like that are standard. On Tex's band, I worked the stop watch, and I would clue Tex on what to signal. Or if he weren't on the stand, and the band needed some out-of-tempo direction at the end of a tune or something, I would do that. Lou McGarity used to do that for Goodman some. We trombonists don't possess any special talents, its just that we were down front and could be seen by the other guys.[18]

Oh, those little naps do help. *1939*

Miller fishing, with wife Helen (in neckerchief) and friends. *1939*

Blow, Glenn, blow. *1939*

Early Sax Section: L to R: Stan Aronson, Bill Stegmeyer, Will Schwartz, Hal McIntyre, Tex Beneke. *1939*

A couple of kids named Rolly Bundock and Tex Beneke. *1939*

GLENN MILLER AND HIS ORCHESTRA APPEARING NIGHTLY
AT GLEN ISLAND CASINO

NO COVER CHARGE AT ANY TIME

MINIMUM CHARGE: $1.50 Weekdays, $2.00 Saturdays, Sundays, Holidays and Holiday Eves.

MENU

(Effective until 10.00 P. M. Only)

PRICE OF ENTREE INCLUDES COMPLETE DINNER

Fruit Cup Melba — Seafood à la Russe
Cranberry Juice Cocktail — Tomato Surprise

Fresh Vegetable Soup Basque — Consommé aux Perles
New England Clam Chowder — Cold: Chicken Broth in Jelly

Cauliflower Mornay — Beans Panaché
POTATOES: Hashed in Cream, Baked Idaho

Mixed Green Salad

Meringue Melba — Stewed Fresh Fruits
Fruit Pies — Ice Cream — Ices
Cheese and Crackers

Coffee — Tea — Milk

ENTREES

1	Grilled Block Island Swordfish Steak Hôtelière	1.50
2	Casserole of Spaghetti with Meat Sauce, Italian Style	1.50
3	Brizzola Steak Sauté Bordelaise	1.75
4	Minced Turkey à la King in Chafing Dish	2.00
5	Roast Prime Ribs of Beef, Pan Gravy	2.00
6	Whole Broiled Fresh Killed Squab Chicken and Bacon	2.25
7	Broiled Double Lamb Chops	2.25
8	Broiled Whole Live Maine Lobster	2.50
9	Broiled Sirloin Steak, Maître d'Hôtel	3.00

ALL BROILED ITEMS COOKED ON OUR CHARCOAL BROILERS

Thursday, July 13, 1939

July 13, 1939

Glen Island Casino. *July 1939*

Glen Island Casino and the sea wall. *July 1939*

Bunny, Paul's late wife. Glen Island Casino. *July 1939*

Dick Fisher, P.T., and Bill Finegan. *July 1939*

Mickey McMickle. *July 1939*

Bunny with Bill Finegan. *July 1939*

. . . and with handsome Dick Fisher. *July 1939*

Marion Hutton and Bunny at the sea wall. *July 1939*

Marion Hutton and Will Schwartz at Glen Island. *July 1939*

Calm down, Ray. *July 1939*

Al Klink gives Tex Beneke a light. *July 1939*

**Chummy MacGregor says,
"God Bless You, Lightnin'."** *1939*

**Rolly Bundock,
the bathing beauty.**
July 1939

Ray Eberle strikes out. *1939*

**Cheering section for our ball game at Glen Island.
Includes two Mrs. Millers and one Mr. Miller.** *1939*

P.T. and his big feet.
1939

Glen Island afternoon broadcast. Get a load of P.T.'s music stand–Marion Hutton. *1939*

Hal McIntyre climbs into the rumble seat. *1939*

P.T. with Bullets Durgom and his car. *1939*

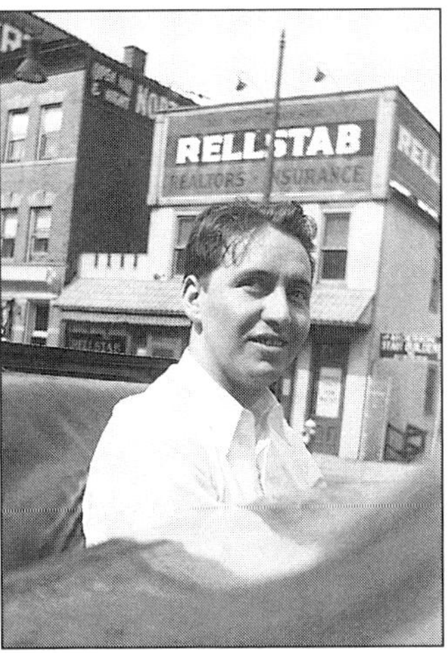

Hal in the rumble seat. *1939*

Glen Island Casino. Sax section: L to R: Tex Beneke, Tenny Tennyson, Hal McIntyre, Will Schwartz, Al Klink. *1939*

Ray Eberle. *1939*

Glenn happy with Al Klink, of course. *1939*

Paramount Theatre in New York City.
1939

Paramount Theatre, New York City
L to R: Johnny Best, P.T., Tommy Mack, Al Mastren, Glenn. *1939*

Marion at the Paramount Theatre. *1939*

Paramount Theatre, New York City. *1939*

With us during our first stay at the Paramount Theatre in New York City. *1939*

Pictures from Paramount Theatre used to advertise Bach Brass Instruments. *1939*

Metronome

MODERN MUSIC AND ITS MAKERS

DEC. 1939
25c.

Glenn Miller
AND HIS ORCHESTRA

Glenn would like to have been a baseball player. Here he is batting left-handed. *1939*

Marion Hutton. *1939*

Ray Eberle. *1939*

P.T. on the road somewhere doing his favorite hobby. *1939*

The Meadowbrook fans! *1939*

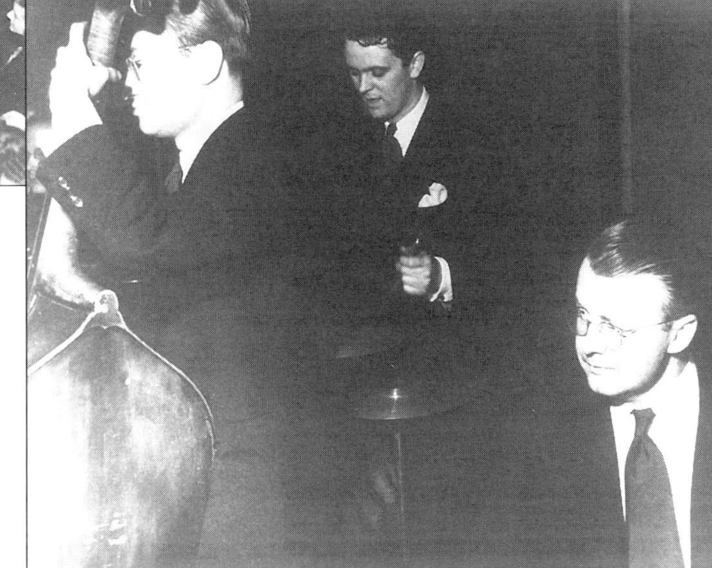

Rolly Bundock, Mo Purtill, Chummy MacGregor at the Meadowbrook. *1939*

The smile that captured a following—Ray Eberle, Meadowbrook. *1939*

Mickey McMickle and Al Mastren, Meadowbrook. *1939*

The Meadowbrook. *1939*

Marion mugging, Meadowbrook. *1939*

The Meadowbrook, the place to be. *1939*

Now where is my table? *1939*

Meadowbrook parking lot. *1939*

Glenn would sit and chat with fans any time he could. *1939*

Chesterfield program–
Glenn explains life to the Andrews Sisters.
1940

Advertisement. *February 28, 1940*

Musical Achievements of Glenn Miller's Civilian Orchestra

5

There are lots of things we did that I'm proud of, that I look back on as thrills, as achievements. I'll play excerpts for you as reminders.[1]

❶ **"Moonlight Serenade"**

There are often comparisons with the great service band. Glenn had to have achievements with the civilian band in order to have the service band.

You had to sell a million records to have a gold record. This was the first gold record, the one that started that whole concept; Glenn had others later. There was one back in 1927 on "My Blue Heaven" sung by a fellow named Gene Austin. This next excerpt was the next one–1941.[2]

❷ **"Chattanooga Choo Choo"**

Glenn had more top of the chart hits than Elvis Presley and the Beatles combined–what a track record!

On October 6, 1939, we played in Carnegie Hall, now there's a great treat! If you listen hard, you'll hear Gene Buck, the President of ASCAP, introduce us. Goodman's "Sing Sing Sing," done earlier, was picked up on and sent on a *telephone* line to a radio station and put on an acetate. It was later cleaned up and printed logically. I don't really know if Glenn's efforts were sent in by telephone then put on acetate or not, but I wouldn't be surprised.[3]

❸ *tape of Buck introducing us* **"Moonlight Serenade"**

"Little Brown Jug" was one of the numbers we played at Carnegie Hall. You can tell that we really weren't nervous or intimidated, but I guarantee you, we were thrilled. I can hear Legh Knowles' voice, the guy who started this yelling sort of thing. Glenn liked it because it sort of showed energy and enthusiasm.[4]

❹ **"Little Brown Jug"**

Another achievement was making movies. As most of you know, in 1941, we made *Sun Valley Serenade*; and in 1942, we made *Orchestra Wives*. I already played an excerpt for you from "Chattanooga Choo Choo" from *Sun Valley Serenade*, so it's only fair that I play "I Got a Gal In Kalamazoo" from *Orchestra Wives*.[5]

❺ **"I Got a Gal In Kalamazoo"**

For Glenn, at first an unknown band, to get a record date with RCA was an achievement mainly because of what it led to–so many more dates, so many more records. We recorded 272 sides in record studios, this of course doesn't include all the records made from broadcasts or anything like that. There were four of us who were on every Bluebird record. Now this next

"By the Waters of the Minnetonka" 6

excerpt is "By the Waters of the Minnetonka," off an air shot from the Paradise Restaurant at 49th and Broadway. Glenn was brave; he wanted to make a two-sided record on it. Nobody was buying two-sided records. Even Goodman's "Sing Sing Sing" had to have a break to turn the record over, so they used a drum solo by Gene Krupa. So Glenn had Tex play a low register clarinet solo, long enough to turn the record over. Tex hadn't played jazz clarinet before–or since. We also had a Debussy piece called "My Reverie" and Jelly Roll Morton's "King Porter's Stomp." Well, he got into RCA, not much income at first, but later it paid off handsomely.[6]

What an achievement to land the Glen Island Casino for the summer of 1939, and the Meadowbrook Supper Club both before and after. You were on the air so often that if you looked up and there was no microphone, you wondered what was wrong–was President Roosevelt giving a speech or something? These places were jobs where bands were made–all that air time!

When Glenn got the arrangement of "In the Mood," written by saxophonist Joe Garland, Glenn saw possibilities. Glenn has been criticized for cashing in on Garland's efforts. In the first place, by the time Glenn finished altering the arrangement, Garland himself would never have recognized it.

I'm told that Glenn got $175 in royalties. Then later a new contract was made up and he got his due amounts retroactive, now that had to work out well for him. Meanwhile, Garland, a talented fellow, and his estate, cashed in quite beautifully. Garland also wrote Les Brown's theme, "Leap Frog."

"In the Mood" 7

At the Glen Island, Glenn tried out his ending on the dancers; they loved it. It quickly became a hit. I see on cruises that if you want to crowd up the dance floor, there are two tunes from the whole swing era that will do it–"Moonlight Serenade" and "In the Mood."[7]

"Pennsylvania 6-5000" 8

It was a true achievement to land the plum job of New York City as a regular winter location, the Hotel Pennsylvania.[8]

How about landing the Chesterfield program for an achievement, we started on it in December of 1939. To show some class, some professionalism, Glenn recommended Harry James to replace him instead of one of the bands in which he had a personal financial interest.

"Juke Box Saturday Night" 9

This tape is of our last Chesterfield show. Listen to handsome and talented Ralph Brewster as he both sings the high part and speaks the low part of the Ink Spots.[9]

"Tuxedo Junction" 10

Wasn't breaking the record at the Savoy Ballroom in Harlem an achievement? Here's "Tuxedo Junction," Erskine Hawkins' theme song. He played the Savoy quite regularly. Would he feel badly with our playing his theme there while breaking the record? Heck no–he loved the royalties he was getting.[10]

The first time at the Paramount Theater in New York was September of 1939. The kids screamed so much when the pit went up for each show that it was a real thrill to not even be able to hear yourself play–take that any way you want to.

Another achievement was the tremendously successful "Sunrise Serenade" starting about October of 1941. Our good friend, Tom Shiels, was greatly responsible for this achievement. The kids poured into the Cafe Rouge at the Hotel Pennsylvania. They were charged one war stamp or defense stamp, whatever it was called, for 25 cents. Glenn gave away to military camps many, many records of all bands and phonograph/radio sets. The only people not happy were the waiters because the kids would buy a coke and sit and listen or dance, so often to "Sunrise Serenade."[11]

11 **"Sunrise Serenade"**

Glenn had the top selling records for many, many weeks. He wanted to record "Stardust," but the RCA big wigs said, "Nothing doing, we are up to our chins in 'Stardust' records." So, Glenn said to them, "Just hear the first eight bars, that's all." They did, and said immediately, "Let's record it." So here is the first eight bars that sold them on making the record.[12]

12 **"Stardust"**

Glenn's achievements kept adding up from a time early in 1938 or so when he felt like folding. He called us into his hotel room in Boston and told us that he had nothing, that if we had anything at all, that we as individuals should go to it. We responded with fond accolades about the band and how it was the best band we had heard and all. Glenn said, "OK, guys, we go on."

Then he went on to win polls like the Martin Block poll in 1940 when he got over twice as many votes as Tommy Dorsey who was number two. Glenn's achievements included pulling in 7,000 people at the Hollywood Palladium twice.

He was obviously America's busiest band–140 playing situations in two weeks. We did seven shows a day at the Paramount (that's 98 performances), and at the same time, two sessions a night at the Pennsylvania six nights a week (that's 24 more), six Chesterfield programs (three for the east coast and three for the west coast each week, no tape in those days), plus three rehearsals a week. If you add that up, I think that does it–140. Of course, he broke records every place.

Please don't get the wrong idea from my talk here. This is not a bragging situation, this is a talk about the achievements of Glenn's civilian band, and these achievements are due to one man alone. What I am saying is that I was purely lucky to be along.

Also I am a great admirer of the military band to be sure, it was as fine a musical group as there ever was. But without the accomplishments of the civilian band, Glenn might not have had the reputation and prestige that allowed him to put together that great, fabulous band in the service.

Off on another track–consider that there was a fine movie made about Glenn and his band–Jimmy Stewart and June Allyson were featured in *The Glenn Miller Story*.

"Too Little Time" (13)

This next tape is the love theme from that movie, it was written by Henry Mancini and called "Too Little Time." I'll just do a little bit of it for you because I'm playing the solo out-of-doors at Disneyland with Tex Beneke and His Band. There is no balance, just live, no retakes.[13]

"Moonlight Serenade" (14)
with Glenn saying goodbye

Now here was a goodbye to the public from our last Chesterfield show at the Central Theater in Passaic, New Jersey.[14]

At 20th Century Fox Studios, Hollywood, California. *1941*
L to R: Trombones: Paul Tanner, Jim Priddy, Frank D'Anolfo, Glenn Miller; Trumpets: Johnny Best, Ray Anthony, Billy May, Mickey McMickle; Saxes: Ernie Caceres, Tex Beneke, Hal MacIntyre, Al Klink, Will Schwartz; Bass: Trigger Alpert; Drums: Mo Purtill; Piano: Chummy MacGregor; Guitar: Jack Lathrop; Singers: Ralph Brewster, Hal Dickinson, Ray Eberle, Chuck Goldstein, Bill Conway.

6 A Personal Look at the Fellows in the Band

The first thing that happened with this presentation was that lovely helpers gave to each person, as they came in the door, a photograph of the band. It was not only a nice souvenir, but also a big help in my presentation. Along with the photograph, everyone was given a list of the names of each fellow in the band and where they were located in the picture. (See photo at left).

I didn't bother saying things about myself at this point, enough had been said and ego has its limits. Also, I didn't talk about Glenn as a member of the band–as he *was* the band. So, I started with my trombone buddies as they were down in front on the photo.

JIM PRIDDY

Good buddy, neat, first class in every way.

I took him with Betty to be married across some state line because she was under age.

We had a cabin together near Chicago when we worked at the Sherman Hotel–whenever anybody visited, Jimmy hid Betty's clothes in another room.

No trombone parts for him at first, so I wrote them.

Whenever Jimmy and I rode the band bus, we had a scheme where we got off the bus first in case there was a shortage of rooms with twin beds and shower.

I took him to my dentist who told me that working on Jim was tough because Jim's knees were in the way.

FRANKIE D'ANOLFO

Rock of Gibraltar, steady, had studied trombone well.

A friend of mine drove Frankie's car to California for me–everything was fine until he got to Long Beach and drove it through a gas station glass window.

After Glenn broke up, Frankie went with Lombardo.

trombones playing sweetly 1
"Its Always You"

Still around now, enjoying his grandkids.[1]

JOHNNY BEST

Brought a real jazz feel to parts of the arrangements.

I saw him once playing a Louis Armstrong trumpet cadenza in a Japanese train station.

I heard John compliment Billy May on the way he played like Cootie Williams while Billy complimented John on his Armstrong feeling.

John had to be careful–kidding around back stage could get him in the next show.

I heard trumpet players at Disneyland complaining that John was using up all the air.

John fell off a ladder very late at night while watering his avocado trees. He was found 24 hours later. It was doubtful that he would live, then doubtful he would not be paralyzed. Today John gets around in a wheelchair and plays trumpet really well.

Believe it or not, John is a bit shy, even today.

When John was with Bob Crosby, he walked into a Holiday Inn where a sign said, "All you can drink for a dollar." John immediately said, "I'll take two dollars worth." [2]

RAY ANTHONY

Youngster brought up from Al Donahue's Band, only about 19 years old then.

Considered very cocky, especially by McMickle.

Only guy Glenn ever fired twice.

BILLY MAY

Loose, funny, sparked the band with his playing and arranging. He was very talented.

Enthusiastic.

Sensational ear. He proved on a Charlie Barnet record that he can play anything you play.

Greatly influenced by Cootie Williams (Ellington's Band).

I first asked this big fellow if he ever played football–I doubt he had ever seen one.

Rather outgoing–acted as an MC at Willie Schwartz's funeral.

Glenn promised Billy's wife an orchid if Billy would let his fingernails alone–Glenn won.

He had to keep cutting off his knit tie as it kept growing.

Went from booze to coffee to ice cream.

Do you like the intro on "Serenade In Blue"? Billy wrote it after others failed.

MICKEY McMICKLE

Most consistent lead trumpet ever, bar none.

Nice guy, but had a temper.

Threw his trumpet across the room at a record session when a valve stuck.

Was hired to play jazz solos, replaced Lee Castle. Then because of good strong consistent upper register, he replaced Bob Price on lead.

When Bobby Hackett joined the band, he was having gum trouble, Bobby said Mickey was a great help to him. Bobby also said he would give his arm to play like McMickle; Mickey said the same thing about playing like Bobby.[3 & 4]

3 *brass* **"Danny Boy"**

4 *brass* **"Running Wild"**

ERNIE CACERES

Everybody enjoyed Ernie.

Good jazz clarinet player, good baritone sax.

By fooling around and kidding backstage, he got put on an arrangement singing, I remember, "Jingle Bells."

Got some of the guys loaded on an air-conditioned bus with Tequila.

TEX BENEKE

My old buddy, Tex–most of us called him "Cuz" because he seemed to have cousins by the dozens.

I played in his band for six years. We were friends, but I tried to quit, he wouldn't let me (kept offering me raises, that'll do it).

I tried to teach him one of those "stammer quotations" but it lost so much with a Texas drawl.

At first, Tex demanded $2.50 more than our pay. Glenn, of course, kept it a secret.

Once, Glenn and Tex put on an act–ending up with Ernie offering to quit.

Tex was recommended by Krupa who later tried to get him away from Glenn with more money. Tex said no.

Easy going, relaxed, everybody liked him.

Tex and Margurite went with the Tanners on a cruise to Virginia Beach on our first four-day vacation; barely got back in time for a rehearsal.

Had a ham radio he used in his car on one-nighters.

Could repair lighters, his horn, etc.

Was pushed very hard by his first wife.

We got Tex to hire a sax player once who was a scratch golf player.

excerpt of Tex's solo ❺ **"Stardust"**

The Texas contingent in Tex's band couldn't seem to drive on ice and snow–resulted in lots of new car grills.[5]

HAL McINTYRE

A real gentleman, All-American.

Recommended to Glenn by Benny Goodman.

At first, Hal played a little lead clarinet and also some jazz solos on clarinet.

Glenn backed Hal's band.

When Hal left, he was replaced by Skip Martin. Skip was playing baritone sax with Benny Goodman, so Glenn made a trade–Glenn got Skip, who was also an arranger for lead alto sax, and Benny got Alex Fila, a fiery type trumpet player from Glenn; Glenn really didn't like Fila. Sounds like baseball teams, right?

AL KLINK

A real gentleman, Al certainly liked Tex as a friend.

Al felt he should play more solos, Tex felt Al should play more solos.

Al was recommended by Legh Knowles.

Glenn woke Al up in the middle of the night in Al's bedroom and offered him a job.

I shared a house in Hollywood with Al, Priddy and wives. They lost money on the food bill.

Glenn took care of everything when Al's mother was in the hospital; same with Chuck Goldstein's dad.

When the band broke up, everybody wanted Al–Tommy Dorsey, Goodman, *The Tonight Show*, records, etc.

WILLIE SCHWARTZ

The Jersey Cupie Doll, sometimes Peck's bad boy–lovable.

At first, McIntyre played some lead clarinet.[6]

His (Willie's) tone was not to be imitated.

Willie played louder and stronger than other clarinet players, yet he could play *very* delicately.[7]

6 *excerpt featuring Willie on clarinet* **"Berkeley Square"**

7 *saxes playing sweetly* **"Stardust"**

Willie, Rolly Bundock and I shared an apartment while at the Glen Island.

He fell in the lake at Green Bay, Wisconsin.

Was always up to mischief.

TRIGGER ALPERT

Everybody loved him; a real spark, gregarious, enthusiastic.

He was a swinging bass player right out of Jimmy Blanton (Ellington).

Glenn got him from Alvino Rey's Band.

He was bright, very affectionate.

He was very attached to his parents, especially his mother.

Glenn had a tune written for him to sing, "Nobody Ever Wants Me."

He now does portrait photography in Miami, does very well. He was into photography in the band.

MO PURTILL

Mo only looked happy if the Yankees won.

Mo loved working with Norvo, said it was more subtle.

But he came to Glenn out of Tommy Dorsey.

Played exactly as Glenn wanted all the time.

Made a tremendous difference from others Glenn had tried out.

Complained because the guys never made any mistakes, said it caused us to be too stiff. (I doubt anybody ever accused Lightnin' of that).

CHUMMY MacGREGOR

I found out immediately that Chummy was a really first-class stammerer, so at first, I was afraid to talk to him.

An old friend of Glenn's from 'way back.

When the band first started, Chummy even did some of the copying, even wrote an occasional arrangement.

He drove one of the cars (called "Sudden Death").

He kept the financial books for Glenn. He kept on making out the salary checks to the end.

He deducted money off our checks for our ties for example, so we teased him about staying up all night sewing on designer labels.

He wrote our substitute theme–"Slumber Song"–when the ASCAP forbade us from playing "Moonlight Serenade." They even forbade us from improvising for fear a part of an ASCAP tune would slip into a player's thoughts. (ASCAP stands for American Society of Composers and Publishers.)

Much earlier, he had a booze problem, took a successful cure and all (it worked). All those years, his mother never even knew about it.

JACK LATHROP

Odd situation with Jack, I think what Glenn wanted was a clone of Johnny Mercer or Hoagy Carmichael.

Glenn expected Jack to organize a singing group (maybe out of the band), it never happened.

He lasted a little while, he didn't impress Glenn too much as a player, but he was sort of cute; the boy next door, sort of.

RALPH BREWSTER

The first night the Modernaires were with us (that was at the Hotel Pennsylvania), they left early to catch a train home. Glenn was mad, gave them a lecture the next night.

Good looking singer, the ladies liked him. He happily married Bonnie.

Good musician, played trumpet.

Unlike Hal Dickinson and Chuck Goldstein, Ralph could read music.

HAL DICKINSON

Married to Paula Kelly. I told Paula once that I never really knew how to act with Hal, sometimes he was outgoing, sometimes rather aloof. She said, "Tell me about it."

Hal wrote good "extra lyrics" for the Modernaires.[8]

8 *Dorothy Claire singing* **"Perfidia"**

RAY EBERLE

Bob Eberly's kid brother, there was also a younger brother who sang. Walt?

For some reason, Glenn called him "Jim," said he looked more like a "Jim."

Ray was a really nice fellow, great sense of humor, the ladies loved him, very romantic.

He was as strong as an ox, used to handle kegs of beer for his father's business.

His first few vocals were pitched too high, we all wondered about that.

Ray had a difference of opinion with Glenn about movie salary, so Ray left. Skip Nelson came in the next night from Chico Marx's Band.

Ray joined Krupa right away.

Ray started a band, and even though Glenn had a contract, he never took commissions.[9]

9 *tape of Ray singing* **"A Nightingale Sang In Berkeley Square"**

Ray's daughter has done a book on Ray.

CHUCK GOLDSTEIN

A real extrovert, but with lots of feeling for other people.

Actually, he was a ham, a likeable ham, and the audiences enjoyed it.

Chuck sang in a falsetto voice on top of the group unless there was a girl singing, then he sang the bottom part.

BILL CONWAY

The silent type, but always with a great sense of humor.

Wrote the arrangements for the parts for the Modernaires–*very* talented. Listen to what they sing in the middle of "Serenade In Blue," nobody else has gotten the harmony out of that part, just Bill.

People not in the photograph

MARION HUTTON

We loved her *like a sister*–really pretty.

At first, because she was 17, I understand that Glenn and Helen were her legal guardians.

Glenn was a father image for her.

Glenn first called her "Sissy Jones"–that didn't last.

Married Jack Philbin and had a son. Later divorced I guess because she married Vic Schoen.

Marion went on to college and got an MA in psychology.

PAULA KELLY

Dorothy Claire came in when Marion took a sabbatical; then pretty, perky Paula Kelly replaced Dorothy.

She was married to Hal Dickinson, but no politics at all involved.

Marion came back and picked up where she left off.

P.K. Junior sings with today's Modernaires–and well too.

BOBBY HACKETT

We were all thrilled when Bobby joined the band.

Mickey said he'd give his right arm to be able to play like Bobby. Bobby said exactly the same thing about Mickey.

Glenn was criticized for putting Bobby on guitar, but what hardly anyone knew was that Bobby was having gum trouble and just couldn't blow his horn at all at first.

Bobby playing delicately (10) **"Rhapsody In Blue"**

Later, he didn't play loudly enough to be in the trumpet section. He said Mickey really helped him so very much.[10]

Bobby's classic solo (11) **"String of Pearls"**

His classic solo on "String of Pearls" was an exercise he had invented for guitar according to Bobby.[11]

ROLLY BUNDOCK

Solid bass player.

Had me meet his prospective bride to show her there were sober musicians.

Wouldn't talk in front of Clare Chatwin in Tex's Band because they both had a lisp.

Left the band to study at Julliard.

Was #158 in the draft which meant he was drafted immediately.

DOC GOLDBERG

Followed Trigger in after a short stint by Mike Rubin.

Great bass player. Glenn knew of him from Will Bradley's Band; he had made good trio records with Ray McKinley and Freddie Slack.

Doc did very well with pictures, both stills and movies.

Went into the Merchant Marines, I think; I know he became an exercise instructor.

ZEKE ZARCHY

Excellent player, good honest warm person with sharp sense of humor, outspoken without being unkind.[12]

12 **"Swing Low, Sweet Chariot"**
trombones swinging, Billy May soloing, saxes swinging, Chummy MacGregor soloing

7 Inside Glenn's Biggest Hits

I sent letters to a couple dozen of my literate friends–do I have a couple dozen? They had problems separating the *most popular* from *their favorites*. Then they had the problem of putting them in order. It took a lot of pressure off me. My wife, Jan, said that I would get a lot of static on the order of the records, but I just figured I would shift the blame to my friends.

We recorded 272 tunes in regular record studios, all were put out but one–"WPA"–it would have been politically incorrect lyricwise. Glenn decided against it.

Then there were hundreds of tunes, I suppose, taken off radio programs and made into commercial records. Two things about them–I doubt that Glenn would have okayed them at all because they are so seldom perfect as far as balance and blend are concerned. The other thing is that the musicians were never paid for these. They are called "pirate" records.

First, I'll read to you the list of winners. It shows the diversity of records that were big hits. Remember, I liked the ballads best, but look at all these up-tempo tunes–I guess people thought it was an excellent band to dance to. The list from top on down was:

1. Moonlight Serenade
2. In the Mood
3. String Of Pearls
4. Chattanooga Choo Choo
5. I Got a Gal In Kalamazoo
6. Tuxedo Junction
7. American Patrol
8. Little Brown Jug
9. Pennsylvania 6-5000
10. Serenade In Blue

#1 MOONLIGHT SERENADE

This was actually a harmony exercise for Dr. Joseph Schillinger. About the Schillinger method–it was good if you were hurried; this system should not be overused. I studied under Jesse Crawford, a disciple of Schillinger, then Eddie Sauter got me with Stephan Volpe. The tune creates an atmosphere–people will dance, romantically.[1]

❶ *first strain of* **"Moonlight Serenade"**

We recorded it in April of 1939, I think, before going into the Glen Island Casino. The record company put it on the opposite side of "Sunrise Serenade;" actually, "Moonlight Serenade" was the "B" side, but its popularity just kept growing.

Some record pundits decided it had to have lyrics because it was recorded and published. So first, George Simon tried some–"Now I Lay Me Down To Weep," then "Gone With the Dawn." Glenn thought they were too sad. Then Glenn went to Mitchell Parrish of "Stardust" fame. Parrish wrote "Wind In the Trees;" then, because it was on the opposite side of the record from "Sunrise Serenade," he wrote the lyrics to "Moonlight Serenade." A funny thing but all my part said on it was "Theme."

I was asked to do, and I did, a theme song for a band not too long ago. I was told it reminded them of "Moonlight Serenade." That was O.K., I wasn't writing them a tune *per se*, just creating a mood.

But for a short while, "Moonlight Serenade" wasn't the theme. ASCAP was having a strike against the networks and we couldn't play any ASCAP numbers, which included our theme. So Chummy MacGregor wrote a piece called "Slumber Song." Glenn published it with a non-ASCAP company which he also had, and we used it until we could go back to "Moonlight Serenade."[2]

❷ *second strain of* **"Moonlight Serenade"**

#2 IN THE MOOD

While we were at the Glen Island Casino, Joe Garland brought it out to us. Glenn has been criticized about the profits. Glenn was paid $175 at first for doing the record, later the agreement was modified greatly.

Glenn, being creative, changed the original to the point where Garland would have only recognized the first part. Glenn had an idea for false stops at the end. Then he tried it on the dancers at the Glen Island–they loved it.

Glenn played a gag on me–also did it on "Pennsylvania 6-5000."

"Moonlight Serenade" and "In the Mood" are the two pieces that will get people on the dance floor anywhere.

It was offered to Artie Shaw, but it was 6 or 7 minutes long and evidently he wasn't capable of editing it down feasibly for the 3 minute 78 rpm records we were all making at that time.[3]

❸ **"In the Mood"** *intro and first strain repeated*

Good tune, usually at a good tempo for dancing sort of jitterbug style. We recorded it while we were at the Glen Island, August of 1939.

#3 A STRING OF PEARLS

Don't believe the movie version.

This was another exercise of the Dr. Joseph Schillinger system. He called this particular method "A String Of Pearls." I heard Glenn say that Schillinger would be happy that Glenn called the piece by that name.

It is a standard arranging issue where the melody stands still and the harmony moves.

Glenn sat Jerry Gray down at the piano and said, "Do this," and showed him a string of pearls. Then he said, "Have the improvised choruses use the blues chord progression, then get Bobby Hackett to improvise a real classic solo and you've got a hit." Jerry did it exactly that way, and got credit and royalties as composer.

About Hackett's solo–I heard Bobby say that it sounded like a guitar exercise that he made up for himself. I've heard the solo scored in harmony for four trumpets, and at another time for five saxes, I'm told.

Tex on lead alto–Babe Russin in and out. Tex alternated alto solos with Ernie Caceres while Al Klink played tenor solos with Babe Russin.

"String of Pearls" 4 *first strain, then through Hackett's solo*

Recorded it in November of 1941, but we had been playing it for a while to the best of my recollection.[4]

#4 CHATTANOOGA CHOO CHOO

Of course, this record started the whole scene of "gold records." In 1927 however, a fellow named Gene Austin recorded "My Blue Heaven" and sold a million–that was before the depression and before gold records.

It used to be that there were two tunes to a record; you had to give both of the tunes credit for the sales I suppose. Today it is impossible as so many tunes are on one record.

"Chattanooga" 5

I have "Chattanooga" on an antique music box.[5]

Glenn put the clarinet on high F on the end–which the lead trumpet eventually got credit for.

It was a Jerry Gray arrangement, the tune was written by Mack Gordon and Harry Warren.

"OOch OOch Agoonattach." That's what Tex called it.

"Chattanooga" 6 *intro and first part*

Tell about the Russian woman wanting to know about the train effects–trombones and saxes in the introduction.[6]

#5 I GOT A GAL IN KALAMAZOO

If you've got a hit in "Chattanooga" from the first movie, then you just follow it up with sort of a sequel in the next movie. It's the same type and worked very well.[7]

Whenever I have to spell it, I have to sing it.

It was a good show piece for Tex and the Modernaires.

A Jerry Gray arrangement.

Recorded in May of 1942, after the second picture.

7 "I Got a Gal in Kalamazoo"

#6 TUXEDO JUNCTION

Recorded in February of 1940.

This was the theme song of trumpeter Erskine Hawkins.

Of course, Glenn altered it considerably–originally there were two musical thoughts going on–a saxophone line and a solo trumpet part; Glenn put them together at the same time.

There was a pretty good "cover record" right away, by Gene Krupa.

Glenn put the trombones with their plungers in front and also at the end–sort of a featured sound. Then he undoubtedly used a more logical tempo than either Hawkins or Krupa. So Glenn's sold extremely well.

Of course, it was the trombones with the plungers that made all the difference–right? When Jimmy Priddy joined the band, there was no part for him. So I saw what notes Glenn, Frankie, and I were using and filled in another note for Jimmy. I liked those notes better than mine so I gave him my part and kept the new one.[8]

8 "Tuxedo Junction"
intro and through first strain

#7 AMERICAN PATROL

Really shows a spotlight on Glenn's patriotism. It sort of points up the drum and bugle corps.

With Ray McKinley and with Jack Sperling with Tex Beneke, the arrangement became a show piece for drum solos later on.

We recorded it in April of 1942 so you can see the War was on everybody's mind, we were still in Hollywood at the time.

No particular problem recording it, just a good straight ahead arrangement.[9]

9 "American Patrol"

 # 8 LITTLE BROWN JUG

The tune first saw the light of day around 1860; no, we didn't record it at that time.

Here's an odd situation–a very simple tune, a very simple straight forward arrangement by Bill Finegan, about a three minute tune–and yet it took us about 6 hours to do it. For some unknown reason, we just couldn't get every second of it satisfactory to Glenn.

For those who believe everything in the trade papers, George Simon said that the trumpet solo was by Clyde Hurley, actually it was by Mickey McMickle.

We recorded this Bill Finegan arrangement before going into the Glen Island Casino, it was April of 1939.

"Little Brown Jug" ⑩

Legh Knowles used to do a lot of yelling on this piece, then that got picked up by Jimmy Priddy and others. Miller loved that, it showed enthusiasm.[10]

#9 PENNSYLVANIA 6-5000

Of course everybody knows that this was the phone number of the Hotel Pennsylvania in New York City.

It is a Jerry Gray arrangement, and it sold 40,000 copies in the first week–really caught on.

Glenn pulled a gag on me. It gives you a chance to hear one of my so very rare vocals.

"Pennsylvania 6-5000" ⑪

We recorded it in April of 1940, but we had been playing it on the air I believe, helping it to catch on with sales so fast when it was released.[11]

#10 SERENADE IN BLUE

Glenn recorded this in May of 1942, it was involved in the movie *Orchestra Wives*, surely *one* of the prettiest tunes we ever did.

An interesting aspect was the introduction. Glenn had both Bill Finegan and Jerry Gray write intros; Glenn specified that he wanted a sort of "classical" sound. And he had two very talented arrangers try but neither satisfied him.

So what does Glenn do but turn to a fellow who was considered to be a jazz trumpet player and swinging big band arranger–Billy May. Billy wrote an intro that worked perfectly for Glenn and went straight into Finegan's arrangement of the rest of the tune. I talked about this recently with Billy, and he said that it's amazing what you can learn by listening to classical records.

The arrangement is such a perfect example of the woodwind section with the lead clarinet plus giving Bobby Hackett a chance to spread his charm on the fill-ins.

Another thing–lots of people have arranged this beautiful number, but only one group–the Modernaires–has ever gotten the harmony out of the middle section that they did; I don't know why others haven't copied that.

12 "Serenade in Blue"

Incidentally, I love the way Pat Friday sang it in the movie.[12]

Well, those are my ten, folks, I'm sure you'll agree with my "experts" on *most* of them.[13]

13 "Moonlight Serenade"

Notice only one 'n' in Glenn.
1939

8 George Gershwin

I am to talk to you today about two *very* successful American composers: George Gershwin and Cole Porter. They were not only very successful musically, both writing music that became standard repertoire of the highest level, but furthermore, they both became extremely wealthy.

If I'm to talk about each of them, then I'll stick to Gershwin today.

Now I don't know exactly what Michael Feinstein is going to tell you (or has told you), but I know that he is a talented singer and piano player. Now I don't do either, so I'll steer my talk down an entirely different path. As there is no way for me to sing at all, I'll emphasize what directions some of the music went instrumentally.

Most of the music that Gershwin wrote was to be performed vocally, except of course "Rhapsody In Blue" and "Concerto In F." But the songs that he composed were so flexible that instrumentalists latched on to them *very* securely.

Gershwin's dates are from 1889 to 1937. He was influenced by Irving Berlin and Jerome Kern because they wrote songs that communicated so well. But Gershwin's sense of rhythm and harmonies were well ahead of his time.

The blues were an inspiration for him as can be heard throughout "Rhapsody In Blue." The long gliss on the clarinet in the very beginning could be heard accomplished by early blues players, and even the wa-wa gimmick on the trumpet was definitely because of listening to the black players around the early 1920s. I'll play a taped excerpt of "Rhapsody In Blue" for you in a couple of minutes, and I'll point these items out for you.

Gershwin's **"Rhapsody In Blue"** (1)

"Rhapsody In Blue" is Gershwin's most famous composition. He wrote it in 1923. Now I'll play a tape for you of Gershwin's rendition of the work. Gershwin is at the piano with Paul Whiteman's Orchestra in Carnegie Hall or Aeolian Hall in the Carnegie Hall Building on February 12, 1924. I haven't taped the whole work for you because of its length. But I have enough here for you to get a real feel for it and for his piano playing. And the realization that this performance helped make him a wealthy man.[1]

I was called to play in an orchestra to accompany Oscar Levant doing a performance of that. Also a buddy of mine did the solo for a couple of weeks in Radio City Music Hall when they did a salute to Gershwin (Ray Barr).

Gershwin wanted to do something a bit more of what people would think of as "classical" or "symphonic;" so he wrote his "Concerto In F." Ambitious, but I guess not as sensational as "Rhapsody In Blue." He studied very conscientiously with a fellow named Karl Goldmark who wrote operas, chorales, and orchestral and chamber works. All this time of course Gershwin was very successful writing music for Broadway.

While we still have "Rhapsody In Blue" in our minds, let me go on to another story. I suppose you figured I'd get Glenn Miller into this talk somehow. Well, Glenn and Gershwin knew one another in the early and mid thirties. They were both studying from the same teacher, a fellow named Dr. Joseph Schillinger. His approach to music was quite mathematical. You did most everything from graphs. It was OK if you were real busy and had a lot to write in a hurry. You could use a graph to get you started, then drop it and go off with your imagination in whatever direction the graph suggested. I only know this because I studied the system. But I studied from a student of his, an organist named Jesse Crawford. I did get disenchanted, however, because he wasn't as sharp with mathematics as he should have been. I would ask a question, and by the time he figured out the answer, I already had it. So I switched to a fellow named Stephan Volpe. You had to be recommended by Eddie Sauter. If he told Volpe to work with a person, then you were in. You remember Sauter? Goodman's Band and the Sauter/Finegan Orchestra.

At any rate, Gershwin and Miller were friends. Now Gershwin died in 1937, and everybody wanted to record their version of "Rhapsody In Blue." But the estate flatly refused. They said that the work would be in little pieces. After all, recordings in those days were only three minutes long. The ASCAP and the copyright people determined that Porter's estate had the entire say about the work for fifty years after Porter's death. Now if you have noticed almost to the day, United Airlines put out a commercial using that work, or pieces of it; because the fifty years after the composer's death was up in 1987, and they got on it immediately. I would suspect that they had the music already scored and everything ready to go.

Now then Miller went to the estate in 1942 and suggested he do his version of the work. They agreed to it right away saying that they knew he would do a real nice job of it. And he really did. I'll play the tape for you now, one of my favorites of Miller's records. You'll hear some lovely fill-ins by trumpeter Bobby Hackett, nice lush work by Tex Beneke on tenor sax, the sax

Miller's ② **"Rhapsody In Blue"**

section with clarinet lead as would be expected. I'll try to point out these items to you.[2]

Now a curious coincidence, Gershwin wrote "Porgy and Bess" in 1935, it was the first American opera performed at La Scala in Milan. Now the coincidence–I was working on my doctor's degree at UCLA, and most people getting such a degree feel that the dissertation is the hard part. Well, they told me to write a piece to be performed by a symphony orchestra and by a 100 piece concert band. Now the committee knew I had some things published, so I was directed to not bring in anything that was published.

Well, I had needed some music to perform as a trombone soloist, so I had chosen to use "Porgy and Bess" as a resource. I had previously written a nice legit concerto using some of this material. There was so much really good material from that opera that I could have done a whole different concerto with entirely different pieces in it. I had been performing this concerto all over Europe and everywhere. I was no dope, I knew that the music itself was enough to garner real good acceptance. Naturally I couldn't publish it because of the rules. So I brought it in to the committee all spruced up for both types of performance organizations, and I had it made.

Well, one thing more, the biggest compliment I ever got on my playing–there is a big introduction, then I come in and play the first line to the beautiful tune "I Loves You Porgy." Then I'm on a high note and the orchestra comes in. Well, I was doing it with the Honolulu Orchestra, and in a rehearsal, they played the introduction then I came in and went up high–then instead of them all coming in, there was nothing but silence. Well, the conductor stopped and said, "What happened?" They all just said in unison, "We wanted to listen." Now there's an absolutely beautiful compliment!!!

"Porgy and Bess" ③

I'll play for you just a tiny excerpt.[3]

Now just a little more on the explanation of the fact that Gershwin's music is so terribly flexible. Take a simple tune like "I Got Rhythm." The chords are easy and the form so natural that the jazz guys have composed hundreds of pieces off just that format. In case of doubt in a jam session, they just go straight into it, and play for hours.

Let me play a short sample for you–with a bit of a story. There was a concert in New York City, in 1945. It was a charity concert for the musicians' union or something. It was in the winter and the weather was just terrible. Well, the concert was going along, but suddenly a small group of excellent players couldn't get there on time. It was late at night, but the powers that be looked back stage and found two guys–but two really fine improvisers, Don Byas, a tenor sax player from the Basie Band, and Slam Stewart, a superb bass player. So they talked these two giants into coming out on the stage, just the two of them, and playing something. So they did–and with no choice, they automatically decided on "I Got Rhythm." Well, they barreled right into it and they went through chorus after chorus, three or four for the tenor, a couple on the bass, back to the tenor, and so forth. They finally decided it was enough, and played and played while pleading for help and pretty much bleeding to death. The audience saw the problem immediately, and loved them for their artistry, their courage, their endurance, and everything else. The gist of the story here is to show you that Gershwin's creativity and flexibility with this simple tune went any direction that music people wanted to take it. It served them well.[4]

❹ *Play first 2 or 3 choruses of Byas and Stewart on* **"I Got Rhythm"**

But besides that, there's a list of Gershwin's beautiful tunes that goes on and on. Consider "Embraceable You," "A Foggy Day In London Town," "But Not For Me," and on and on.

Now to close off this session, let me put on one more tape that will probably bring nostalgia back for all of us. How could you beat Nat Cole singing "Embraceable You?"[5]

❺ **"Embraceable You"**

9 Cole Porter

Artie Shaw's 1
"Begin the Beguine"

Now this time we're going to talk about Cole Porter. The tape I had on was Artie Shaw's record of "Begin the Beguine." Porter has stated that this was his favorite composition. It was written for a fairly unsuccessful (by comparison) show called *Jubilee*. Victor records called Shaw in to record Rudolf Friml's "Indian Love Call." Shaw said that his fellows loved "Begin the Beguine," and had been jamming in their free time and all. Shaw said that they would record Friml's work if Victor would let them record "Begin the Beguine." Shaw said it was a turning point in his career.[1]

Paul Smith's 2
"Night and Day"

Now let's go on to another absolute classic of Porter's. I want to show you the great flexibility of his works, how the performing musicians fell in love with these tunes and adapted them to their own style. This first one is "Night and Day." Now here is a very creative, a very inventive piano player friend of mine named Paul Smith, one of the best ever. He is using "Night and Day" to express himself in his own way.[2]

Now a little bit on Cole Porter. Remember the authenticity of facts on Porter depend a bit on what author you read.

He came from a wealthy family and was never in any financial difficulty. He entered Yale then Harvard. In Harvard, he entered the school of law but soon switched over to the school of music. It is said that he served in the French Foreign Legion. It is said that he taught gunnery to American soldiers during World War II. He married a wealthy lady and also inherited a million dollars from his grandfather.

Now what we are sure of–he wrote both the music and the lyrics, thus cashing in on double royalties.

His songs in shows were so influential that the shows started to be called after his tunes. For example, the show *Gay Divorcee* became known as the "Night and Day" show. *Taking a Chance* became known as the "Eadie Was a Lady" show. *Paris* was the "Let's Do It" show, and *Fifty Million Frenchmen* became "You Do Something To Me," and *The New Yorkers* became "Love For Sale," and on and on.

Now in the way of showing you more of what the instrumentalists will do with Porter's works, let me play for you an excerpt of trombones adapting "What Is This Thing Called Love."[3]

❸ **"What Is This Thing Called Love"**

Next I'll give you a *short* sample of my expressing myself on "Love For Sale." Would you believe I played this as a solo once where they changed the title on the printed program to "Amor a Vendre." They had to in order to get away with the title, I guess nobody at that school spoke French.[4]

❹ **"Love For Sale"**

How about a little of the greatest jazz player ever, Louis Armstrong, as he does an excerpt from "You're the Top."[5]

❺ **"You're the Top"**

Let me show you the great variety of Porter's songs by reciting just a little portion of a list. They are sort of swinging things, some real love songs, and some sort of novelty pieces.

"I Get a Kick Out Of You"
"Blow Gabriel Blow"
"I've Got You Under My Skin"
"Don't Fence Me In"
"Easy To Love"
"It's Delovely"
"Get Out Of Town"
"I Concentrate On You"
"Friendship"

There are plenty of tapes of performers taking advantage of Porter's talents on his tune "Just One of Those Things." So, I'll close off this chat with again referring to Louis Armstrong.[6]

❻ *Armstrong singing and playing* **"Just One of Those Things"**

10 Dixieland

Two kinds of Dixieland jazz–Early New Orleans and Chicago Style. The differences have diminished today and so most people (including the players themselves) just say Dixieland.

The reason for the diminishing of differences is because today's players have lived through the many stages of jazz that have taken place since the Dixieland styles were the only way to play. They have heard, and mabe even played, Swing, Bop, Cool, Funky, and so forth. All this becomes part of their own musical personalities, their own means of expressing.

Now let me show you very simply these differences: the early players marched along (with spirit) and they did this in a flat four rhythm.

tape of Early New Orleans ❶

tape of Chicago Style ❷

Now the players just sort of play whatever comes naturally to them.[1]

Then they started to hire piano players. These ragtime players had been playing "um-chuck." They influenced the rhythm. (Change in instrumentation).[2]

Now let's jump up to about 1927–Babe Ruth hit 60 home runs; Lindbergh flew the Atlantic Ocean; Gene Tunney and a long count finished Jack Dempsey; Jack Teagarden arrived in New York City from Vernon, Texas; the "Jazz Age," as F. Scott Fitzgerald called it, was really cooking; the Flapper era was in.

This brand of Dixieland jazz that caught on so definitely became called Chicago Style jazz even though the pioneers, the innovators, were surely New Orleans bred. Even though the gangsters ran Chicago with Eliott Ness chasing Al Capone around, it was definitely a happy time for the public. In fact, usually the musicians call Dixieland "happy music." Remember all this came on before the depression, people really celebrated the good times. And they still do. When people hear Dixieland music, it feels happy, even frivolous to them, time to have a good time, to loosen up.

Of course, the Dixieland bands played what they and their followers knew, and as a consequence, they played a lot of church music. What a lot of people don't realize is that much more of the beginnings of jazz came out of religious services than out of the red light district. In the houses, mainly, there were piano players playing ragtime. Some Dixieland standard tunes were church tunes, tunes like "A Closer Walk With Thee."[3]

3 "A Closer Walk With Thee"

And that all-time favorite, "When the Saints Go Marching In."[4]

4 "When the Saints Go Marching In"

Once upon a time there was a band called the Dorsey Brothers Band. They still felt like clinging to Dixie a bit even though the band was larger. The brass section was a bit unusual–one trumpet and three trombones. The one trumpet player (George Thow) ended up with Lawrence Welk. One of the trombone players was also an arranger–his name was Glenn Miller. Glenn had organized a band for them. Then when the two brothers couldn't get along, Jimmy kept that band and Glenn helped Tommy use the Joe Haymes Band. But the point is that the Dorsey Brothers Band had a boy singer named Bob Crosby.

Now when a group of fellows from Ben Pollack's Band got started, they needed a leader. This was a cooperative band, run mainly by a fellow named Gil Rodin. They weren't as enthusiastic about Bob Crosby's singing as they were about his attitude, enthusiasm, and his family connections. So, this band came up when bands were getting bigger, and it was known for its big band Dixieland; exactly what Bob Crosby had been weaned on with the Dorsey Brothers Band.[5]

5 "Palesteena"

In spite of the fact that we went into the era of big bands, Dixieland never slowed a bit. Some of this is because talented people like Bobby Hackett and Jack Teagarden could get together.[6]

6 "That's A-Plenty"

Good players like Al Hirt made good records.[7]

7 "Down By the Riverside"

The public liked it, they thought it was fun, they still do, and, the musicians enjoy it.

Almost all the big bands had a small band within the band. We all know about Goodman's trio, quartet, and so on. We know of Artie Shaw's Gramercy Five. But most of these little bands played Dixieland–Tommy Dorsey's Tailgate Seven, Bob Crosby's Bob cats, and so on.

I personally am glad you continue to enjoy Dixieland jazz because I sure do.

Let me finish this little talk with some real good music by Pete Fountain.[8-10]

8 "Muskrat Ramble"

9 "12th Street Rag"

10 "Won't You Come Home Bill Bailey"

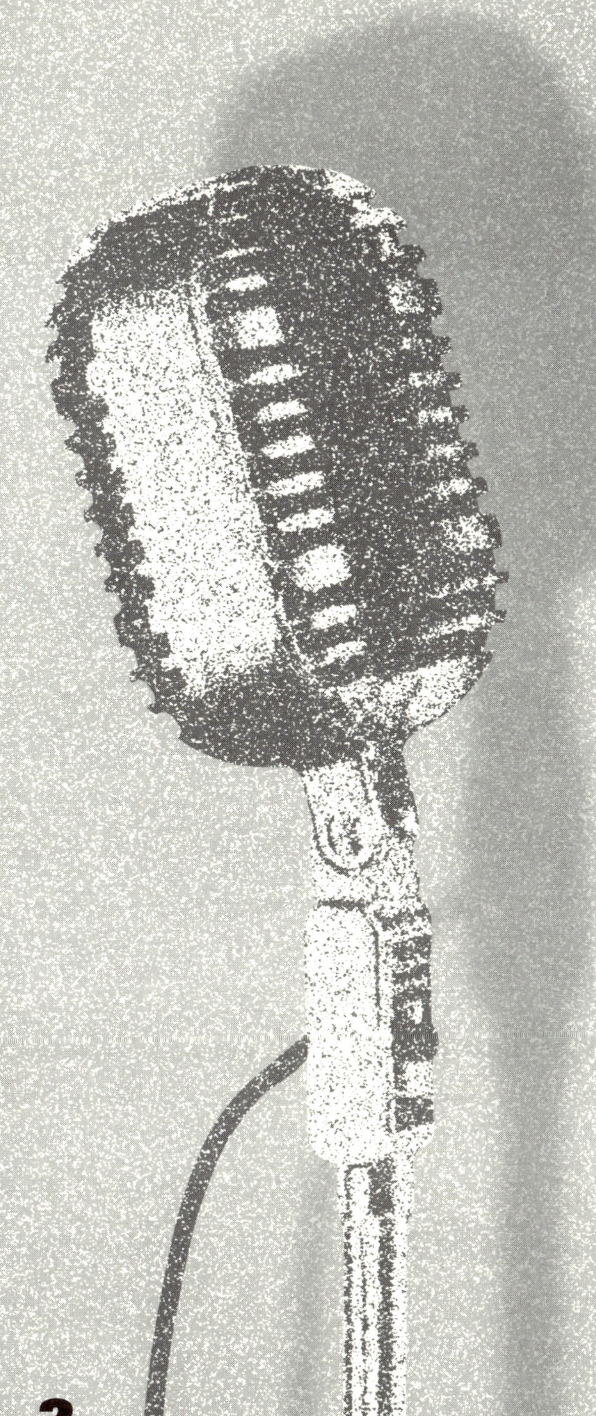

PART 2

INTERVIEWS

Just One (More) Question 11

It Never Fails:

At the end of every presentation,
At the end of every interview,
At the end of every anything …

And what would YOU ask?

Questions you always wanted to ask but never had the chance.

12 First Interview with David Heagerty

DH Just to ask you a couple of intro things, and then we'll get into some of those questions that I sent you.

With us is one who played a special role in the Glenn Miller Orchestra, Doctor Paul Tanner, a jazz author and jazz authority who contributed some great trombone sounds in the Miller Band 1938 to 1942.

PT Thank you very much, glad to be here.

DH Here with us again on our annual salute to Glenn Miller is Doctor Paul Tanner who was an outstanding member of that famous orchestra's trombone section from 1938 to 1942. Nice to have you with us, Paul.

PT Well I'm glad to be here. Thank you.

DH We want to welcome again Doctor Paul Tanner who played great trombone in the Glenn Miller Orchestra for four years from September 1938 until that historic band broke up in September 1942. Again, it's nice to have you on our show, Paul.

PT Thank you very much.

DH Paul, I believe you played in all of Glenn Miller's Victor Bluebird records.

PT That's right, all of them.

DH How many were there?

PT Well, I don't know, must have been three or four.

DH At least.

PT No, there were …

DH About three or four a week if I remember correctly.

PT In fact, when we'd have a record session, the standard thing to do was to record four tunes. But some times you only got in three, some times five or six. But we had so many record dates that we had no way to keep count. I have to look it up in the John Flower book or some place.

DH What about Paul Tanner, tell us about yourself. Where did you grow up and what happened to you in your formative years?

PT Well, I was born in Skunk Hollow–Skunk Hollow, Kentucky; you know where that is? That's the truth though, it's right across the road from Pumpkin Ridge where my brother Slim was born. So everybody knows where it is. You know, I went and found it once; and it's not a town, it's a house. It was called Pole Cat Hollow, then they cleaned it up and called it Skunk Hollow. But I left there when I was about six inches high and went to Delaware, Virginia then Delaware. My dad was in education at that time. He became the superintendent of the state reformatory there in Delaware. So I was raised in a boys' reform school. And that's actually where I learned to play, the guys in the reform school got me started on the trombone. They showed me the slide positions and everything,

DH That was your original instrument, the trombone?

PT Well, yeah; there are six brothers in our family. My dad went to Cincinnati Conservatory as a piano student. That was after he graduated from Mankato State in Minnesota, and played four years of college football before they used padding. So, he was a piano player. We all had to work up a certain amount of proficiency on the piano; then after that, we could take off on any instrument that we wanted to. I worked real hard on the piano because I wanted to get to the trombone before any of my other brothers did.

DH Did you?

PT Yeah, sure did.

DH Your brothers are musical too?

PT There were six of us, they all tried to be professional players, it ended up that three could and three couldn't. Two of them are still playing very well today. But David, the others guys either kind of wanted to start at the top or they didn't have the ambition to practice or something.

DH Practice is tough.

PT Practice is tough.

DH How did you get into the band business as a professional?

PT Well, my brothers and I formed our own band and we went out on the road. We played a lot of gambling clubs in the south in Atlanta and Florida and places like that that had gambling clubs. So we made a lot of friends but we didn't make any money, so the band eventually had to break up. I went with somebody and kept on going.

DH What was your path to the Glenn Miller Orchestra?

PT Well, my brothers and I were playing in a place in Georgia and we just didn't have anything else to go to. Then Frank Dailey came to town. Frank Dailey owned the Meadowbrook in Cedar Grove, New Jersey; and whoever played there was on the air constantly, they got a lot of air time. So my brothers and I thought, well, we'll get Dailey to come out and hear us, and if he puts us in the Meadowbrook, we got it made. If he doesn't put us in the Meadowbrook, we'll break up. That's all there was to it. So he came out and heard the band, and all he said was, "Well, I'll take the trombone player." So there I go, and the band broke up. So I went up with Frank. And he sold his band to Buddy Rogers. Did you know that?

DH No, I didn't know that.

PT Well, he sold his band to Buddy Rogers.

DH Is that *the* Buddy Rogers?

PT That's right, Buddy Rogers, the movie star, had a band. Rogers said, "OK, that's just fine. I'll buy the band." But he wanted it the way he heard it. Now he heard the band before I was with the band, so Frank Dailey had to hire two or three guys back again that he had let go and had to let go some of us that were there. So there I was in Cedar Grove, New Jersey, and no job.

Well, if you are in the East in the summertime and you're a young musician, the thing for you to do is to go to Atlantic City. Because in Atlantic City, there were a half a dozen name bands that came through there every week. Sometimes they're looking for somebody. Besides that, Atlantic City, in those years, this was 1938, was loaded with small clubs. And you could walk into some club and play, and maybe they would feed you, and eventually maybe somebody would hire you. So some musicians talked the owner into hiring me in this joint I was in, a place called The Swing Club. And what it was was a strip joint. I got to where I only recognized the girls from the back. Here I am playing pretty tunes like "In a Persian Market" and all kinds of nice things, and the girls are stripping. Like I say, I only recognized them from the back.

Glenn came to town, he had just started organizing his band, the band that he kept; he did have a band before that. So he was looking for a trombone player. I never found out who it was, but somebody told him, "Why don't you go down to this joint and hear this kid play?" I was a kid once. So he came on down there. And here's Glenn and his wife–the wrong people in that kind of a scraggy joint. She's sitting there with white gloves on and the girls didn't have anything on. So he listened to me play some pretty things with high notes and all. And when we took a break, he called me over to his table. I knew who he was, because he was doing what I wanted to do, big time trombone player and arranger. So, he called me over and said, "I want to talk to you about your high register." So he told me a couple of very nice things. Then he asked, "How long are you going to be here?" I was making fifteen dollars a week, that was pretty good for me. In fact, the owner paid me fifteen dollars a week, but I had to pay five dollars to the union; so each of the other five guys in the band each contributed a dollar. Bless them, they were only making eighteen dollars, and it brought mine back up to fifteen. So Glenn asked, "How soon can you come with me?" And I said, "I could come right now, I'm packed already, 'cause this is all the clothes I've got." I had my white suit on, that was all I had. And I showed him, I had my toothbrush in my pocket. His wife, before she passed away, told the story about that; she said that it took me a half hour to say that because I stammered so badly. I couldn't hardly talk then, you can see I make up for it now.

DH Yes, you do.

PT I babble on, don't I?

DH It's great, you're doing fine.

PT So this was in the Summer of '38, I came with him then. He had just started, so I only missed about a month or so. So there I am.

DH I think when you joined the band, there were just three in the trombone section, weren't there?

PT Well, there was Glenn, there was Al Mastren, and myself. My first night with the band was at Wildwood, New Jersey. They left Atlantic City and went on to Wildwood, and Glenn told the guy he had to go home. And here I am. I moved very slowly then, I get around fine now, but that's how come I got the name Lightnin', because I moved so slowly. Glenn really pinned that on me. But the guys in the band–you know, I walked up to the front door of the ballroom; the guys were getting out their instruments and everything. All around the ballroom there were chairs, folding chairs; and the guys had taken the trouble to push back the seats of every folding chair except one, knowing that this slow lazy cat was going to walk up to that one chair and sit down. And so I did. I walked up to it and sat down, and they had fixed it. I collapsed. All six foot-three of me all over the floor, arms and legs flying! The guys in the band just cracked up! But you see, you don't mind being the butt of a gag; at least, you're recognized. They all laughed. Glenn said, "Get out your horn, Lightnin', come on up and play with us." So I did.

And there were only three trombones. The very first night I was with the band, I was standing up there and I was at a microphone with Glenn and Al Mastren; we were faking three part harmony on some dumb thing like "Flat Foot Floogie" or something and Tex was on some other mike playing a solo and we were faking three part harmony. So that endeared me to Glenn a little bit that I could do that. But you see, I had been arranging, so I knew chords and things like that. So I got off on the right foot with him, and it lasted about four and a half years. It worked out well.

DH That's great.

PT I do babble now, don't I?

DH After the Miller Band broke up, Paul, what happened to you, where did you go next?

PT When Glenn broke up, the whole trombone section went with Charlie Spivak, and that was a lot of fun. It was a good band. It had—Davey Tough was playing drums, Willie Smith was playing alto, Neal Hefti was in the trumpet section, Nelson Riddle was playing trombone, so we went to four trombones, so it was a good band. And Charlie was such a good player. But you know, it was a funny thing, Glenn's band was so precise, and it was kind of fun being with Charlie because it was so loose. The first thing we did was to play a stage show, play a theater with him. And here the trumpets are down in front so Charlie could stand there and play with them, and the trombones are in the back. Well, I went to Charlie right the first show and said, "Charlie, if you want us to play with the trumpets during the ensemble, we can't hear them because they are in front of our bells, our trombone bells, so we couldn't hear them to follow them." So Charlie said, "Do you want me to put the trumpets behind you?" I said, "Yeah." So, the next show, the trumpets were behind us, and I heard the trumpets. And after Glenn's section with McMickle and Zeke Zarchy and Billy May and Johnny Best,

I went back to Charlie and said, "Put the trumpets down in front of us again." But Charlie was a good guy. A beautiful sound. I was a loud trombone player; so Charlie, during one show, turned around to me and played one of those pretty solos straight at me and pretty nearly blew me off my chair. He said,"You think you can play loud?" He just wiped me out completely. Charlie was a good guy. So, after Charlie, I went into the army. I knew I was going to go in, the army knew I was going to go in, so they said "Gotcha." So I went into the army. Then when I came out of the army, I went with Les Brown. I stayed with Les until Tex got started with the Glenn Miller Band again. Then I stayed on the road with Tex for six more years. So actually, including the time I was in the army, I was on the road for seventeen years, that's a long time.

DH Did you play at all in the service?

PT I played all the time. They offered me that Officer's Training School, so I called my dad who was a colonel in the army. And I said, "What do you think I ought to do?" He said, "You want to play afterwards?" I said, "Sure." So he said, "Then don't take OCS, keep on playing." So that's what I did.

I thought I had a deal set up where I was going to be the head of a jazz band at this big air force base in Delaware; and my wife was the head of the rationing board. So I went ahead and volunteered. I wasn't all that eager, but I knew I was going to go in, so I figured I'd get a good thing set. So I asked Glenn,"Please don't request me because you'll goof me up." So he said, "OK, but you will play for me after the war." So I said, "Yeah, that's right."

So I went on in. At the very time I went in, they were organizing a band, an orchestra, to be in New York City, and it took precedence over everything else. So, my duty, I had to do basic training, but then after that, all I had to do, I had an apartment in New York City, and I played propaganda radio programs, I played movies, I played V-discs, I played every kind of music. That's all I did. I'd call up on the phone and say, "Where am I supposed to be?" They'd say, "Well, you're at CBS at two o'clock." And that was it, that was my army career.

DH You did that the whole time?

PT Yeah, the whole time I was in.

DH When you left the Miller civilian band, who else went with you?

PT Jimmy Priddy and Frank D'Anolfo. The three of us went on over there, and Nelson Riddle was already there.

DH That gave you a very strong trombone section.

PT Oh, we had a lot of fun. And we made a lot of connections. When I finally quit traveling and came out here to Los Angeles, here's Nelson Riddle already doing well, Billy May's out here doing well, Neal Hefti is out here doing very well, Sonny Burke who was doing an awful lot of writing for Spivak, was already vice-president of Decca. I couldn't miss; these guys kept me so busy, I didn't have time to do everything. And yet I enrolled as a freshman at UCLA.

DH You did?

PT Yeah. Well, two days after I got my union card, I went on the staff of the American Broadcasting Company, and I stayed there sixteen years.

DH And did studio work for ABC?

PT Yeah, also I did freelancing every place, but I had that income from the staff. Some times they didn't even use me and they had to pay me for a full week. But what they do is that they pay you for the privilege of first call on your time. But besides that, I enrolled at UCLA. I had to drop out for three years because the ABC staff said, "We're going to need you every day now from ten to two. It was a terrible show that was on at that time and they wanted the staff orchestra to play for it; so it was bad enough to where it lasted three years. And just as soon as it went off, I went back and finished up and got my bachelor's degree. And as soon as I got the bachelor's degree, I went straight on the faculty. Then I went and got the Master's and the Doctorate,

DH Gee, that's great. And how long were you at UCLA?

PT I taught there twenty-three years. That was on the faculty, that doesn't include being an undergraduate. I didn't even know they had a retirement system until I had been teaching about ten years. It's a nice thing, it really is; it worked out fine.

DH And you authored a book, a textbook, I understand.

PT Yeah, actually I've got fifteen or twenty books; but they're technical things, how to do this on the trombone. And I put together a lot of exercises and things like that. But this book that you're talking about is a textbook on the history of jazz, and it's doing very well. I got a great deal of help from a talented young fellow named David Megill, just a very bright man, and a lot of fun too.

DH Did you have a particular style of play, Paul, or was there anybody that you kind of modeled yourself after as a young fellow when you were just getting into the business?

PT There are an awful lot of them. Naturally, I tried to imitate the last guy I heard. I still think that Jack Teagarden is the best thing that ever happened to jazz trombone. But then for other guys playing, there is no way to beat Dorsey or Will Bradley. I'll tell you a funny story about Bradley who's real name is Wilbur Schwichtenberg. People don't know nearly enough about Bradley. I remember that we played Madison Square Garden, and they put our band, and Tommy Dorsey's Band, and Will Bradley's Band together. All these bands were together, like all the trombones together, all the trumpets, like with Berigan and all were together, all the saxes. The problem was what to do with the three drummers. Now there was McKinley who was working for Bradley, and Buddy Rich was working for Tommy Dorsey, and we had Mo Purtill. Well, Buddy Rich of course was so good, but such an ego that it was kind of hard to like him, but he was such a good drummer. They flipped a coin and Rich ended up in the back row with the coin flip and everybody was glad. Of course, also, he would push the band from back there. Well, Oliver Nelson or Sl Oliver or someone had written a thing for three trombones, a terribly hard thing. And Dorsey and Bradley and Miller were to play it as a trio, and the band was to play an accompaniment for them. And when Glenn came back, it was such a terribly hard thing, I figured Dorsey was going to play lead. Glenn said, "Bradley rescued us! He played the lead for us so we could get through it." That's the opinion they had of Bradley. Of course Miller knew his playing from the Ray Noble days. He had organized the Ray Noble Band for him.

DH Was he a pretty good player, Glenn?

PT A very good player, a very underrated player. You see, he didn't feature himself because he knew that if he featured himself playing ballads, he'd end up second to Tommy Dorsey, and he knew that. And if he featured himself playing jazz things, he'd end up second to Teagarden, and he knew that; and he loved the way those guys played. So, that wasn't for Glenn to end up second. But the guy, you know, he played in tune, he had a good register, hardly ever missed a note, good interpretation. I don't know what people would want from a trombone player when they say that maybe he wasn't so good a trombone player. He himself didn't think he was as good as some other guys, but boy, he was a good trombone player. He was the best trombone player in his band, I'll tell you that.

DH I understand that you have a very excellent register, or had one when you were playing.

PT Well, I stopped playing maybe ten years ago.

DH You don't play at all now?

PT No, I don't even have a horn now. I sold it to a Japanese fellow who walked in here a little while ago and asked me how much I wanted for it. So I autographed it and sold it to him–at a slight profit.

DH Good for you.

PT He was a good guy. I said, "What are you going to do with it? You don't play trombone." He said, "Put it on exhibition in Tokyo somewhere." So, I said, "OK, fine." I don't even have a horn now.

DH I heard that when you joined the band, or shortly after you joined the band, that you were known for your high register. But that they placed you in the section, so that you were kind of in the lower end. And somebody said that this broadened your range considerably. Do I have that right?

PT Yes. That's what I said. In fact, I was concerned at first, and I went to Glenn and asked him about it. He said, "Look, nobody needs a lopsided trombone player." Because I didn't have a very good low register at all and I did have a high register. So he said, "Nobody needs a lopsided trombone player, I'm doing this as a favor to you." He was right. I never did lose the upper register, but I did build up the low register. The only time I used it with Glenn's Band was–I remember a couple of times we did stage shows where we had to play this tune called "Smoke Rings," things like that that had a very high trombone solo. So I was the guy that played it. Now that wasn't something we would record. We just played it for a stage show.

DH Paul, anything that you might have recorded that would feature that high register?

PT Well, I've done a lot since then, but nothing with Glenn's band.

DH Did you kind of mix your career of being a professor and also playing? Were you able to do that as you went along?

PT At first, when I went on the faculty, I would have conflictions that were unbelievable. I had to figure out which way I am going to go when there's a confliction. At first, I went with the playing. Then later on, I got terribly involved in teaching; and I figured that when I had a confliction, I owed allegiance to the university, so I stuck with that. But the people who hired me, like Nelson Riddle and people like that, understood and it was perfectly all right. You do recording at all wild hours. I saw to it that all my classes were in the morning, so I was free in the afternoon and evening. I knew that sometimes, like a date with Frank Sinatra, started at eleven-thirty at night. I was already in bed. Nelson called up and said to come down to Capitol, this was when Sinatra was recording for Capitol. I said, "OK." Sinatra wants to record. I put on some clothes and dashed down there. According to the union scale, at twelve, your scale is doubled; and then after three hours, you have to multiply everything you're doing by three. So here I am starting at eleven-thirty, and by two-thirty, I'm starting to get six times my salary. You know something, I didn't care, I'd drink coffee all night, it was all right with me. And we went through a whole gang of different tunes. And would you believe it, Sinatra sang one thing after another. He's a real good guy to work for, he loves the musicians and everything is just fine, without a complaint. But he went through several tunes, never did record a note. And we looked back there in the back, and there he's got a girl friend sitting back there who he's singing to. That's what the whole thing was about. That's a beautiful thing. But then I've done some work with the Beach Boys that, you've probably heard of a piece called "Good Vibrations." I invented an electronic instrument and, anybody could have done it 'cause I have trouble changing a light bulb. But I invented this thing and I was the only guy who had it. I've since sold it, because this was before synthesizers. They called up the house and they talked to my wife. They said, "We need Doctor Tanner tonight." She said, "He's got a record date tonight." And they said, "How late will he be?" She knew who I was working for and she knew that the guy I was working for never heard of overtime. So she said, "He'll be recording from eight to eleven tonight, and then he's through." And they said, "Ours will start at eleven-thirty, so come when he can." And those guys, they don't care about the clock. It doesn't mean anything to them, they just record when they feel like it. Brian Wilson had this whole set-up in his home, a sixteen track thing and he had an engineer on call who just worked for him, that's all he did. So we go there and we record all night long and just put pieces together. Then they'd call you back in a few nights and put some more pieces together; and the first thing you know they've got a thing called "Good Vibrations." Somebody made a buck on that one, but it's a good record, it really is. It's a versatile record.

DH What about records? How did you feel about? Did you enjoy the record making process?

PT Most of the time, yes. With Glenn, you had to be a little more careful because he was such a perfectionist, you were a little more careful. You get with other guys, and as I got older, I got a little looser. You start to relax. You just play the best you can, that's a habit you get into. You play the best you can and that's the best you can do. And that's the feeling you get; instead of "God, I hope I don't make a mistake." No, you just hope you're playing well, that's all

DH Well, technology had something to do with that too, didn't it? I mean, when you were back in the Miller days, if you made a mistake, you had to do it all over again and so forth?

PT Oh yeah, in fact that thing that they invented called "direct to disc," that's the way we did it in the ancient caveman days. But it's true, if they had to make another take, you hoped that they didn't do it because of you. Now I've seen it happen where they had to do it because of me. I remember one time we were recording something with Glenn. The brass section were in cup mutes up around a microphone. Now I don't know if it was "Danny Boy" or what we were recording. And I'm playing along and my fingernail hit the bell of my horn as I went by, you know, and so I didn't think anything about it. The guy in the booth started screaming at the drummer, "Don't play a cymbal there, my goodness, what are you doing!!!" And I never told him. Poor Mo.

DH Did you notice a lot of differences in playing with Glenn and with other bands?

PT Oh yeah, surely.

DH With Charlie or some others?

PT Oh yeah, it was a lot looser with other bands. With Les Brown–Les was fairly subtle and held down a bit. Les is the kind of fellow who can let himself get real loose. Spivak's Band, the guys would get real loose anyway, that's the kind of players he had in that band, it was very relaxed. And then after I got out here, you were treated differently, you were as if you were a real good player. Like one time I told Nelson Riddle, "Gee, it's awfully nice of you to have me on the dates." He said, "What do you mean? I just get the best guys I can." Which is really nice. He even took me on some trips with Nat Cole. And he would take Lester Young's brother, Lee, Lee Young playing drums. And he'd take me along to hold the thing together because he had written some dastardly trombone parts. And we would go to San Francisco and places like that to play concerts with Nat Cole; and he knew the trombone parts would be taken care of and also the rhythm section. He'd also take Bill Miller on piano, 'cause Bill played so much like Nat Cole that he played a lot of Nat Cole solos on Nat Cole records when Nat was singing and couldn't get to the piano. Bill Miller would play them and everybody would think they were hearing Nat Cole. And that's a pretty good thing for Bill because Nat was a fine player.

DH I think that Legh Knowles told me once that he was Bill Miller's roommate with Red Norvo.

PT I bet that was a scene, because Bill is a little spooky. All due respects to Bill if you are listening.

DH Yeah, he had some rather interesting stories to tell.

PT Bill, in the army, walked around with these two great big white dogs on leashes. If you think that's not G.I., you're right. He couldn't hardly salute when he was holding on to these two dogs. A fine player. If you have run out of questions, I haven't run out of stories.

DH Sweet? Swing? Vocals? Instrumental? Did you have any preferences?

PT That's fairly easy, the ballads. Things like "Rhapsody In Blue," "Spring Will Be So Sad This Year," which didn't even become a hit, I thought it was one of the prettiest things I ever heard. "Serenade In Blue," things that Bobby Hackett played, things like that, those had to be my favorites. The sax section was absolutely gorgeous, and then you put in somebody like the Modernaires; boy, they were good, really were. A lost art I guess.

DH Yeah, there were people like Tommy Traynor, people who are doing the Modernaires now were at that last night and just some fun things, "Juke Box Saturday Night."

PT Paula Kelly Junior?

DH And Paula Kelly Junior, yep.

PT You know it's very seldom a girl gets called "Junior."

DH Yes, it is.

PT PK is very nice and so is Paula, Paula is a gem.

DH You didn't have very many ladies in the band, did you?

PT No.

DH Marion Hutton, I guess, and her replacement.

PT Yeah, that's right, when Marion decided to have a baby, somebody else got to get in.

DH I think Paula was one of those, she replaced Dorothy Claire as I recall.

PT And gosh, the girl who sang "Wheel Of Fortune."

DH Kay Starr?

PT Yeah, Kay Starr came in and she did "Baby Me" and a couple of things like that. I liked Kay Starr; in fact, I still do.

DH Did you ever perform with her after that?

PT Well, no, no I didn't. But she was on one of those Glenn Miller reunion things. And she sings well today. But Glenn stole Dorothy Claire from Bobby Byrne, trombone player. Then Dorothy didn't work out. The thing that Glenn did–if he had Marion Hutton there who he knew wasn't the world's best singer, OK; but boy, you couldn't have a prettier girl on the bandstand. Now it's pretty rare when you get a pretty girl like Helen O'Connell who can also sing well. But Marion sang better as she went along, and before she passed away, she was singing pretty well. But she was such an attraction; guys would stand around and just drool at this pretty girl. But Ray Eberle was a good singer, Skip Nelson was a good singer, and the Modernaires were fantastic.

DH I wanted to ask you a little bit, Paul, about the arrangers in the band. Miller had a reputation of being a great arranger himself, and some of the people that he had doing the arranging were certainly highly regarded folks. I just wondered what your thoughts were on that aspect of the band.

PT Well, Glenn certainly was a fine arranger. But he just got too busy. He was unbelievably busy taking care of business. He was a fine business man as well as a fine musician. So he hired two people who were just excellent. He hired Bill Finegan and Jerry Gray and they were the mainstays. He would buy other stuff, but they were the mainstays. Jerry

Gray, he showed himself off to Glenn with Artie Shaw's "Begin the Beguine." And Glenn said, "Wow, we ought to get this guy to write for us." So he did; and you get "String Of Pearls," "Pennsylvania Six-Five Thousand," a whole gang of other things. But Bill Finegan was the guy who floored me. The first thing that Bill sent to the band, I remember, we were up in Boston, we rehearsed it. I think it was "My Blue Heaven." It was so over-arranged I couldn't believe it. He had everything in there, he had the kitchen sink in there. You know, everything but the kitchen sink, he had the kitchen sink in there. What Glenn had to do was to go through the whole thing bar by bar and take stuff out. He just over-arranged, he was trying to show Glenn what he could do, so he threw everything in. And then Bill wasn't very happy about being told what to do and what not to do because he was a very creative fellow. He knew that he was writing well. And he went right straight out of that writing stuff for Tommy Dorsey and anybody. He teaches now back at Connecticut, at a university back there. But he was a fine arranger, especially with ballads, he is just excellent, such beautiful harmonies he came up with.

DH Do you remember some stuff that he did, some particular tunes?

PT Most of the ballads were Bill's. And he would get together with the Modernaires and check out what chords they wanted to use and so forth in the accompaniment behind them. Most of the ballads he did.

DH How about Billy May?

PT Well, Billy was a wild man, and he still is. He could do things that would show off a lot, that would give the band some kind of "tang" it didn't have before, some kind of spice that it really needed, especially that's the way Bill played. He played kind of wild after being with the Charlie Barnet Band for a while. So he wrote some very interesting things that would really swing well. In fact, when people would say sometimes that the band was stiff and didn't swing, they didn't hear some of the things we did, especially later on in the band, "Johnny Comes Marching Home," and "Volga Boatman," they moved very well, they really did.

DH Who were some of the members of the Miller Band who, in your view, were unusually gifted or talented?

PT Well, of course, we had the best lead trumpet there was, Mickey McMickle. Then Billy May added a lot of spice to the trumpet section.

But then you also had reliable guys like Zeke Zarchy in there. And then there was Johnny Best, you couldn't get any warmer sound, like Louis Armstrong lines with Johnny Best. So the trumpet section was loaded with talent. And then in the saxes, Wil Schwartz with that sound he got on the clarinet. Then Glenn was always able to get good lead alto players. After McIntyre left, a couple of guys came in and tried, but they were just too scared to play, that's all, because they were good players. But Al Klink was a fine jazz tenor player. People say that he didn't get enough to play. He got enough to play in that as soon as the band broke up, everybody wanted him. He went immediately with Goodman and people like that, so they heard him. And, of course, Tex was very talented. I liked Tex better on ballads, such a good ear. And they had Ernie Caceres in there, a good jazz clarinet player, good baritone player, lots of talent in there.

DH Rhythm section?

PT They kept time and that was their job. In a ballroom with ten thousand people in it, you need four guys to keep time; and that's what they did, and they did it well. A guy named Trigger Alpert on bass, he kept things moving very well; he and Mo were good friends. Mo Purtill got criticized a lot. He wasn't a Buddy Rich. The thing people don't know about Mo is that he did exactly what he was told, and he did it well. And he just kept time, that was their job, nothing flashy.

DH How about the singers? You mentioned some of them, did you have any favorites among them?

PT The Modernaires of course. Paula Kelly, I had a crush on Paula. She was awfully good in there. What a lot of people don't know about the Modernaires is that Chuck Goldstein sang the lead part in falsetto before guys started singing falsetto; now everybody, all the Rock singers and all sing falsetto. But nobody was doing that, and Chuck sang falsetto and sang the lead over the Modernaires. Then when Marion would sing with them, Chuck would sing the bottom part, very flexible guy. You know, when the Modernaires first came with the band, the first night that they were with the band, we were at the Hotel Pennsylvania on the job until say one o'clock. Well, along about twelve-thirty, Glenn looks over and says, "Where are the Mods?" I had to tell him, "They caught the last train to New Jersey." So they left. Man, did they get a lecture the next night! "This is a job, this is a business. You were hired until one o'clock. You work out your transportation however you want to, but you are on this job until the job is over. This is what it's all about." So they never left early again. But we went out of the hotel, and the first thing we did was on the train, a train ride somewhere. And the Modernaires were new to us. We had heard them with Paul Whiteman and bands like that doing things with Jack Teagarden like "Aunt Hagar's Blues" and things like that. Just great things, "Jamboree Jones," things like that. And so the first night out on the train, those poor guys were in the men's room on the train, and they sang all night long. Tex sang Teagarden's parts and they sang a capella all night long. The rest of us just stood there and we were gassed by it because they were so good, so in tune. So, I thought they were so good.

DH Did Paula Kelly stay with them throughout the whole tenure from the time they joined the band until it broke up?

PT No, she was with her husband Hal Dickinson, but she wasn't singing in the band.

DH She wasn't?

PT No.

DH How about as part of the group?

PT No.

DH No?

PT No, not until Marion was off having a baby.

DH Well, afterwards, when Marion came back, she got her job back, huh?

PT Yeah.

DH Did Paula continue to perform with the group or what?

PT No, it was a four-way group, four guys. What they had Paula for was to sing Marion's parts, like on "Chattanooga Choo Choo," things like that.

DH Right.

PT But Paula is so good, all you've got to do is listen to a record called "I Know Why," and things like that. That's a good tune too.

DH It's wonderful.

PT Ray was a good singer, Ray Eberle.

DH He had never sung before, before he joined the band? Is that the story?

PT In those days, they often hired a guy's brother. If a guy was good, they figured his brother was good. The Dorsey Brothers were crazy about

Bing Crosby, so they hired Bob Crosby, he sang with them. Then Bob Crosby went out with his own band. Glenn hired Ray Eberle because Bob Eberly was so good. And then there was Marion Hutton; Betty Hutton was a big star, so he hired Marion Hutton who was a lot prettier than Betty Hutton. She didn't have that voice, but that happens. Glenn hired the trombone player that he started out with who was in my chair, Jack Jenny's kid brother. And he didn't play worth anything according to Glenn, so he let him go right away. But Ray had this problem. Bob Eberly was really a good singer, fine singer, so people compared Ray to Bob. Well, Ray did exactly what he was told. Glenn would say "Sing it this way," and that's the way Ray would sing it. That's what he was paid to do. And if he varied from that, Glenn would let him know about it. That's all there was to it. So he was a good singer, then they got in Skip Nelson. Glenn "borrowed" him from Chico Marx's Band, and he was in there the next night after Ray left. Chico Marx said, "Take this guy."

DH And he was pretty good, was he?

PT He was a good singer, a good singer, a little on the Billy Eckstine side. There was a fellow later on with Tex, Glenn Davis, who sang a lot like Billy Eckstine.

DH Who were some of the fun guys, the cut-ups, the comics, the guys who kept everybody loose, who were those guys?

PT Well, we didn't have an awful lot of that.

DH I guess you wouldn't with Glenn.

PT No, Willie was about as loose as anybody. I remember when one time we were playing in Green Bay, Wisconsin. And we got there early, and here we were on a lake in canoes. We all knew what was going to happen. So, I said to Willie, "We'll take your clarinet," (he carried his clarinet with him). So, I said that we'll take it in our canoe. And sure enough, Willie tips over. Now he had on his outfit to play in that night, and he here is, he's sopping wet. So, the manager, Johnny O'Leary, had to go out and he bought him a shirt and a pair of socks, and had his pants and coat pressed the best he could, and bought dry underwear. But he couldn't do anything at all about the shoes. So, every time Willie took a step, you'd get "squash, squash, squash, squash." And Glenn never let him up for it either. But he didn't give him a bad time, just teased him. Well, things like that would happen to Willie. Peck's Bad Boy. They called him "the Jersey Cupie Doll."

DH Have you kept up with the guys who played in that band over the years?

PT Well, this is not a very nice thing to say, but they're disappearing. The guys are all in their mid-seventies. But also, as you know, I live about a hundred miles south of Los Angeles, so I don't see them too often. Every now and then, I'll come across Zeke who is still very active–Zeke Zarchy. I called Willie the other day. I see Tex now and then because he lives up the road here in Costa Mesa. In fact, for a while, I was doing all Tex's work with him. But other than that, I don't see the guys very much. Whenever you work with Tex, you usually see Rolly–Rolly Bundock. Other than that, you drift apart, you've got different directions going. But you know, musicians are weird–every time they see one another, even if they haven't seen one another in four of five years, it's like they hadn't seen each other since last week. And they are a bunch of huggers, they hug each other and are so glad to see each other, it's like a real family thing.

DH Was there a lot of camaraderie?

PT Oh yeah, there certainly was–an awful lot of good guys. In fact, David, Glenn would investigate a guy, his personality and all before he'd hire him because he didn't want somebody in there who was going to be a bad guy. He would also look into what kind of a wife he had, because she could stir things up, and he didn't want that going on in his band. Otherwise you get a thing like the movie "Orchestra Wives" we made. But I remember one guy that he fired that, he loved the guy's playing, but there was a guy named Clyde Hurley, a real good trumpet player who played real "down home" Texas style. This concerns Legh Knowles. The first trumpet player, McMickle, had to take off to have a cyst taken off his lip, so they got in Zeke Zarchy. Now Zeke is an excellent player, good lead trumpet player and everything else. Well, when Mickey could come back, Glenn just couldn't see letting Zeke go. So, he let Legh go. Here we are on a train ride. Clyde Hurley is sitting there on the train and he's griping like mad about, "What a terrible thing to do to Legh, such a nice guy and everything, just a terrible thing to do to him." And he didn't know that sitting right around back to back with him was Glenn. Glenn heard all this going on and so he spun around and said, "Clyde, you're that unhappy, take two weeks notice." He just let him go just like that. Clyde was a griper, that was about all that Glenn could handle. But everybody loved Legh, we all felt badly about it.

DH Who were the stars in the band, if there were any, Paul?

PT Well, you know, Glenn made a star out of Tex, cause he sang and played solos. He wouldn't have played so many solos probably if he hadn't also been a singer. Glenn loved Teagarden and he wanted somebody like that, so Tex was as close as he could get to it. But Tex was also a fine player, an excellent player. Criticized here and there; that's too bad, because he was a fine player, especially on ballads. He could find pretty notes that the only other guy who could find them was Bobby Hackett. But Tex was probably the big star in the band. He started to feature some things with Billy May and started featuring some things with Johnny Best. But other than that, it was usually Tex, because he was a singer. And Glenn didn't want big stars in his band. He had had that with the band he broke up. He had some good, good players in that band, but he broke the band up because they were a bunch of drunks. So he didn't want that going on, he figured he'd get a bunch of young fellows and mold them into a good successful musical outfit that would play well and behave themselves up to a point, as long as they were working. And that's exactly what he did. Now, if you were off the bandstand, you could do whatever you wanted to do. But on the bandstand, you had to take care of business. He had a thing at the Meadowbrook once where he called us backstage. The people were awfully nice to us (the public), and they liked to buy you a drink, things liked that. So he finally had to lay down the law. When you had those band meetings, you knew you were in trouble. So he called us into the back room and said, "Look, we've got to lay down a rule here, one drink per night on the bandstand." Al Mastren, the trombone player, said, "Does that include me too, Glenn?" And Glenn said, "You're the reason for the meeting." So Al said, "Well, I can't handle that." So he left. But since then he's sobered up, and Al's playing well and he's teaching well and he's doing fine in upstate New York. Nice fellow, he was real good to me.

DH Bobby Hackett?

PT When Bobby came on the band I was one of the most thrilled people in the music business. I had stood, when I was starving to death, I had stood outside a club that Bobby was working in in Boston. It was cold. And there would be a grate in the middle of the cement where the bad fumes and everything from out of this club that was downstairs, letting the bad air come out. But I could stand there and the warm air would go up my pants and I would hear Bobby Hackett playing trumpet down there. I thought it was worthwhile to put up with the smell coming out of the place. So when Bobby came on the band, I told him it was such a gas, and he said, "I'm gassed to be on the band." He was such a nice fellow. And when he played–the problem was that he played guitar most of the time on the band. And he picked up the trumpet and played. So whenever he played you had a gang of gems coming out. We wished he'd play more. Glenn tried him in the trumpet section, but Bobby just didn't play strong enough to play in Glenn's trumpet section. Bobby told me that he would give his right arm to play like McMickle; Mickle told me that he'd give his right arm to play like Bobby Hackett.

DH It seems almost like a paradox that here was this guy who could play this great sweet stuff and yet not be strong enough to be in the section.

PT He could play with drive, all you had to do is listen to the dixieland things that he did with Teagarden and other players like that. He could move it along, but he couldn't play very loudly. And he practiced all the time, practiced constantly, but he just didn't build up any strength in his lip. But he really had an ear. Of course, part of that ear was because he was a good guitar player. I don't mean a soloist on guitar, but he knew his chords so well. That went right over into his trumpet playing. He knew what notes were going to sound right, and he found them every time. Such nice phrasing, nice tone.

DH You kind of touched on it earlier, what quality would a fellow have to have to be successful in Glenn Miller's Orchestra? What kind of things was he looking for?

PT Well, you had to have a good work ethic. I enjoyed going to work, that helped me. But you know, I realized what a neat thing it was to be able to make such a good living doing something I thoroughly enjoyed doing and would have done for free if I had to. Now that's a good thing. I did that for about fifty years, and was so gassed to be in the top paying band, and here I am loving every minute of playing. So that was the first thing. If you were tired, or you were sick to your stomach or something like that, then that's the thing you had to put up with, and we had this famous saying, "Smile, damnit." So be happy. He knew that the people were there to have a good time and didn't want to look up there and see somebody who was sour, so you had to be a pleasant person. And you had to have good ears, and listening all the time, not only to what was going on around you, but what you were doing. So you would play in tune and blend nicely with what you're supposed to do. So you had to be very conscientious. You had to be ambitious.

Can I tell you one other story about Bobby Hackett? We're out here working on a picture called *Orchestra Wives*. It was a lot of fun. That was the second one we made. Jackie Gleason was on the band, he kept us in stitches pretty much. Here he is working Slapsie Maxie's all night long and out there early in the morning working all day long. And as a bass player, he can't play a note, Doc Goldberg did the playing for him. But Bobby and I–when they shoot a camera angle, sometimes you are in the picture, sometimes you aren't. Sometimes, they want some action, so they have you walk into the picture; sometimes you are in it and they have you walk out of the picture. Then they move the camera angle and you're walking into it. Bobby and I would get back there in the back and we would be smoking cigarettes as we are walking out of the picture. Then they'd change the camera angle and we'd walk into the picture smoking pipes. But it all ended up on the cutting room floor. We figured that Hollywood lost another chance at Edmund Lowe and Victor MacGlegan. They had their chance. Bobby was lots of fun.

DH What about that Miller sound? How do you describe that?

PT Well, let's see, it's the reed section. He based his style on the woodwinds, clarinet playing lead over the saxophones. You see, I used to tell my students at UCLA that the bands all had the same set-up. They all had a trombone section, a trumpet section, which made the brass section. They had a sax section and a rhythm section, and singers. And the students couldn't figure out how come they didn't all sound alike. Well, each band had to have it's own identifying feature. Like Tommy Dorsey, being probably the best ballad trombone player, would feature himself on that. Benny Goodman, being the clarinet image of the world, featured himself on clarinet, and so forth. What Glenn figured he should do is something a little different, and he searched for this sound. Now when I first joined the band, I rode in Glenn's car. They had three cars that traveled. One was "Sudden Death," that was the piano player's car, it didn't have any brakes or anything. One was the "Viper Special" which was the guys who were getting a little high as they were going down the highway, not even using the road at times. And the other was Glenn's car which was called "Solitary Confinement." So Glenn himself told me the story of getting that sound that he got. He said he was with Ray Noble's Band and there was a trumpet player in the band named Pee Wee Irwin, a good trumpet player, a very flexible trumpet player. So Glenn wrote some things for Pee Wee to play over the saxes, and they came off very well. Pee Wee left the band and they got in Charlie

Spivak. Now Charlie with his great big enormous beautiful sound was not flexible at all, so these things didn't come off. So what does Ray Noble do, he hired a fine clarinet player named Johnny Mince. He came on in the band and Mince played these things that Pee Wee had played over the saxes. Glenn heard that sound and said, "My God, that's what I've been looking for." Never wrote another note of it for Noble, saved it for himself. When he had the band he broke up, he had Irving Fazola playing lead clarinet, good big sound. But he got the right guy when he got Willie Schwartz. And when we made the theme song, "Moonlight Serenade," an awful lot of people couldn't believe that it wasn't Goodman or Artie Shaw or Fazola or somebody because they never heard of Willie Schwartz. Here he was about nineteen and he's playing a solo on there that is absolutely gorgeous. Of course, I heard a little Japanese girl play that solo just beautifully last year over in Japan. These high school girls play Glenn Miller music, they play it so nicely it's unbelievable. They play "Moonlight Serenade," they play Willie's solo note for note, all the little turns and everything. This little tiny girl stands up, she's so teeny, plays beautifully.

DH Comparing the Miller Band, there were other great bands of that day, Benny Goodman, Artie Shaw, Dorseys, probably a couple others like the black bands, Ellington, Basie; many will say that the Miller Band was maybe not on a par with these bands, and yet, among those who were around in those years, if you had a vote, the Miller Band would probably get the vote, that's my sense of the thing.

PT Well, David, they did have votes, they had contests constantly. And I remember one time in the middle of a contest, we had slipped up a little below Benny Goodman, and then we went back up. But at the time that we were a little below, they were doing a thing in Carnegie Hall and we followed them in. This was not the big 1938 concert they did, but it was another one and we followed them in. Chris Griffin from Goodman's trumpet section, hollered over to me, "How do you like being second?" Then of course we went on up. But we admired all those bands. I remember Glenn asked me when I was first on the band what bands I like. I told him it was probably the last band I heard. I admired Lunceford, Dorsey, Ellington, Basie, Shaw, Barnet, all those bands were great bands, there's no getting away from it. But Glenn knew how to please the public, and he did it without sacrificing the music. He didn't go for gimmicks, and he still knew how to please them. Too many of the other guys sort of did some things that didn't quite catch on. And one of the big examples of that is Shaw. He had such a good band, and yet you can't name a lot of Shaw classics. And you can't name a lot of Goodman classics. That's a shame because they were just great bands. All you've got to do is listen to "Sing Sing Sing" and you're a Goodman fan whether you were before or not. Exciting band.

DH One interesting comparison I think is if you go through books that list all the tunes that were on the charts those days, and tunes that were number one on the charts, the Miller Band for the time it performed overshadows all other bands; and some of the bands that you think are really great suffer by that comparison.

PT Well, David, after a while a band builds up automatic sales on records, and Glenn did that. He built up automatic sales to the point a big hit for Tommy Dorsey was "I'll Never Smile Again" with Frank Sinatra singing on it. Now Don Haynes, Glenn's manager, told me that they never play Glenn's record of it, no one talks about Glenn's record. And yet Dorsey's was the big one, but it didn't sell as many as Glenn's. Glenn had those automatic sales, whatever comes out and says "Glenn Miller" on it, people are going to buy it, and he had that going all over.

DH The band was certainly busy, wasn't it? Was it busier than other bands?

PT I jotted down a thing because I thought maybe you'd ask me that. Let me see if I can put my finger on it. We played one hundred and forty sessions in two weeks, now who does that? This is in two weeks–we were working at the Paramount Theater in New York–we did forty-nine shows a week, that's seven shows a day, forty-nine shows a week. At the same time, we did two long sessions a night at the Hotel Pennsylvania at the same time, and that was six nights a week. We did six Chesterfield programs a week because there was no tape in those days, so you played it once for the east coast and once for the west coast. So we did six Chesterfield programs a week, we did that three days and there were three rehearsals. So that comes to seventy performances a week, we did that in two weeks, that's one hundred and forty performances in two weeks. Glenn got sick, but we weren't allowed to. He was in the hospital. We're still doing the Paramount and all, so some leaders came up and substituted for him. Tommy Dorsey came in and substituted for him, Gene Krupa came in, Charlie Barnet came in, and Dick Stabile came in. And then anybody who was in town would come on in and sub for him. When he ran out of leaders, then he went to radio announcers. Paul Douglas would come in. So when he ran out of them, he went to politicians. We told them all you've got to do is raise your hand and lower it, because we're not going to pay any attention to you after that. The guys all knew the tempos, knew how fast the things were supposed to go; we were going to listen to the drummer anyway. So just raise your hand, bring it down, then turn around and smile, sign autographs, do whatever you want to do. It was a lot of fun. But we did work hard. There for a while, we had four days off a year. Of course, we did have Sunday off from the Hotel Pennsylvania; but other than that, Glenn gave us four days a year. Which is not very much. One night, we were playing the Pennsylvania, and Glenn had a thing for us to play the following Sunday if the guys wanted to do it. Now he never said anything like that before; because if there was a buck to be made, Glenn was going to make it. So he said, "I know you're working hard, but you want to do the Sunday thing?" They took a vote, the guys decided no, they didn't want to do it. So we did it anyway, because Glenn wanted to do it. That was his crack at democracy. But we really did work hard. We were young.

DH When you joined the band, Paul, back in the middle of '38, they hadn't made it, had they?

PT Oh no; in fact, David, at one point, Glenn was going to break up the band. He called us into a hotel room in Boston and said, "Look, I don't have anything at all for you guys. If you have anything, go to it." And here I am, a kid, I said, "Glenn, it's the best band I ever played with. Let's practice or rehearse or something." So he said, "OK, if you guys feel that way, straight ahead." And within two years, he was a millionaire. Not because of me!!

DH Well, because of you and fifteen or sixteen other guys. Did the band evolve and change much from the time you joined it until the time it broke up?

PT No, it got a little smoother. We got a little quicker finding out just exactly what Glenn wanted, how to do it and everything, that got to be an easier thing for us. Other than that, it didn't change too much. He worked out what he thought were the weak spots and emphasized what he thought were the strong spots.

DH Were you ever rehearsed much with that kind of schedule you had?

PT Yes. When we were at the Pennsylvania, we rehearsed all night one night a week. I mean all night, to nine or ten o'clock in the morning. After the job was over, we'd take a break long enough to clear out the hall, clear out the dining room, and then we'd start rehearsing. And arrangers would bring things in and we'd try them over. We had a lot of rehearsals while we were at the Glen Island, afternoon rehearsals.

DH Why do you think the band really made it?

PT Why?

DH When.

PT I think, well, when I knew they had it made–we were playing some place, and they told us that we were going to go in the Meadowbrook. And from there you're going to go to Glen Island for all summer. Then you've got to come back to the Meadowbrook. I thought my gosh, we'll be on the air, every time we look up there'll be a microphone, and so we got it made. Because all you had to do was to have all that air time. And then he started recording some things that made some difference–the theme song, "Sunrise Serenade," "In the Mood," things like that and they caught on. Plus those three engagements–Meadowbrook, Glen Island, and the Meadowbrook–you couldn't miss if you had anything on the ball at all.

DH "In the Mood" was not a big favorite with the players, was it?

PT Oh, it was OK, I didn't mind it. He tried it out at the Glen Island with the false endings and all. He played a dandy gag on me. He had me, at the hotel, sit on the outside because he knew I would talk to the people out there; you know, go ahead and chat with them and not be grumpy about it. So he knew I was listening and that I would do what I was supposed to do all the time. So, you know on "In the Mood," those endings can go on and on, there is no set number of times. But the time before the loud part, he gives Mo Purtill the sign, so Mo hits the cow bell and we know that the next time we blast away. Well, I'm looking at these kids, talking to them, and he tells the guys, "Hold it down, we're going to fix Lightnin'." He has Mo hit the cow bell, so I stand up all by myself and blast away on "In the Mood." I was so embarrassed. Fortunately, I didn't miss the note and that was a good thing. He did the same thing to me once again on "Pennsylvania Six Five Thousand." I stood up and yelled "Pennsylvania." He knew from then on that I was no singer.

DH You didn't do any singing?

PT No. He had an idea at one time but then he heard me and threw that idea out in a hurry. I said, "I can't sing at all." He said, "You're right."

DH Club dates like the Paradise and the Meadowbrook and Glen Island and Cafe Rouge, those are fun to play?

PT Well, yes, because you sort of sat down for a little while, and you could send your laundry out. The Paradise, the funny thing about that is they fired Glenn because they didn't think the band was handling the show well. And then they tried to hire him back later on and they couldn't afford him. He thought that was just great. He liked things like that. For example, when I first joined the band, they were playing the Million Dollar Pier in Atlantic City. But the real place to play was the Steel Pier in Atlantic City. That was the class place, and yet he was playing the Million Dollar Pier. So later on, after he was really doing well and could pack them in, he went back and played the Million Dollar Pier just as a favor to the guy because the guy hired him before he was making it. He thought that was really nice and that he owed him. Glenn would never let the promoters lose money on him. If it rained really bad that night and the crowd was really poor, he skipped his income and everything. He protected the promoters constantly; whereas, a lot of guys wouldn't do that. On the other hand, he would send a guy in ahead of time and say, "OK, if I'm getting three thousand dollars and fifty percent, how would you like it if I were making less guarantee and a bigger percent?" And the guy would say, "Of course, I'll do that because of less guarantee." But Glenn knew he was going to pack them in–in that case, the promoter would lose every time. But some of the promoters tried to hype Glenn. He was the first guy to start to carry around the ultra violet ray. You stamp people's wrists, you can only see it under that light. I remember the band boy carrying this thing in every night. He was the first guy to start doing that because they were selling tickets at all the doors and they weren't counting all the tickets. He put a stop to that. He put one of his guys on every door and had the ultra violet ray going. "I don't mind playing for you, but you're not going to cheat me."

DH Was there any place or city that was a particular favorite of yours?

PT Well, I always had a lot of fun in New York. It was a bit different than it is now. Now it can even be a little dangerous. But in those days, it was a lot of fun. We enjoyed it. One of the biggest thrills I ever had was at the Paramount Theater when the stage comes up and all these kids start to scream. You know, the stage is an orchestra pit; so you go in and the people are way up here. Then the stage goes up and you're way up here somewhere. When the stage goes up and the people start to scream because you're there and it's really a thrill, goose pimples–people screaming because you're playing the trombone. Either screaming at you or for you. Of course, you come out to Hollywood and make a couple of movies, that's a big thrill.

DH I bet it was. Did you enjoy those movies?

PT Sure, had a lot of fun. We asked them, David, not to pay us until after the movie was over. We were doing the Chesterfield programs, and that was plenty, just fine. So we said, "Don't pay us until after the movie is over." Boy, everybody took their money and went right to Detroit and bought a car. It was a lot of fun. I told somebody, Hedi Lamar or somebody, I said what a thrill it was for us to come out here, and she said, "Well, it's a thrill for us to be able to hear you." Which was very nice.

DH There were some great tunes in those movies.

PT Yeah, there were even more than what ended up in the movie. Some of them didn't make it, there were some good tunes.

DH Those guys who wrote those tunes–I think were great–Harry Warren and Mac Gordon. Some of them were my favorites, "Serenade In Blue," and you mentioned one a while ago, "I Know Why."

PT You know a funny thing about "Serenade In Blue" is the middle of that. So many people have played it and never gotten the depth of harmony out of it that Bill Conway did for the Modernaires. He was a guitar player, but he was with the Modernaires, and he rehearsed them and taught them their parts. He got harmony of that middle that no one had ever before or after and made it a gorgeous sound. Bill was very talented.

DH When the band broke up, September of 1942, was it in Glenn's mind or in the minds of everybody that was performing then that after the war, that you'd get back together again?

PT David, I don't know how many people know, but Don Haynes–I was so friendly with Don Haynes, his wife and my wife (my wife has passed away and I'm remarried now), they had a book store together. So Don and I were Coolie labor. But he told me that Glenn, after the war, had a seven year contract with the Paramount Theater in New York, he had a seven year contract with the Statler Hotel chain, he had a seven year contract with Twentieth Century Fox and a seven year with the Victor record people. Glenn said to me, "You gonna play with me after the war?" I said, "Where do I sign?" And I didn't even know about those contracts. But he had an awful lot going for him. I forgot your question.

DH Well, it was whether you'd get together after the war.

PT Glenn figured he would have a band because you can see from these contracts that he had. He was going to have a band. Considering the band that he had in the service, I don't know what the band would have been like, it would have been a great band. But I doubt it would have done so many one-nighters, just too big to do one-nighters. The finances would have been overwhelming to cart that big band around. I know guys like Kenton had problems, the Sauter-Finegan Band had a lot of problems because they got so big. But Glenn could have done a lot of work out here. He could have done a lot of work in New York City, could have done a lot of work in Los Angeles in the studios and he would have done very well. He would have had a great band.

DH What do you think, you know, here it is fifty years later, and...

PT And I'm only in my twenties.

DH The band still has a sense of popularity and has a certain timeless quality to it; I'm sure that's more true among people like myself.

PT Well, David, it reminds a large population of people of good times they had. When an awful lot of movies and TV shows want to depict that era, they very often play something of Glenn's or an imitation of something of Glenn's, so his sound reminds them of a certain era. As a consequence, you can't sell nostalgia short, that's a saleable product. It's still very thrilling for a lot of people to be all of a sudden fifty years younger.

DH What about today's technology and so forth, do you think that would have been a boon to Glenn Miller?

PT I thought about that. He would have solved his balance problems that he sometimes had because now everybody's got a microphone. I don't think he would have gone for that, but he would have gone for a lot more microphones. You know, when you're out playing ballrooms, you very often had only one microphone. The singer used it, and if somebody like Tex plays a solo, he walks down to the microphone, and the leader makes announcements over the microphone. So he would have solved his balance problems. He would have gone for some electronics, I suppose, but not for loudness for loudness sake. I don't think he would have done that. But I think he would have experimented some. He could have gotten some other pretty ethereal things going that hadn't occurred to him because the technology wasn't there. That's quite possible. But I think he would have looked it over very carefully, and used what he thought would be of use to him, and just not bothered with some of the other things, like distortion was such a popular thing for a while. He wouldn't have gone for that, I'm sure.

DH What were some of your personal favorite tunes that the Miller Band did?

PT They were usually the pretty tunes, "Rhapsody In Blue," "Serenade In Blue," "Spring Will Be So Sad This Year." But then on the other hand, the up tempo tunes were fun. "Volga Boatman," the trombone part was like a union test. You know, you've got four guys who have to play this thing without one error out of the four guys. It was a treacherous thing anyway. So that was kind of fun to get through. So I didn't mind the up tempo things at all, I enjoyed them.

DH How did you feel when you heard that the band was going to break up?

PT Well, it was a sad thing because these people are your family, they are the only family you know. You lived with these guys constantly, day in and day out, they are your friends, your family. But then, on the other hand, it's always exciting to go to something new. Most of us were in our mid twenties, so we knew we were going to be drafted. I was in my mid twenties and didn't have any kids. Uncle Sam said, "I want you." So most of us knew that was coming up. It was kind of fun trying some other musical direction.

Time caught up with that interview, remember we were on radio. However, we did pick up on a new interview almost immediately as you will see in what I have labeled as Second Interview with David Heagerty.

Second Interview with David Heagerty 13

DH There's our theme again, "Moonlight Serenade," I'm Dave Heagerty here with our genial co-host, John McCloud, the effervescent program director here on KLIU to bring you Part Two of our Ninth Annual Salute to Glenn Miller. How you doing this evening, John?[1]

❶ "Moonlight Serenade"

JM Oh Dave, I'm just dandy, and I'm excited we're in Part Number Two. What's happening this evening in our salute to Glenn Miller, Dave?

DH Well, as always, John, quite a bit, we've got a lot on tap; some great Miller medleys by the highly popular civilian and Air Force Orchestras and our special guest this evening, Doctor Paul Tanner and his introducer Legh Knowles, the former trumpeter and recently retired wine executive. We'll have some special features and a few surprises perhaps, all brought to you by our sponsor of all nine Miller salutes, the William Lyon Company, California's leading home builders.

JM That's wonderful, Dave. Do you think we'll have time to play any songs this evening?

DH Sure, John, thanks to our expanded 1990 program, at least fifteen tunes. That's about three more per evening than ever before counting the occasional medley that we play.

JM I'm keeping my fingers crossed, Dave. Well, shall we roll them here?

DH Yeah, let's do it. let's start our show with two recordings from Glenn Miller's famous 1939 appearance at Carnegie Hall in New York City. We'll listen to the pretty "Stairway To the Stars," then another ballad, "To You," with vocalist Ray Eberle featured on both.[2 & 3]

❷ "Stairway To the Stars"

❸ "To You"

JM Ah Dave, those were both very nice tunes to listen to.

DH You're right, John. I've always found those Carnegie Hall recordings particularly interesting. The first, "Stairway To the Stars," was one of eighteen tunes that topped the charts in Glenn Miller's all too short five year civilian career as a leader. It features Tex Beneke on tenor sax and the maestro Glenn Miller on trombone. That and our second selection,

"To You," showcases the vocal talents of the popular Ray Eberle. John, let's take a brief pause for a helpful word from from our good friends at the William Lyon Company, California's leading builder.

JM Good evening, we're back on 1590 AM KLIU. You mentioned earlier that our guest tonight is Doctor Paul Tanner, Dave.

DH That's right, John, he played lead trombone in the Miller Band and made all of their Bluebird recordings from 1938 until the band broke up in September of 1942.

JM Do we have Legh Knowles here again to introduce him?

DH Indeed we do, John. Legh who came into the Miller Band a little later in 1938 is standing by on one of our pre-recorded cartridges. Let's catch some of his impressions of the talented Doctor Tanner.

We're delighted to welcome once again our good friend Legh Knowles. He's here to introduce our special guest, Doctor Paul Tanner. Legh is a recently retired chairman of the Beaulieu Vineyard. And like Paul, he joined Glenn Miller early on in 1938 where he contributed so much to the band in its trumpet section.

Legh, it's just great to have you with us once again.

LK Well, Dave, its awfully nice that you remember to include me in all these times. I'm just very happy to be part of this and part of anything you do to tell the truth.

DH Great. What comes to mind when you recall Paul Tanner in the days you fellows were making big band history with Glenn Miller?

LK Well, several things I can remember. But one was the fact that I used to sit in back of Paul. And here was a guy playing a lot of wonderful notes who was probably one of the greatest high register trombone players there was. Here's one guy who could play like Jack Jenny and even before him years ago, George Troop. And of course, in a situation like this where the leader was a trombone player and wants to have, whether he likes it or not, the image of playing the lead parts, Paul played the other parts. That's what I remember about Paul. He was a real great trombone player and paid his dues all the time he sat in the section.

DH What is the advantage of having this high register give somebody like Paul, Legh? What did that mean in terms of the band?

LK Well, if you ever heard Billy Rauch play "Smoke Rings," or hear Paul Tanner play "Stardust," or hear Tommy Dorsey play some of his wonderful things high, and you heard that pretty sound, a lot of guys didn't have the ability, the capacity, the physical make-up or the talent to play that, the high register. But Paul had it. Cy Zentner, people like that, Paul could play and he never had a chance to do it, which is really quite a different thing for him.

DH Why didn't he have the opportunity?

LK Well, because Glenn would have to. They would write the parts for, at the beginning, for three trombones, then for four trombones. And the tendency was to let Glenn, the leader to be the leader. And I'm sure that given the choice, Glenn would have split that thing around between several of the guys. But he couldn't do it, he played most of the stuff, but not all of it. I heard Paul play one night in the Cafe Rouge, we were playing dinner music, and I don't know what it was, I think it was "Stardust," but it could have been "Smoke Rings;" and my goodness, he played so pretty. Great guy, I remember that about him, that is one of the many things I remember.

JM Boy, as he always does, Legh gives us a lot of insight into our special guest.

DH Yeah, he sure does. Let's hear from Doctor Tanner himself, as he recalls his active career as a musician, key member of the Miller Band, and professor at UCLA, spanning some fifty years, John.

With us is one who played a special role in the Glenn Miller Orchestra, Doctor Paul Tanner, a jazz author and jazz authority who contributed some great trombone sounds in the Miller Band from 1938 to 1942. Welcome to our Glenn Miller Salute, Paul, its great to have you with us.

PT Thank you very much, glad to be here.

DH What about Paul Tanner; tell us about yourself, where did you grow up, and what happened to you in your formative years?

(All this was amply covered in David Heagerty's first interview, so it must be skipped at this point. So I'll pick it up at the end of a long reiteration.)

JM Well, I can tell Paul is going to be a great guest, Dave. Now you said he's on all of Glenn's RCA recordings. Why don't we play a couple?

DH A great idea, John. Let's listen to a couple that I think Paul would like. The Harry Warren, Mack Gordon movie tune "Serenade In Blue," one of Glenn's best in my book. Then one we've never played before in any of our nine Glenn Miller Salutes, "Spring Will Be So Sad When She Comes This Year." [4 & 5]

4 "Serenade In Blue"

5 "Spring Will Be So Sad When She Comes This Year"

JM Well, those were definitely interesting tunes, Dave.

DH Yes, the first, "Serenade In Blue," is one of my real Miller favorites. It features Pat Friday and Ray Eberle on the vocals backed up by the Four Modernaires with Bobby Hackett on cornet and Tex Beneke on tenor sax. It was a hit tune in the 1942 film, the Miller Band's second flick, *Orchestra Wives*. The last selection was "Spring Will Be So Sad When She Comes This Year." It's interesting, it comes from a radio air check in Hollywood when the band was in California in the Spring of '41 to do the first movie *Sun Valley Serenade*. Ray Eberle does the vocal honors again supported nobly by the Modernaires, our prior guest here, Tex Beneke, on tenor sax, and the late great Willie Schwartz on clarinet.

JM Well they were just great to listen to, Dave. But a question, what was going on in the world back then? We opened time capsules for 1937 and 1938 in Part 1 of our Glenn Miller Salute last week.

DH We'll look into the years '39 and '40 this evening. Nineteen thirty-nine was a momentous year, John, and a year of war on many fronts, the Imperial Japanese aggression in China raged all year. The bloody civil war in Spain entered in March. World War II began September first with Nazi Germany invading Poland, a conflict that would last six long agonizing years. The Soviet Union took Eastern Poland and invaded Finland in November much to the dismay of neutral America. Finland was very popular here because they were the only nation that had repaid its World War II debt to us. Pan American Airlines opened transatlantic between Europe and the U.S., and Igor Secorsky built the first successful helicopter. World Fairs opened in New York and San Francisco on Treasure Island. We'll review 1939 for sports and entertainment a bit later in the show, John.

JM Well, why don't we swing away from that grim news of yesteryear and play some of the more memorable Miller music, Dave?

Miller's Medley 6

DH Coming up, John. Let's spin one of those favorite Miller medleys and the Tommy Dorsey standard, "I'll Never Smile Again."

Miller's Medley [6]

"If I Had My Way" (Miller) is the old tune that means it is medley night tonight.

"All the Things You Are" (Paul Douglas) is new and comes from Jerome Kern's "Very Warm For May."

"Oh Johnny" (Miller) Marion Hutton borrows from Orin Tucker. Bonnie Baker's sensational version of "Oh Johnny."

"Blue" (Miller) For something blue, the well-known "Blue."

"I'll Never Smile Again" (with Ray Eberle).

JM Oh there was a lot of good music there, Dave.

DH Yeah, indeed, John, and I think the medleys are fun. Often they were preceded by Glenn Miller or one of his announcers saying "Something Old, Something New, Something Borrowed, Something Blue," and were hallmarks of his broadcasts and club dates. This set offered "If I Had My Way," the old tune, "All the Things You Are" the new tune, "Oh Johnny Oh Johnny Oh" with vocal by Marion Hutton, the song borrowed from Wee Bonnie Baker and Orin Tucker, and the blue tune "Blue" as in "Blue and Broken Hearted." The last song, "I'll Never Smile Again" made famous by Frank Sinatra and trombonist leader Tommy Dorsey, features Ray Eberle and Glenn Miller along with our special guest Paul Tanner in the trombone section. John, let's take care of some of the bills and break for our friendly sponsor, California's leading home builder, the William Lyon Company.

JM Well, we're back this evening on 1598 AM, KLIV. You mentioned Paul Tanner, Dave, do you have more of your interview with our special guest and your introducer, Legh Knowles, with some of their views of the popular music scene when the Miller Band was in its heyday?

DH You bet. We'll catch up with Legh, and then hear from our special guest Paul Tanner again. What do you remember about him as a guy? I mean what kind of a person was he?

LK Well, he was a guy who was just straight. He believed, he had a no nonsense approach to it. You know, it was a given in Glenn Miller's Band that you play the job perfectly. I don't care who was in the band. I think Billy May said it, he said, "Whoever it was, anybody in that band was a pretty solid musician, because Glenn didn't hire secondary musicians." So Paul played the job the best way he could all the time, and he played it marvelously. He did that but, at the same time, he had a different element which I heard a guy refer to last night as the Glenn Miller Band "processing." We call that "visual awareness."

DH Why don't you elaborate on that?

LK Well, if you watched Paul, he looked just like the greatest thing in the world was happening. He was really enjoying himself. He looked good, he looked happy, he looked like the music was inspiring him. He moved around, he smiled, he was a good-looking guy, he is a good-looking guy. *(Editor's note–A decidedly flattering comment made by a slightly myopic friend.)* Anyway, that's the way he struck me. He really made the band pep up. Glenn believed in that stuff, and Paul was really sensational.

DH Was he a guy that was well liked by the other members of the band, Legh?

LK Oh sure, sure. You know, that's one of the things about Glenn Miller's Band. Somebody, I don't know who it was, said it meshed their personalities, I never saw anybody talking down anybody else. Everybody seemed to get along fine. Somebody said that was Glenn's talent for the human resources. I don't know about that, but Paul, you would never have any trouble with him, not at all. He'd greet you in the most gracious way and treat you so good. All the guys were that way. But Paul particularly was a very affable guy. Yeah, he does a lot of things. I have another thing. May I? We had a well-known guy named Hal McIntyre. And he used to think he had an expression called "grovering." He was referring to Grover Whalen who was the greeter for the city of New York who met all the emissaries and dignitaries and squired them around, he knew who they were. Well, you know Paul was kind of like that, and to tell you the truth, so was I. In other words, on our side of the bandstand, we'd play some place, you'd notice people waving and we'd be waving back. Because both Paul and I were interested in people. I hope he agrees with this. We're interested in people and we knew where they had come from, who they were, when they heard the band the last time. And we could tell them a lot of things about themselves, these people in the audience. And crazy Hal used to say, "You guys are grovering all the time." Of course, I used to do it for another reason though, because when there was an intermission, they'd always buy me a drink. I don't think that was the case with Lightnin' or Paul. I never saw Lightnin' drink much to tell you the truth.

DH That was his nickname, Lightnin'?

LK Lightnin'.

DH Where'd he get that?

LK Well, I don't know. I've heard stories. He had it when I got there. Probably because he didn't move too fast. He was kind of a laid back dude. Good guy.

PT Well "Moonlight Serenade" was on the back of "Sunrise Serenade." They were 78s so they only had one tune on each side. And that was probably the big one, and then "In the Mood" came along. We did those while we were at the Glen Island.[7]

7 "Moonlight Serenade"

DH How about those production numbers you did in the movies? "Chattanooga"? "Kalamazoo"?

PT Well, of course, everything is recorded ahead of time. Except with Glenn's band, we recorded a couple of things right off the stage, right off the set. You know, it's a funny thing, while sitting there, you're wasting a lot of time while you're making movies, you sit around a lot while they do lighting and decide what they're going to do. So what Glenn would do for the grips and everybody else working there, and the extras sitting around, you play for them. And they'd get up and dance while they're just killing time. But most of the things are recorded ahead of time and you pretend you are playing. Out of a big speaker, they play at you, you pretend you're playing your part. Of course, if you get a guy like George Montgomery with a trumpet in his hand, then somebody like Steve Lipkin standing off camera, and Montgomery's looking at him doing everything he does. And with Jackie Gleason with a bass, he'd be looking at Doc Goldberg. And Cesar Romero on piano. That was some rhythm section. Cesar Romero was a nice guy. I said to him not long ago when I was at a function where he was and I told him I was in those pictures. He said that was the most fun he's ever had in Hollywood, making movies with the Miller Band. Nice fellow.

JM Boy, Legh and Paul certainly have some great thoughts about Glenn Miller and their fellow bandsmen, Dave.

DH Yes, and their style of recalling their memories is equally fascinating, John. I should mention that since Paul and I did our interview, Willie Schwartz, the great clarinetist, passed away.

JM Well, Dave, as we continue with the show tonight, how about some more of that great Miller music, what do you say?

DH Yeah, we're always ready to oblige with more of that Glenn Miller music, John. In fact, we've got two Miller Orchestra chart busters, a pair of golden records. First, the unusual song written by arranger Jerry Gray around a hotel phone number, "Pennsylvania 6-5000," and then the rousing movie production number "I Got a Gal In Kalamazoo."[8 & 9]

8 "Pennsylvania 6-5000"

9 "I Got a Gal In Kalamazoo"

JM Oh Dave, those were really good tunes.

DH Yeah, each of those sold over a million records, John. First we played "Pennsylvania 6-5000," the Jerry Gray composition named for the phone number of the Hotel Pennsylvania where the Miller Band performed so successfully over so much of the band's tenure at its Cafe Rouge. Former special guest trumpeter John Best and tenor sax star Tex Beneke are show-cased when current special guest Paul Tanner and introducer Legh Knowles are making their presence felt in Glenn Miller's scheme of things. Our second tune, "Kalamazoo," was the big production number in the band's second movie *Orchestra Wives*, filmed in the Spring of 1942. It features Marion Hutton, Tex Beneke, and the Modernaires on the vocal, but it's clearly Tex's song. The movie version offers some very spirited dancing by the Nicholas Brothers, still active nearly fifty years later. With Mo Purtill on drums and Billy May with the muted trumpet. Another smash hit by those great movie songwriters Harry Warren and Mack Gordon. Let's pause, John, for another word from our friendly sponsor, the William Lyon Company, California's leading home builder.

JM Well, we're back on. Hi, John McCloud on 1590, KLIV, and we're back with Dave Heagerty, your host for our Ninth Annual Salute to Glenn Miller right here on KLIV. Dave, how long did our special guests play with Glenn Miller?

DH Well, John, both joined Glenn in 1938. Legh left in 1940, and Paul stayed right to the break-up of that great civilian band when Glenn Miller accepted a captain's commission in what was known then as the Army Air Corps in September 1942. Let's see, John, if we can get some more humorous incidents with former fellow members of the band. And I wonder is there anything that comes to mind in regards to Paul that might have been a little funny?

LK Well, no, he was just a guy. It was his presence that was funny. You know, someone would say something, and the way he would react would be very funny. He wouldn't have to say anything or do anything, he had a terrific presence, you see. If he wanted to appear funny, he appeared funny. If he wanted to appear enthusiastic, he appeared enthusiastic. If he wanted to appear that this was a beautiful, beautiful sounding ballad, he appeared like he was playing a beautiful sounding ballad. Or if he wanted to indicate that the band was swinging, this would be the toughest part as far as I'm concerned because that band didn't swing that much. But he made it kind of look like it did swing. That's a major contribution in that band.

DH How was Glenn Miller as a person?

PT Well, he was a very fine musician. He was a tremendous businessman. He was a perfectionist. He was extremely patriotic. Everything. You do these war bond things and things like that, and he was really serious. He was really patriotic. He didn't have to go into the service. He just went in to bring a piece of home to some guys who had been dragged away from home, that was his whole idea. And he fought the red tape like mad to get that in. But he was always strict in that this was a business and you do your part as best as it can be done or someone else was going to be there tomorrow night. So that was always on your mind. But you got in the habit of doing the very best you can and that gets to be a habit, then you don't think too much about it. You're just doing the best you can. The rest is up to someone else.

DH Was he tough to the point of being unfair?

PT No, I don't think so. He climbed on my back more than once, it was because I needed it, I wasn't moving the trombone slide well or something. But he was very good to me, I didn't have any problems with him.

JM Well, these guys have some very, very interesting observations about Glenn Miller and his band, Dave. It's sure fun to go down memory lane with our two guests, Legh Knowles and Paul Tanner, Dave.

DH It sure is. I bet it puts you in the mood for some of that highly listenable music, John.

JM It's funny you should mention that, I was just thinking the same thing. I love that highly listenable music, Dave, you bet.

DH Our next two tunes are about as listenable as they get, John. First, we'll play the melodic "Begin the Beguine," our first and only Air Force Orchestra action this evening. Then we'll complete the set with another version of "Stardust," always one of our real favorites. This one is from a November 1941 Cafe Rouge broadcast. It presents an exquisite Bobby Hackett solo with some awfully good trombone work from our special guest Paul Tanner as noted by Legh Knowles.[10 & 11]

10 **"Begin the Beguine"**

11 **"Stardust"**

JM Well, those were sure listenable tunes, Dave.

DH Indeed they were, John. The first one, "Begin the Beguine," as we mentioned before we played them, was done by the famous Glenn Miller Air Force Orchestra, and it featured your old friend Peanuts Hucko on clarinet.

JM My favorite name.

DH Right, and George Ockner, the symphony violinist.

JM Doesn't exactly have the same ring as Peanuts Hucko.

DH Doesn't quite, really doesn't. Then the last tune in the set, "Stardust," one of our great favorites. This version was done in 1941 at the Cafe Rouge and featured the great cornet solo by Bobby Hackett. Of course, our good friend and special guest, Paul Tanner, was featured in the trombone section.

JM Boy, music from that period based on those two tunes certainly had something going for it.

DH Yes, as you and KLIV have proven time and time again over the past decade, John. It might be appropriate to take another look into our time capsule for 1939.

JM All right, Dave, I'm ready. What was going on back in 1939?

DH As we've said on previous shows, John, 1939 was absolutely the greatest year ever for the movies. No other year in my view even comes close for the quantity of quality motion pictures. Just a few of the more than fifty I could rattle off are *Gone With the Wind*, *Goodbye Mister Chips*, the major academy winners that year. Then there were just so many others such as *Stage Coach*, *Gunga Din*, *The Women*, *Young Mister Lincoln*, and *Gulliver's Travels*. Some great comedies too like *You Can't Cheat An Honest Man* with W.C. Fields; the Marx Brothers' *At the Circus*, and *Flying Deuces* with Laurel and Hardy. The year got off to an auspicious start locally with a Saint Mary's twenty to thirteen win over Texas Tech in the Cotton Bowl. Texas A & M became the national football champ. Oregon won the first NCAA Basketball title. Joe DiMagio earned the MVP title for the Yankees. The Glenn Miller Band was really coming into its own, too, with twenty-four hits that made the charts; seven of these would become number one. In the *Metronome* poll, the Miller Band was ranked fifth in the swing category and fourth as a sweet group. *Down Beat* had the band second in both ranking. So much for 1939, John, we'll take a look at 1940 in a little while.

JM Well, Dave, we look forward to your golden anniversary review of 1940 up ahead. Dave, meantime, how about—

DH How about some more music, John?

JM Funny, you took the words right out of my mouth, Mister Heagerty.

DH Great. We've got another pretty pair that made the charts. First we'll have "Adios," then the equally harmonic "Falling Leaves." [12 & 13]

⓬ **"Adios"**

⓭ **"Falling Leaves"**

JM Boy, two stand-out instrumentals there, Dave.

DH Yeah, I sure like those. The first, "Adios," John, recorded at Victor studios in Chicago, had Mick McMickle on trumpet, also Doc Goldberg on bass, and the leader, Glenn Miller, on trombone. We followed that with "Falling Leaves" with the star of the band Tex Beneke on tenor sax, from an air check at the Cafe Rouge in December of 1940.

JM What was happening back in the year 1940, Dave?

DH Well, again, John, the war was everywhere but here in the western hemisphere. Certainly very much in the news though and on people's minds here in America. With the sudden collapse of France and the Nazi Germans over-running Western Europe, and with Britain's back to the proverbial wall, I think we all had the feeling the war would eventually engulf us as well. Despite to the contrary, rhetoric in the 1940 presidential campaign, Wendel Wilkie, our last dark horse candidate, gave Franklin Roosevelt a real run, but FDR rallied to win an unprecedented third term. National defense and the draft brought home the realities of World War II. On that unhappy note, we'll leave our time capsule of 1940 for now. But we'll come back to look at the sports and music in our golden anniversary year, John.

JM Well, do we have anymore 1940 Miller music, Dave?

DH Indeed we do, John. We've got "Call of the Canyon," with Ray Eberle, the Miller Band recorded it in 1940 in August of that year. And then to the particular tunes from the band's epic Glen Island Casino extended engagement in the spring and summer of 1939. This one features none other than Kay Starr in a spirited rendition of "Baby Me." [14–16]

⓮ **"The Call of the Canyon"**

⓯ **"Baby Me"**

⓰ **"Moonlight Serenade"**

Well, this seems to be about all I have from Mister Dave Heagerty. He must have gone into his theme song from there.

14 Interview with Edwin Klitch

There are, of course, different ways of doing interviews; there are even a variety of ways to accomplish this over the phone. A fine gentleman named Edwin Klitch called and suggested his way of putting spice into his radio show. I was quite interested to see if he could pull it off logically, and he surely did. He sent me a list of questions, all neatly numbered. Then I sat down with a tape machine and answered said questions in order. I labeled each answer (number one, etc.) then sent the tape to my new friend. He edited mine to take off such nonsense as "number one" or whatever, and interspersed my responses with his own voice asking the questions. Worked fine, congratulations, Edwin. However, dear readers, later in this session, you will see that the interviewer strayed far from his original plan.

EK Something I've been looking forward to for a very long time. Way back, way back in, I think it was December, I wrote a letter to Mr. Paul Tanner. Our good friend Earl Blair in Rouzerville, you've heard us mention him, had told me about Mr. Paul Tanner and Mr. Skeets Herfurt, being available. And I wrote to both of them, Mr. Tanner responded. I wrote in effect, "Dear Mr. Tanner, a big band fan, Earl Blair of Rouzerville, gave me your address for which I thank him most profusely, and I'm putting it to speedy use. I'm also enclosing a copy of our latest *Al Ham* magazine. I know a lot of you friends have received those. And this *Al Ham* includes a bit of a sketch about me. I'm very interested in hearing the latest in the life of one of Glenn Miller's greatest musicians, and I'm wondering if I might solicit a conversation or two via cassette with you." I told him I do a band show here on Sunday, also do a lot of things with Miller, we told him about Gene's Norman's program of the reunion of the Glenn Miller band which Paul Tanner participated. That was April, 1954, in the LA Shrine Auditorium. But anyhow, I wrote him a nice letter. He responded as graciously as he could. He's a very, very gracious sounding man and he is a very talented man. This being Paul Tanner. And on December 28, last year, he wrote back, "What a nice letter to get from you. Thank Earl Blair for me next chance you get. I'll be glad to tape conversations on the air with you. I have the equipment, but I've never done this, so I don't know the procedure." Now you can rest assured all we're talking about right now is being taped. So I can send a copy of this to Mr. Paul Tanner, or Doctor Paul Tanner, we might add. He taught at UCLA for twenty-three years after he had done a lot of things. And he answers in this letter some of the questions I had written to ask him if he would respond. Well, that was the genesis really of the program you're going to hear with Mr. Paul Tanner very, very shortly.

Now, the band goes back, the band we're talking about that Paul belonged to was the 1938 Glenn Miller Band. Glenn decided to really get going because he had had a real blast. He was unhappy and the band was playing along. And our immediate area too was involved with this sad story. The Glenn Miller Band, to which Paul Tanner did not belong, had been having—

(Editor's note–At this point, Mr. Klitch saw fit to quote from George T. Simon's fine and informative book, Glenn Miller and His Orchestra. *It set the scene for questions that followed.)*

"...successive dates in Reading, Pennsylvania; Auburn, New York; Easton, Maryland; and, finally, on New Year's Eve of 1937, in York, Pennsylvania, seemed absolutely meaningless. For Glenn, his once-promising career had deteriorated into a barrage of backbreaking one-nighters through snow and over icy roads; never sure about arriving at any of them; wondering which guys would show up sober and which guys might not show up at all; worried about his wife who had just undergone a major operation; growing more and more frantic about where the next money was coming from; faced a future with no engagements that might bring some semblances of recognition, all encompassed by an ever-gnawing awareness that, musically, and commercially, his band was going absolutely nowhere.

"And so, on New Year's Eve, at the Valencia Ballroom in York, Pennsylvania, Glenn Miller gave his men their final notice. They played one more date, on January 2, at the Ritz Ballroom in Bridgeport, Connecticut, and that was it. Glenn had worked terribly hard, driving himself into a state of complete nervous exhaustion and a feeling of almost uncontrollable desperation. But all his expertise, experience, patience, musical knowledge, and commercial sense still hadn't been able to add up to anything except failure.

"He returned to New York, broke and depressed, not knowing what he was going to do, where he was going to go, or if he would ever again lead a band."

(Editor's note–At this point, Mr. Klitch resumed using his own very kind and lively resources to continue on.)

EK Well, early in 1938, Glenn Miller decided to form another band, this was early in the springtime. He didn't stay inactive too long. And that band opened at the Raymor Ballroom in Boston on April 16, 1968, correction, 1938, April 16, 1938. But he didn't have all these good musicians that he wanted, and from time to time, little things would happen to raise his spirits like a trombonist that he discovered in a week in August of 1938 when the band was playing in Atlantic City at Hamid's Million Dollar Pier. It was losing money in those days we understand, the take for a week at Hamid's Million Dollar Pier, twelve hundred a week. But he played there just so he would get air time from the Million Dollar Pier. One evening after work, Helen and Glenn went into a night club that turned out to be a strip joint. But there they found a trombone player that turned out to be one of the band's mainstays and who, with his wife, became one of the Miller's dearest friends. His wife at that time being a lady, a very pretty lady, named Bunny. Paul Tanner, who later became a professor of music at UCLA, he'll tell you about this, was then a shy gangling musician out of Skunk Hollow, Kentucky. Skunk Hollow he said. And he was sitting in a semi-permanent band called Marty Caruso. "These guys in the band liked my playing, so they chipped in and they hired me, at fifteen bucks a week." But, you'll hear this matter of meeting with Glenn Miller from Paul Tanner in his own words. Without any further ado, friends, here now is my interview, not my interview, but the way we worked it, my questions of Paul and his responses to my questions. Let's listen.

I'm so grateful to Paul Tanner, Mr. Paul Tanner, for responding to the questions. We have a variety of questions touching on his whole career. I sent him a series of questions and he just responded to each question as I asked them to him. So, I'll ask the question and then play Paul's response in that manner just as though he's still here. So, my first question for Mr. Paul Tanner, Paul, would you please touch on your early musical training.

PT Well, my early musical training. At first, I learned from my dad, and then more by doing than any other way. I don't recommend this, I recommend studying under good teachers, of course. I had bad musical habits that I had to undo, but I did listen well and that was a real big asset I'm sure. The only formal help was from some all too brief contact with talented personnel from Curtis Institute. You must remember that I went out on the road at about sixteen years of age, not much time for early study.

EK Paul, how did you meet Glenn Miller?

PT Well, let's see, the band that my brothers and I had, which incidentally we started while we were in high school in Wilmington, Delaware. Well, we finally had to break it up. We made lots of friends, but not quite enough money to survive. Well, in those days, about 1938 I guess, in the summer, if a musician was out of work, he'd do well to head for Atlantic City. There were just dozens of small clubs to try to get a job playing, plus the fact that a half a dozen big bands went through there every week playing at the piers. So, off I went to Atlantic City. I jammed around in a few clubs, then one night I mosied into the Swing Club where some nice guys from Chester, Chester, Pennsylvania, these fellows were working there. I sat in and played with them, five fellows, and they were good too. They went to the owner and asked him to hire me. Well, after the union tax, I ended up with ten dollars a week. So what did these thoughtful young players do? They each chipped in a dollar of their eighteen dollars so I could stay at fifteen dollars. Well, Glenn had just started with the band he kept, and he was badly in need of a trombone player. He was playing at the Million Dollar Pier then in Atlantic City. Well, somebody, and I never did find out who, told him to come in and hear this young guy. So, in came Glenn and his wife. Well now, I've got to explain. This was a club where the ladies disrobed. Boy, you sure memorize your music in a hurry, I tell you that. Well, I saw Glenn, and of course, even though the public didn't know him yet, I knew all about him. He was doing exactly what I wanted to do, he was a big time trombone player and arranger. Well, I was playing some nice, pretty high solos for the ladies to do their bit. I was really embarrassed. It was a nice club but it still wasn't what you wanted to bring your wife into, you know. At any rate, when I took a break, he motioned to me to come to his table. He asked me if I could pack up and leave. I said, "Pack what? I'm packed." I showed him I had my toothbrush in my pocket and that was it. So he said, "Well come with me." And that was that. The fellows from Chester knew all along that would happen, and they were happy for me. One more thing about my conversation with Glenn, I was such a stammerer that Glenn's wife Helen said that it took me about a half an hour to even say my name. Truthfully, I know I do stammer some now, I guess I do, but I couldn't hardly talk until I was about seventeen. Well, I went with Glenn that night and stayed until the band broke up. He broke up his band in 1942. I usually stay with jobs until the jobs go away.

EK Paul, how did you miss getting with Glenn and that great Army Air Force Band that he put together?

PT Well, when the war came our way and the draft was nibbling at our toes, I got a real nice offer from the New Castle Air Force Base. They had Walter Hendl to conduct the concert band and asked me to lead the jazz band. Well, we had bought a house in Wilmington, and my wife got a job as head of the rationing board. So, I asked Glenn not to request me, you know, he would goof up what I had going. I had already made a deal with him where I was to work for him after the war. But he was just fine, he understood that I would be with my wife, and he saw that as a priority, you know. Incidentally, that deal fell through, but a better one turned up anyway. My wife and I were never separated except for my time at basic training.

EK Paul, the band, you said you were with in '38, the big band that he reformed, the band that lasted. What were your reactions almost four years later when Glenn Miller said goodbye to the band on September 24, 1942, that's when he went into the Army Air Force, and what'd you say, what'd you feel when he said so long to the band at the Central Theater in Passaic, New Jersey?

PT Well, when Glenn broke up the band, it was very shattering, yeah, it really was. These people were your friends, your family. You not only worked with these people, you lived with them. And you knew that you would never see some of them again. As far as Glenn was concerned, I looked forward to working for him again. As far as the music was concerned, I also looked forward to doing some of that later on too. But even though we were a little excited about going on to the next phase of our lives, it was really pretty weepy. It would really have been devastating if we could have been able to see into the future, of course. You know, Glenn was really good to me and I'll never stop appreciating it.

EK Paul, when you joined Charles, Charlie Spivak, after the band broke up, what was that like? Spivak had a great reputation too, but was he anything like Glenn Miller?

PT Well, no, Charlie was not at all like Glenn. Charlie was a good guy and an excellent trumpet player. But there never was a leader with the overall musical knowledge that Glenn had. And he knew just what he wanted and he knew how to get it. Charlie's band was fun though. I was a bit shocked at first because along side of Glenn's band, Charlie's band was very ragged or something. But he had Davey Tough on drums, he had Willie Smith on alto sax, Neil Hefti and Nelson Riddle were there and all, it had to be fun.

EK Paul, what was your army tour of duty like? Getting into this subject right now, but it sounded like that Charlie Spivak gang was a great organization for you and you apparently enjoyed it; but following that now, what was army tour like?

PT Well, when the draft made it obvious that I was going to be in the service, I volunteered in order to be sure that I would be there in time for this real nice situation at the New Castle Air Base. Well, at that very moment that I was being inducted, a unit was being formed in New York City that simply had priority over anything, if you were what it was that they wanted, of course. They wanted musicians who were experienced on radio, records, and movies. And there I was. So, I was sent to New York. And after I did my basic training, even though I was in the army, they had me do nothing but play trombone. And to make music arrangements, of course. We did all kinds of propaganda radio shows, we did movies, and of course, we did lots of V discs.

EK Paul, when you returned to music, first with Les Brown and then with Tex Beneke, was it different from the period before the war; if so, how was it different?

PT When I knew I was being discharged from the service, I went over to Frank Dailey's Meadowbrook to see Frank. I had not only worked there with Glenn, but also I played in Frank's band. So we were friends. I knew that Frank cashed the salary checks for the bands, so he would know what bands paid well. He told me that Harry James paid well, but that the trombone section was sort of locked up. He said that Louis Prima was doing well, but he didn't think I'd be happy in that band. So the ideal band for me, a happy band that played good music and paid well–Les Brown. Frank also knew that Les was at that moment at the

Sheraton, pardon me, at the Sherman Hotel in Chicago. So I wired Les. I got a wire right back saying that he needed a lead trombone immediately. Well, if you know the army, they dragged their feet letting me out. And wires went back and forth with Les. Finally he said, "Just come as soon as you get out." Well, I got out of the army in New York on Saturday and joined Les in Chicago on Sunday. I walked into the lobby of the Sherman Hotel and I saw Les who immediately said, "Paul, I'd like you to meet my girl singer, Doris Day." Well, now remember, Ed, I was very young then, very young. Doris sort of looked me over, then blurted out, "I'm going shopping with you." I said, "Oh, groovy." Then she said, "Are you married?" When I said, "I sure am." Then she said, "I'm going shopping alone." The end of a beautiful romance, Ed, I didn't even make it to her book. Well, I had signed to work for Glenn for a year after the war. So when Glenn didn't come back, his office still held me to my deal, which was just fine with me. So I went with Tex Beneke who fronted the Miller Band. At that time, Tex and Les Brown were both in New York, and their hours didn't conflict, so I worked with both until I had to leave town with Tex. And I stayed with Tex for six years on the road. Well, back to part of your question, it was different. But mainly because there was only one Glenn Miller Band and everything was so first class somehow.

EK Well, I think you're right. And quality. My good friend Pete Callas who was with us here when we put these questions together for Paul Tanner, both of us agree with Paul, it really was a first class organization. So, in continuing my questioning with Paul Tanner, I asked him, "Paul, what did you do for ABC for sixteen, seventeen years; you said you were with ABC, the American Broadcasting Company for that period of time, what did you do?"

PT At the American Broadcasting Company in Los Angeles, we had to do everything. The reason for having a staff band on salary is that they will play for you with a minimum of rehearsal. And it could be dixieland, could be big band, bop, classical, or whatever. You might be accompanying the San Francisco Opera. I played lead for them and because of that, lots of other offers would come in, but I surely wouldn't leave. It was a plum of a job, and I loved it.

EK Well, it sounds that way too, a network job for sixteen, seventeen years. OK, Paul, tell us a little bit about your history of jazz classes. Now this was at UCLA, and apparently, you did it for a long period of time, you enjoyed it, and apparently made a name for yourself as a bit of a professor. So tell us something about the history of jazz classes.

PT The jazz classes at UCLA just got so darned big that I had to stop teaching anything else. I would have sixteen hundred students a day, but I got tired and cut it back to twelve hundred, that's all right then. The real reason for its popularity, Ed, was the subject, a real hot, a real alive subject. It wasn't a snap course, there were tough exams I'm told. But they all came to classes. I had great guests who would just walk in, everybody from Stan Kenton to Herbie Hancock to Jon Hendricks; it was just a lot of fun.

EK A lot of fun as a professor at UCLA. Ten thousand record collection, Paul Tanner had a collection of this. I'm curious now of what type of collection, who, who did you have a collection of, how about a few details about your cataloging system. What was the manner of your presentation of this great gift? We understand you gave it away. Are the records being used today? Ten thousand record collection, you assembled over the years and you gave it away. Tell us of this, Paul.

PT The funny thing about having a collection of ten thousand records, when you move, you get the records in first then you try to get in. The records were mainly jazz of course, but all kinds of jazz, going from 1917 on into the 1980s. Naturally, I had plenty of the swing bands, a lot of my favorite singers, and a nice collective batch of classical records. Well, Ed, here's how you catalogue an album. The name of the album, whose album it is, the name of the record company, the number on the record, the name of each tune, who composed each tune, when each tune was recorded, you know, the date, where each tune was recorded, the city, the personnel on each tune, and the soloists on each tune. I did an awful lot of that by ear and logic, Ed, and if you multiply that by ten thousand. The music library at UCLA has this now. They tape everything. Then they put all my data into computers. Then if someone is studying like the difference between Louis Armstrong and Dizzy Gillespie or one fellow's time and another fellow's time, the computer comes up with names of records that each is on and specifies solos also. You know, you could be studying time differences too. You may want to compare the 1940s to the 1950s or something like that.

EK Well, sounds more involved than my collection. My collection is a stack of records sitting in piles around the room. Well, not really. Paul, we'd like to find out from you if you can, who was your best friend in the

Glenn Miller Band? We're hero worshippers right here. We'd like to learn who your best friend in the Miller band was, and how about your favorite musician of all time? You were an outstanding trombone player yourself, who was your favorite musician? What was your favorite song? How about your favorite girl? How about your favorite girl vocalist and boy vocalist? Tell us of those. And another thing, did the Miller Band ever play any dixieland? And what sort of a personality did Ray Eberle have? I know that's a long series of questions right there, but I'd love to hear your comments please.

PT Well, all the fellows in the Miller band were friends, good friends. It's kind of hard to single someone out, but if I had to, I'd probably say Jimmy Priddy. We had so much in common, both played in the trombone section. We roomed together when our wives weren't with us. Ed, I don't think I can name just one favorite musician. It depends upon what kind of music, or playing, or instrument, whatever we are talking about. My favorite song? That changes often. I suppose that right now it could be any Jobim tune. I would suppose that maybe Ella Fitzgerald is my favorite girl singer, and probably Frank Sinatra for the guys. The Miller Band in its very early times doing some one-nighters would occasionally do a little dixieland jamming, but very seldom though. Ray Eberle was truly a very nice fellow, I liked him. He had a great sense of humor. He was a good singer too even though he was always kind of in his brother Bob's shadow.

EK Well, hey, that's a very wise observation, or an interesting observation on a variety of questions there. And Ray Eberle always seemed to be in his brother Bob's shadow. Brother Bob, as we know, having been the great star of the Jimmy Dorsey Band for so long. Speaking about Dorsey, how about Tommy Dorsey, Paul, Tommy Dorsey had his temper and Benny Goodman had his stare, how did Glenn Miller show his displeasure to any sort of musician, huh?

PT Glenn could always show his displeasure very easily, just by a glance; and believe me, he was not shy when it came to reminding anybody who was the boss. But truthfully, it was so rarely a problem with the band. We knew what was expected of us and we knew that if we didn't get fired, he was happy with us. But he could never tolerate anyone in the band or out of the band like engineers or anybody, if they didn't give one hundred percent.

Brass section—Trombones: L to R: P.T., Jim Priddy, Glenn, Frankie D'Anolfo. Trumpets: Charlie Frankhauser, Zeke Zarchy, Mickey McMickle, Johnny Best.
1940

Advertisement.
January 16, 1940

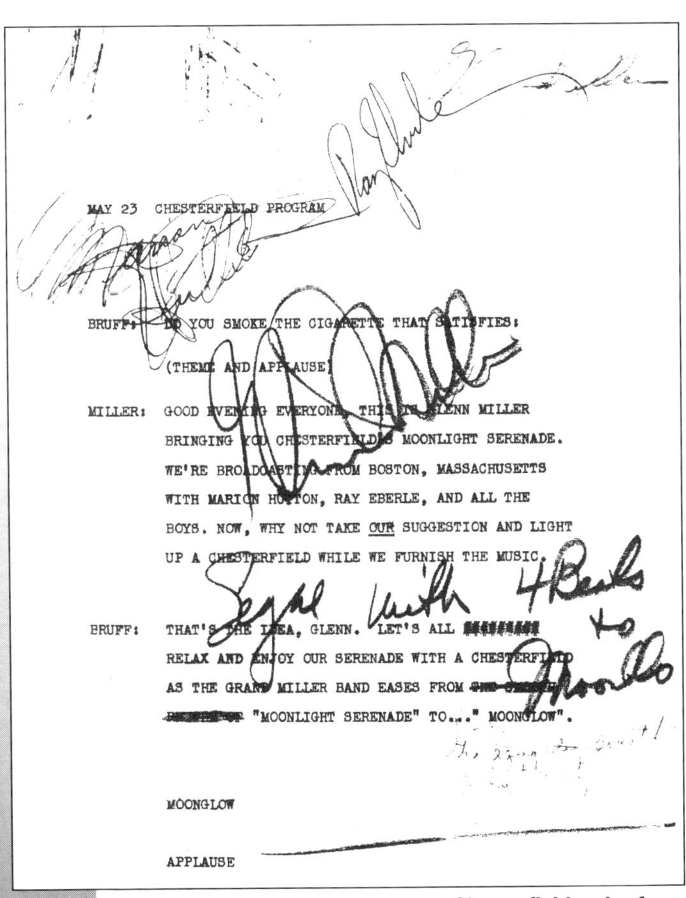

MAY 23 CHESTERFIELD PROGRAM

BRUFF: DO YOU SMOKE THE CIGARETTE THAT SATISFIES:

(THEME AND APPLAUSE)

MILLER: GOOD EVENING EVERYONE, THIS IS GLENN MILLER BRINGING YOU CHESTERFIELD'S MOONLIGHT SERENADE. WE'RE BROADCASTING FROM BOSTON, MASSACHUSETTS WITH MARION HUTTON, RAY EBERLE, AND ALL THE BOYS. NOW, WHY NOT TAKE OUR SUGGESTION AND LIGHT UP A CHESTERFIELD WHILE WE FURNISH THE MUSIC.

BRUFF: THAT'S THE IDEA, GLENN. LET'S ALL RELAX AND ENJOY OUR SERENADE WITH A CHESTERFIELD AS THE GRAND MILLER BAND EASES FROM "MOONLIGHT SERENADE" TO..." MOONGLOW".

MOONGLOW

APPLAUSE

Chesterfield script from Boston, Massachusetts.
May 23, 1940

Glenn and Marion pose for Chesterfield. *1940*

Chesterfield rehearsal. *1940*

Chesterfield rehearsal—Paul Douglas and Glenn make up their "improvisations." Marion's coat hides her on-coming family addition. *1940*

Tex and Marion rehearsing for Chesterfield—"Ooh, what you said!" *1940*

Ray and Marion rehearsing for Chesterfield—"Coochi-coo." *1940*

A Cafe Rouge opening night: L to R: Dick Todd, Dinah Shore, RCA's Leonard Joy, Singer Yvette, Glenn, Eddie Ducin. Yes, the picture is left-handed. *1940*

Glenn autographs for Saint Louis Auditorium fans. *1940*

Tex and Marguerite on the gangplank of SS George Washington, New York City. *August 1940*

Somewhere on the road. Ernie Caceres and Tex Beneke. *1940*

Tex and Marguerite Beneke. *1940*

Cafe Rouge, Hotel Pennsylvania. *1940*

Cafe Rouge–Mo Purtill and Rolly Bundock. *1940*

Tommy Dorsey subbing as our leader at the Paramount, New York City. *1940*

Paramount—Al Klink, Will Schwartz, Hal McIntyre, Ernie Caceres, Tex Beneke. *1940*

Cafe Rouge, Hotel Pennsylvania–"And after the tip I gave him to take all the pictures from the other end." *1940*

Helen listens, watches, and waits. *1940*

Eat when you can, Glenn. *1940*

1940

Tex and Marguerite Beneke. *1941*

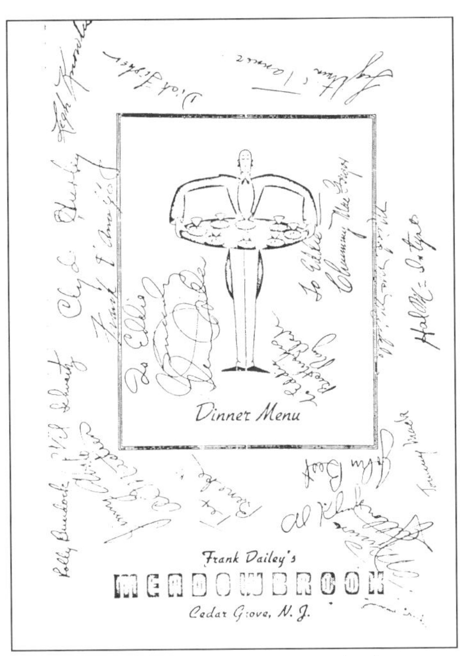

A Meadowbrook menu–autographed to Eddie. (Who is Eddie?) *1941*

A break at the Hotel Pennsylvania soda fountain. *1941*

At the Cafe Rouge, Glenn with Mo Purtill. *1941*

"In The Mood," Glenn, Al Klink, Tex Beneke. *1940*

Modernaires, Glenn, Marion Hutton, Tex Beneke–"Shh, it's a military secret." *1940*

Cafe Rouge, Hotel Pennsylvania: L to R: Jim Priddy, Frank Dailey, Frank D'Anolfo, Marion Hutton, Charlie Spivak, P.T. *1941*

Doc Goldberg digs in. *1941*

"Sure feels good when it swings." Trigger Alpert (bass) visiting Cafe Rouge, Mo Purtill on drums. *1941*

Ray, Marion, and The Mods. *1941*

Billy May. *1941*

Nice to see him happy. *1941*

Ray paying attention to Paula paying attention to Glenn paying attention to details. *1941*

Here's a rare picture–Glenn dancing. *1941*

Glenn, his mother, and his wife. *1941*

A Chesterfield rehearsal. *1941*

***Sun Valley Serenade* set.** *1941*

***Sun Valley Serenade* set, the trained seals make it to the movies.** *1941*

Sonja Heine–a pretty and very talented double. *1941*

John Payne and the wives. *1941*

Sonja Heine, John Payne, Lynn Bari, Milton Berle, Glenn. *1941*

Sonja Heine, Chummy MacGregor, John Payne, P.T., Lynn Bari. *1941*

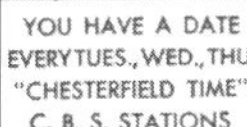

Nicholas Brothers and Dorothy Dandridge. *1941*

YOU HAVE A DATE EVERY TUES., WED., THU. "CHESTERFIELD TIME" C. B. S. STATIONS

GLENN MILLER CLUB BULLETIN

LATEST RECORDING MOONLIGHT SONA[TA] JINGLE BELLS EVERYTHING I LOV[E]

Vol. 1 No. 1 GLENN MILLER RKO BUILDING NEW YORK CITY December, 1941

MERRY CHRISTMAS EVERYBODY

THE WHOLE GANG SWINGS THE JINGLE

If you haven't heard Glenn's arrangement of "Jingle Bells"—you just haven't heard! Here's how they swing into action with this famous Christmas ditty—left to right—The Modernaires—Bill, Hal, Chuck, Glenn (how did you get in here, Mr. M) and Ralph, with Marion, Tex and,—Ernie Cacares, hiding behind the mike and singing into his store whiskers—Picture was snapped in Cafe Rouge of Hotel Pennsylvania—"Jingle Bells" will be a feature of the Christmas Eve Moon-

OUR BEST WISHES FOR 1942

Another year's on the downbeat, and we've gotten out this Christmas newspaper just to thank all of you club members for the swell support you've given the band during the past year. We're mighty proud of the way you feel about our music and we want you to know we'll be in there pitchin' during the coming year. Thanks, too, for your many letters. We read them all and appreciate the time and trouble you take in writing.

When we start on the road again next month we'll be looking forward to meeting new members and renewing old friendships. So, if we come your way, be sure and look us up.

We had hopes of including our new itinerary in the Bulletin. However, our Spring plans all have to wait until we know the "shooting" date of our new picture, and that hasn't been definitely set. After we leave the Pennsylvania, on January 7th, we *may* do a couple of one nighters and visit Detroit, Cleveland, Buffalo and return to New York for a turn at the Paramount before starting for California. Remember, it's not definite.

And, of course, wherever we go it'll be "Chesterfield Moonlight Serenade Time" every Tuesday, Wednesday and Thursday – just as always. That's all except to say "Merry Christmas" everybody and we hope you'll let us know how you like the Bulletin.

GLENN MILLER

Here's Glenn's newest picture. If you'd like an 8x10 in. personally autographed, just drop us a line. But hurry—it's first come, first served.

'Off the Cuff at Rehearsal'

by Paul Douglas

Paramount–who is that playing a solo? *1940*

Well, I'll be . . . *1940*

I know we worked at the Paramount Theatre and the Hotel Pennsylvania at the same time, but I never thought that my inept photography would help prove it. *1940*

Johnny Best with wife, Helen. *1940*

That's a collapsed aluminum chair you see there that simply would not hold Arletta and Billy May at the same time. *1940*

Glenn poses for Chesterfield; sorry, we didn't know they were a health hazard. *1941*

Glenn deciding if Lynn Bari sings as well as she looks. *1940*

John Payne sings soulfully, Glenn conducts, Ernie Caceres plays his part while Billy May looks like a movie tough guy. *1940*

Gene Morrison checks out his girl singer. *1940*

And the boss whips the ball back with poise. *1940*

Glenn reaches for a low fast one. *1940*

Bullets Durgom and Jackie Gleason in Elgin, Illinois. Actually, they're on a set at 20th Century Fox. Wasn't there a president who spent some time in Elgin, Illinois? *1940*

Cesar Romero–a silly shot of a serious lover. *1940*

Cuz and Lightnin' ready for the slopes. *1940*

Back on that ever lovin' road again. *1940*

Whenever and wherever possible–
"Where's the first tee?" *1940*

Glenn and Chummy MacGregor in Hershey, PA. *1940*

I dove and swam better than I golfed. *1940*

John Payne and his chest. *1940*

Chattanooga stock arrangement. *1941*

EK Well, I guess we've heard a little about that. He was a perfectionist. Paul Tanner, what was your favorite ballroom?

PT I don't suppose I have a favorite ballroom. By now, a lot of them are quite run down. The Palladium in Hollywood was very, very pretty, but also it had a meaning. That meant we were in Hollywood.

EK How about Al Klink and Tex Beneke? We have heard stories about maybe they didn't get along too well, and a lot of people said that Al Klink was a better musician than Tex Beneke, but from your point of view, having played in the band with them for a long time, what was your estimate, were they friends?

PT Al Klink and Tex Beneke certainly *were* good friends. I know what the question is all about, and they both said often that Al should play more solos. Maybe Tex didn't say it as often as Al. But you must realize that Tex was really good, and besides that, he was a personality, you know, a good singer, in that particular style.

EK OK, so there's an assessment now by Mr. Paul Tanner of Al Klink and Tex Beneke. My next question that I posed to Paul; and we certainly appreciate his taking the time and answering these questions. Well, it's sort of a multi-layered question once again. How did the band travel when he was with the band? Where did you stay during a stand? Did you stay at a private home, or how were you accommodated in this manner?

PT The band traveled by bus. But I drove my car almost all the time because Glenn had to furnish me a space on the bus, but he did not, by union rules, have to supply space for my wife. We would stay in hotels; there were practically no motels in those days. Glenn wanted us at the better hotels at that, it had something to do with the image.

EK OK, it had something to do with the image. Well I'll tell you, the band had a tremendous, tremendous image. Well, here's my next question, Paul, how often did the band hold a rehearsal, if they did, but I don't think many of us know? How about this?

PT When we were at the Pennsylvania Hotel in New York, we would have an all night rehearsal once a week. The rest of the time we would rehearse at the end of Chesterfield program rehearsals to get us into new arrangements. Of course, it helped that everybody could read well, and we knew pretty much what he wanted.

EK During all the time that you were with the band, Paul, you must have had many many thrills or pride in a particular performance somewhere. Can you maybe share with us what one of these outstanding performances in your mind might have been?

PT I'm sorry, Ed, I simply can't say anything about a favorite performance. When Bobby Hackett joined the band, I was always really enthralled with whatever Bobby played, like on "Rhapsody in Blue."

EK Paul, I'm wondering. Did you ever get into any of the different sorts of jazz? Now you're associated with big bands, I'm thinking about Bop and that sort of music. Did you ever get involved?

PT I think Bop or Rebop or whatever it gets called was a logical move for jazz. The country was nervous, so our music was nervous, you know, a war was going on. Did you notice, after the war was over, we got what was known as Cool jazz? That was very relaxed because the country calmed down. But the draft made it logical to have small bands, and small groups mean lots of improvisation. I was shocked at first, but now it just sounds easy and logical to me.

EK Paul, so far, you've said that in almost every phase of your relationship with Glenn Miller, and your membership in the big band, that you were always at a happy or sort of elated frame of mind. I'm just wondering, did you ever get down or depressed at any time?

PT No, Ed, I can't think of any times when I was really down in Glenn's band. Truthfully, I was glad to be there, I knew I was lucky, good music, good pay, etc.

EK Paul,when you were conducting your instruction at UCLA, did you have anybody of prominence come through your class?

PT Oh sure, having had seventy-five thousand students in the history of jazz, I had most of them that went though the school while I was there. For example, I was one of the fellows who hosted Lou Alcinder, who is now Karim Abdul Jabbar you know, when Lou looked over the place to see where he was going to college. Incidentally, his dad graduated from Juliard on trombone.

EK Paul, one of the fabled members of the jazz fraternity in the big band era, Bix Beiderbecke; did you ever work with Bix Beiderbecke?

PT I never worked with Bix Beiderbecke or Christian, I was too young for Beiderbecke. Bunny Berigan was in Tommy Dorsey's Band when one night in Madison Square Garden, they put together Dorsey's Band, Will

Bradley's Band, and our band. Like all the trombones were together, all the trumpets, and so on. And I really enjoyed Berigan that night. He was so good.

EK From your career with Glenn, it seems I've asked this question before, but I'd like to come back to it right now, can you point out to having *one* highlight in the whole time. One of the things that stands out in your mind the most?

PT I really don't know. I could say playing in Carnegie Hall or making movies or lots of things. Every night was New Year's Eve, Ed. Of course, when you step out on the stage and perform a concerto that you have written and you get appreciated, these are huge thrills and great ego builders. I've done this plenty, even in foreign countries. But, on the other hand, when the pit would go up in the Paramount Theater in New York, and you're sitting playing your part to "Moonlight Serenade," and the reaction of the people just absolutely gave me goose bumps. I've had so many thrills, Ed, I still do have, thank goodness. What a nice pleasure being able to chat with you. I hope you and your listeners have enjoyed it nearly as much as I have.

EK Well, don't go away, Paul, don't go away, Paul. I have a couple more questions I'd like to ask you, I would. And then I'd like, if you would, to respond to some questions that my friend Pete Calas posed to you, and then well, Pete put a lot of good questions to Paul Tanner and he did respond to them. So the other questions I have about–if Paul Tanner was real familiar with the Valencia Ballroom and what did he think of Hal McIntyre, the great sax player who was one of the first musicians to leave Glenn Miller and go off on his own with the help of Glenn Miller. And I asked Paul about the Valencia and this sort of thing, and he just talked. He just talked on a little bit, so we'll just let his conversations to me go. And they'll include my questions, and his responses to my questions and also some of the questions that were posed to him by Pete Calas. So here's Paul Tanner.

PT Ed, I was friendly with Hal McIntyre, he was a charming fellow, like an All-American boy and all like that as far as we were concerned in the band. Let's see, I played in the Valencia Ballroom in York lots of times. But I certainly wasn't with the band that Glenn broke up. I was with the band he kept. You were talking about Mal Hallet, did you know that he kind of had a record? He did six years of one-nighters with no places where he even had a week's stay or anything. Good grief, it was a monstrous endurance contest. I can't place Johnny Metrick, because Jimmy Middleton was the bass player in Les Brown's Band when I was there. I worked at that Pier Ballroom in Ocean City, Maryland, that you mentioned. I worked there when I was still in high school. I worked there for a whole summer, I think 1933, something like that. That TV program that you mentioned that came out of Glen Island Casino, they used some of my home movies in it. Be sure and give my regards to Earl Blair, will you, thank you. Now your friend Peter Callas asked about Glenn's favorite song. I suppose he had one. I don't remember him ever mentioning it. But it probably would have been "Moonlight Serenade." Let me see, were all the musicians alike? Well, no, none of us looked like Billy May I don't think. What Glenn was really after was sort of a clean cut type. But you know, there were young blond Irish types and then there was Ernie Caceres, a Mexican American, and all different types of fellows. But he wanted someone who would keep himself very neat and well-groomed and so forth. Provided of course, the number one thing is he had to play as Glenn wanted. But thanks for the compliment, you're very complimentary about that Cary Grant thing. Let's see, no, no tapes recorded during rehearsals; in fact, Pete, tape hadn't been invented at that time. There are some records out now that were off radio programs, but those would go into radio stations and be put on acetates, but if Glenn heard them now, he would be absolutely furious because there was such a lack of perfection on those things, mistakes on them, bad balances and things like that. Let me see, Glenn made an awful lot of V discs, and they've all been put out commercially now, especially overseas I know. Maybe if you looked at a book by John Flower. It was called "Moonlight Serenade" and it was published by Arlington House. He's got a pretty good discography in there. Or inquire from the Glenn Miller Society in London. I put the address on a note to Ed for you. I don't recall "'Tain't No Good" or the Stage Door Canteen tunes; but "'Tain't No Good," could that have been "'Tain't No Use At All." That was printed off a Chesterfield program, I think. Incidentally, Pete, I know Hagerstown, or at least as it used to be, because I was raised, at least during my high school days, there in Wilmington, Delaware. Well, fellows, this has been awfully nice chatting with you, and you know, send me another tape some time if you have some more questions, I'd be very very happy to chat with you, take care.

EK Isn't that nice. Mr. Paul Tanner, one of the fine, fine trombonists. As a matter of fact, the first trombonist hired by Glenn Miller for the band that he kept as Paul Tanner said. Incidentally that Glenn Miller Society that he made reference to is as follows: it's in London, it's known as the London Glenn Miller Society, The London Glenn Miller Society, in care of Mr. Richard March, as in the month of, Mr. Richard March; his address is 45 Spring Lane, 45 Spring Lane, Woodside, South Norwood, and then there's a combination of letters and numbers, SE 25 45P, England. Here's that address again: The London Glenn Miller Society, Mr. Richard March, 45 Spring Lane, Woodside, South Norwood, SE 25 45S, England. *(Editor's note–he said 45P the first time, then 45S the second time. In my book, I have 45 SP, how's that for confusion?)*

And our thanks, our very, very great thanks to Mr. Paul Tanner for taking the time out. As you can see, he devoted a lot of effort to us here as a result of my questions to him. Well, he looked like a nice trombone player. We knew he was a good one. And well, he's a fine gentleman, too, to respond. That's our program and I'd like to hear from you here. Just send me a card now and this, hey, the Paul Tanner Show, WARK, Hagerstown, Maryland, care of Ed Klitch, and we'll get your remarks off to Paul Tanner. I know he'll love to hear from you. Please let me know here.

15 Interview with Cathy Fife

A young (?) lady named Cathy Fife from KHAT, a radio station in Lincoln, Nebraska, called and we chatted over the phone while she was on the air. This was April 23, 1993.

playing in the background 1 **"Moonlight Serenade"**

CF Cathy Fife with you, it's 10:03 and certainly no secret that our favorite band of all times is the Glenn Miller Orchestra. And every time I hear music like this, I think of how special it must have been back in 1946. I missed the big years, the good years of music as far as I'm concerned. So every time I turn around and see a book that has to do with that special time, I grab on to it and embrace it and am just hungry to learn more. And today, boy oh boy, are we going to learn more. Because we have with us Paul Tanner who has written one of the most wonderful books that I've seen in a long time, *Every Night Was New Year's Eve On the Road With Glenn Miller.* We'll tell you how you can purchase the book, and we'll listen as Paul Tanner shares not only the wisdom of his years with us, but we also have lots of clips from Glenn Miller music. So, welcome Paul Tanner, welcome to KHAT.[1]

PT Thank you very much. It's a pleasure to be here, Cathy.

CF We are just really thrilled to have you, and like I told the audience, anything to do with the Glenn Miller Orchestra, I'm just tickled to death over. We are going to have the Glenn Miller Orchestra right here in Lincoln on the twelfth of May at the Playmor Ballroom. And I understand that people are calling in for reservations right and left, so we're really excited.

PT Is this with Larry O'Brien?

CF Yes,

PT Do you get a chance to talk to him?

CF I haven't yet, but I hope to. What about Larry O'Brien now, he seems to be well-respected among musicians? And as far as ghost bands go, he seems to be right at the top of the list. Everyone seems to think that the Miller Band is very intact.

PT Well, in the first place, give Larry my very best, he's a nice fellow.

CF I certainly will.

PT He's a fine musician, excellent trombone player, and he's done really well playing Glenn Miller music today. I think that Larry's doing a better job than anybody has in a long, long time.

CF I think you're right about that. You were a trombone player as well.

PT That's right.

CF Who are some of the musicians who played at the time that you played?

PT Well, I was with Glenn all the time he had the civilian band. So therefore, anybody who was with the civilian band, I played with.

CF Tell us a little about your personal history. Like for instance, where were you born?

PT Well, you won't believe this, Cathy, but there's a place in Kentucky called Skunk Hollow. It's somewhere between Fort Thomas and Covington.

CF And I trust that has nothing to do with your personality.

PT Well, that's up to you to decide. But at any rate, I left there when I was about a foot long.

CF I love it. Did you know early on that you were going to be musical?

PT Yes. Our whole family was. My dad graduated from the Cincinnati Conservatory. My dad and mother met in a college choir. There were six boys in our family and they all had to take up music.

CF Wow. Why the trombone?

PT Well, because the trombone's out front, Cathy. And being a big ham, that's a good place for me.

CF Now I see, I'm married to a sideman. I'm married to a trumpet player.

PT Well, he sits behind me.

CF Yes. And I'm amazed because he's like you are, he's kind of a ham too, so I'm surprised that he stands for that.

PT He has no choice.

CF That's right. Oh dear. Well, when in school, I suppose you were in the band in school?

PT Sure, absolutely.

CF And what about when you got out of school, what did you want to do for a living, and what did you do?

PT Well, when I got out of high school, I was only sixteen. So I immediately went on the road with my brothers with a family band. Actually, I was on the road for seventeen years.

CF And that's the thing that most musicians dread. They say, boy, I hate those road trips, but you did it for a very long time.

PT Seventeen years. Actually, I didn't know anything different. Of course, I was very young, and I was having a good time and I was learning.

CF Now during those seventeen years, obviously you got married somewhere along the way.

PT Somewhere along the way I certainly did.

CF And band wives–we are a different lot. We come in two varieties. We come the kind like I am, very excited by the music and like to go along whenever. And then there's the band wife who's really disgusted by the whole situation and would just as soon it isn't going on, but that's life.

PT Well, the lady I was married to was thrilled with the band, and she came with me on the road.

CF That's great.

PT She passed away a year or so after I left UCLA, then I was a widower for a couple of years, now I've been married again for about nine years.

CF It looks like from pictures I see of you and your current wife, that you are very happy.

PT Oh yeah, she's very nice, you'd like her.

CF That's wonderful. Well, let's find out how you got from the family band, and what was the name of the family band?

PT The Kentuckians.

CF OK, how you got from the Kentuckians, for crying out loud, to Glenn Miller's Orchestra.

PT Well, the band went broke. I went to Atlantic City and worked in a little strip joint. Glenn took someone's advice and came in and heard me and hired me on the spot.

CF Now as bands go, looking back, it looks like they were the biggie, but of course, they were competing with Dorsey and so many other ones. I mean, did you feel that this was the cadillac of bands?

PT Well, at that time, he was struggling. I knew what he was all about, he was doing what I wanted to do eventually, a big time trombone player.

CF Tell us about Glenn Miller. What was he really like? We see him portrayed in movies and we hear stories. But you knew him.

PT Well, as you know, I did a whole chapter on that in my book. Thanks for the way you spoke about it. I appreciate it. There's a whole chapter in there on what kind of a guy was Glenn Miller. Because he was kind of complex. He was a fine, fine musician, and you didn't get away with anything. He was an excellent business man. He was extremely patriotic. He was also quite athletic. He was fair if you didn't cross him. If you crossed him, he was the devil. But he treated me just fine. I have no complaints at all.

CF I see in the book, I got a kick out of some memorabilia that you have. A picture, you have of a post card, a Glenn Miller post card from December of 1938–it says "Get a load of the one cent stamp."

PT Isn't that something! And you know the card opened up to the size of a large letter.

CF Is that right?

PT For a one cent stamp. Hard to believe, isn't it?

CF Certainly is. Well, we can't wait to talk with you some more. We have music to share, and we have anecdotes to share. We want to know how to get the book. I imagine the listeners can get it through the Glenn Miller Birthplace. Do you have an address, or I do?

PT I've got it in my hands if you want it.

CF All right, you give it and you tell us the cost and so people will know how to send for the book.

PT All right. The lady's name is Mrs. Wilda Martin, and that's at the Glenn Miller Birthplace Society, P.O. Box 61, Clarinda, Iowa. The zip code there is 51632. That's 51632. I can give you the phone if you want it.

CF OK, and also give us the price of the book.

PT Actually don't know.

CF OK, then give us the phone number so we can call.

PT All right. Area code (712) 542-2461. That's area code (712) 542-2461.

CF Well, I have to tell you, Paul, I used your name in vain, I called and there was a machine on. So I said, "I'm Cathy Fife, I'm a friend of Paul

Tanner's," and I said, "I'm going to do an interview with him and I need the book, and I need it as soon as you can get it to me." So I gave them the address and they sent it out, I had it like two days later. Oh, I was really impressed. I have been down there for the Miller birthday celebration; which incidentally, folks, is the first week in June I believe. And it's incredible. I mean the band is there, and you can look at all the memorabilia. Now you've been there before.

PT I've been there three or four times. It's a lot of fun, isn't it.

"Little Brown Jug" ❷

"Chattanooga Choo Choo" ❸

CF It really is a lot of fun, it's really neat. And of course, because it's in the midwest, we can all kind of relate, and it's neat. You just sit tight here; we're just glad to have you today, and we'll be back with more. [2 & 3]

CF We've got Glenn Miller music here this morning because we're featuring a book called *Every Night Was New Year's Eve On the Road With Glenn Miller*. And this book was written by a trombone player with the band, a sideman, by the name of Paul Tanner, who is with us. And if you're ordering books this morning, now the book in the last hour that I told you about Sammy Kaye's Orchestra, it's just a little tiny book with like a cardboard cover and it features a cassette. This one is a beautiful, what I call a coffee table book. This book you would be proud to put on display in your home and share it with your friends and your children and anyone you know who loves Glenn Miller. Father's Day is coming up and your dad or your husband or your brother loves the Glenn Miller Orchestra, this would be a wonderful gift. And they're still making music today certainly. Now Paul, what about the movie making years. Were you with the Miller Band then, I presume?

PT You know I was because I was with the band all the time.

CF And what about the movies? Were you guys excited about being in the movies or was it one of those things like, oh gosh, he wants us to do this?

PT Oh no, we were very excited. We were very excited to come to California, let alone to make movies.

CF And back then, boy, California was the land of the free and palm trees and quite a place.

PT Well, it still is, except for Lincoln, Nebraska.

CF Yep, we don't get your way very often, that's for sure.

PT It's beautiful out here this morning.

CF Oh well, I can imagine. And it's, I don't know, it hasn't been beautiful here, been kind of cold. What about the movie now, how long did it take you to make a movie?

PT About somewhere around ten weeks. That includes the recording which is all done first. Then the picture taking which follows it. And it takes about ten weeks or so. I understand it's shorter today, but that's about what it was then. I'm also in *The Glenn Miller Story* with Jimmy Stewart.

CF Oh were you!

PT Yes, that was in 1954.

CF That's my favorite movie of all times.

PT Well, I know I had a good time.

CF That's why I fell in love with my husband. This is a funny story because after I saw *The Glenn Miller Story,* as a child, I always told my mother that I was going to marry somebody who would love me like Jimmy Stewart loved June Allyson on *The Glenn Miller Story.* She used to say that was just a movie, and when we met...

PT Tell your husband we really tried hard.

CF There you go. And when we met he was a sideman in the band and we got to talking, and his marriage had failed and my marriage had failed. And I said "How come, how come we didn't make it?" He said, "Oh I don't know, I'm a romantic, I just think that love ought to be like *The Glenn Miller Story.* Boy, I'm telling you, I married him right away.

PT Well, you know, Jimmy Stewart was somebody special anyway. He was a good good actor and did an excellent job I think.

CF How much like Glenn Miller was he?

PT Well, not a lot. Glenn was a little more intense like, I suppose, especially when it came to business. But Stewart seemed to be a little softer, a little more compassionate and so forth, and a little more demonstrative with his wife than Glenn was. Glenn was never very demonstrative in public with Helen.

CF So it was a movie. What about June Allyson?

PT June Allyson was very nice. We didn't have a lot to do with her, we had more to do with Stewart than with Allyson.

CF She looked so pretty.

PT Yeah, she was nice.

CF That's neat. What was your favorite part of traveling with the band during those days?

PT Well, I suppose the playing.

CF And what was the least favorite part?

PT Some long nighttime one-nighters, just to get to the next town. But you know, Cathy, It's not as bad as it sounds. If our trip to the next town, now we didn't do one-nighters constantly, you know, but when we were doing one-nighters, if our trip to the next town was one hundred and fifty miles or less, actually I got in a golf game. So, that's not too bad, and we played on the very best courses.

CF Now did you guys play baseball? So many of the big bands played baseball.

PT Yes, but we weren't as good as some of them. We challenged them to golf and they challenged us to baseball. Harry James and Les Brown were very good baseball teams.

CF I hear they hired guys because they were good baseball players not because they were good musicians.

PT Well, with Tex Beneke, we talked him into a saxophone player who was a scratch golfer. Of course, he was a good saxophone player too.

CF Is there any truth to the tale that Tex is on the outs with the Miller people?

PT Well, at one time there was a disagreement about what percentage Tex was to get of the take when he fronted the Miller band; then they did arrive at a parting of the ways. But it's been solved over the years. Most of them are gone now, so there's no problem now.

CF I see a picture of a reunion a couple of years back. I think it was in California where some of you were.

PT Yes, uh huh.

CF Do you get together often?

PT No. In fact, there are getting to be fewer and fewer of us.

CF Did I read that Paula Kelly had died lately?

PT That's right, she did. Paula was very, very nice too, charming person. So actually, we don't get together hardly at all. I talk to Tex every week or so on the telephone just to see how he's doing. That's about it.

CF Now what about Glenn Miller's children, where are they and what are they doing?

PT Steve, the son, has a place in La Vegas and he has real estate investments, I think, and he does very, very well. Jonnie, the girl, married a fellow down here in La Jolla who is a lawyer and they do quite well. They have a lovely home down here, and she has a house full of kids.

CF Oh really?

PT Yep.

CF Well, that's kind of neat. I love it. Who were some of the guys who were really, really outstanding musicians that you played with?

PT Well, you have to start with Bobby Hackett. If it weren't for Bobby Hackett's solo on "String of Pearls," we might not be hearing as much out of "String of Pearls" as we have. Tex was a fine player, he truly was. But then all through the band, like the lead clarinet, Willie Schwartz, no one has been able to imitate that sound. All through the band, it was loaded with a lot of talent. I was just thrilled to be there myself.

CF Didn't Jackie Gleason play bass in *Orchestra Wives*?

PT Well, he was an actor. He doesn't actually know one note from another, pretending to play the bass. He kept us in stitches. He was working so hard. He'd come out there all day long working on the movie, he was a stand-up comedian at Slapsie Maxie's out here in Hollywood and then back there again in the morning. So he was working really hard. But you never knew it, he just kept us rolling.

CF So, you guys probably weren't surprised at all when he finally made it big.

PT No, we thought he was hilarious.

CF He's always so famous for how much he eats and how much he drinks and did he do that back then?

PT Well, we didn't see that very much, because we'd just get a break for lunch and that was it. We had breakfast before we got there and dinner later. And not much boozing on the job, that's kind of a no-no.

CF That's what I wondered too. A lot of times people accuse musicians of drinking so much, and so many times the band leader doesn't allow it, or even the establishment doesn't allow it.

PT Well, I'm sure your husband will tell you. You just can't perform your best if you don't have all your facilities. So, we just never fooled with that very much. Glenn insisted that we give a hundred per cent all the time, and that means that you have to know what you're doing.

CF We were talking to Billy Williams about ballrooms across the United States, and he was pointing out some of his favorites. What were some of yours?

PT Well, the Palladium of course is a beautiful ballroom. Of course, in Lincoln, there was the Turnpike Casino. Do you remember such a place?

CF I don't because it was gone in time, I'm just a child, remember? But people have told me about it. And I'm not a child, I'm a grandma, but I was born in '46. So I'm a little younger than you.

PT A little bit, yes. Nobody was born in '46. there was a war on.

CF Well I was, that's funny. What about now, I always think that there is more big band activity going on on the east coast now than on the west coast. What about that?

PT There are more places to play there and they are closer together. The farther you get from New York, the more spread out the places are, and you have to travel to them, and that's quite an expense.

CF And I was asking Billy about the fact that women are always attracted to musicians. And they always kind of hang around. And he said his wife was always jealous of that, what about yours?

PT Actually, I never saw that to start with, that I think somebody made up.

CF Oh no, no, no, they did not. And I'm looking at your picture and you're a very good-looking man, and I'm sure there was more than one bobby soxer that had the hots for you. You just didn't know it.

PT I met the artist in Japan who did the cover for the book, a very charming fellow, and through an interpreter, he said, "You used to be good-looking." Thanks a lot.

CF Don't you love that? Let's talk about some of the vocalists that came and went. Or did they come and go with the Miller Band? Was there longevity there when it comes to the vocalists?

PT Actually, in the bands in those days, there was longevity all throughout the bands. In the first place, Glenn got himself in a position where he could pay better than anybody else. And so he did. Now the way to keep a fellow is to pay him more than somebody else is going to pay him. So he had his choice of musicians and he had his choice of singers. Now he kept Ray Eberle since the band started up until very shortly before it broke up. And so Ray was in there a long time. Marion Hutton only left to have a baby and then Paula Kelly came in, she was married to one of the Modernaires. And then, he did have the Modernaires. Skip Nelson, who took Ray Eberle's place, was a fine singer, and Glenn got him from the Chico Marx Band. He had Paula sing for Marion and Paula was a fine singer. He had Dorothy Claire for a little while and just on a couple of records . . .

Now would you believe it, that's the end of the tape. Of course, the next two words would have been "Kay Starr."

16 Interview with Malcom Laycock

BBC October 13, 1997, 8:30 PM

Being interviewed on the BBC is sort of interesting to both the interviewer and the interviewee mainly because we each had our own accents. Malcolm Laycock could sound like British Royalty to me while I might sound like a 1930s gangster movie to him. At any rate, he is charming. We were in a tight sort of closet in a tea room of a London hotel, so if you hear tea cups clinking, you'll understand.

Jerry Gray Orchestra 1
"American Patrol"

ML Now it's half past eight, and welcome if you just tuned in, this is Malcolm Laycock with a rather special edition of the Big Band Era tonight. In a few minutes I shall be talking to Glenn Miller's long time trombonist, Paul Tanner. So, for an appropriate mystery it is, one with Glenn Miller connections, see if you can recognize who's playing this.[1]

Glenn Miller Orchestra 2
"Rhapsody In Blue"

"American Patrol," a hit for Glenn Miller, but I'll leave that one with you to ponder who's band it might have been if not Glenn's, and I'll come back to it later. Meanwhile, I'll turn now to Paul Tanner, Glenn's trombonist from start to finish right through the civilian band. Paul was in London this summer and paid a visit to a meeting of the Glenn Miller Society. While he was here, I spent a little time with him and fished out the inevitable tape recorder over a cup of tea in his hotel. Hence, a little clatter in the background. And the reason I've waited until now to introduce you to Paul is that it's his eightieth birthday on Wednesday, and to celebrate, I asked him to pick some of his favorite music for us tonight. He started, as you might expect, with the time he was playing with Glenn Miller, and "Rhapsody In Blue." Now I played this a few weeks ago by Glenn's AAF Band, but here is the earlier 1942 civilian band version.[2]

ML Well, Paul, it's delightful to meet in London as you pass through. We can now hear the voice behind the trombone, can't we.

PT Ah, you certainly can. Incidentally, speaking of being here in London, do you know the tune "London By Night" or "London At Night"? Oh, it's a beautiful tune, it should have become much more popular.

ML Have you ever played it?

PT Well, I didn't play it with Glenn Miller, but I certainly played it, and it's a lovely tune.

ML We've just come out of "Rhapsody In Blue," which you tell me is one of your favorites of Glenn.

PT Absolutely, it's a beautiful piece. Do you know the funny thing about that, no one else was allowed to record that, you couldn't get permission from George Gershwin's estate to record it. But they gave Glenn permission, they said, "We think that you'll do bang-up job, so you can go ahead and record it." And he was thrilled about it because he had studied along with Gershwin from this fellow Schillinger. And he was thrilled to be able to do it and the arrangers really put their hearts into it. It's a beautiful thing.

ML Now you had four and a half years, the whole time in Glenn's civilian band, the second band, the famous one, that shot to fame as it were to use words of all of Hollywood and the films and the sound stages, great excitement. But having said all that, there must be other bands, other pieces of music over the years which you keep finding that you go back to and you listen to through the years, you think "That is really nice, I like that." Can you think of one?

PT Sure, of course every young trombone player had to almost study Tommy Dorsey. And I was a very heavy admirer of Jack Teagarden of course, being from the deep South as I was. Anything that Teagarden played had a lot of heart to it as far as I was concerned. And also I was a great, great admirer of Duke Ellington, most of the things that Ellington did were real thrills to me.

ML Let's go on the Duke Ellington at first, I mean that's a large canon to shoot from. Where would you zoom in on an Ellington recording?

PT Well Malcolm, when I was teaching, I told the students that I had this specific Ellington record that if my house burned down, it was OK, because I had a copy of the record there at the university. It was a gorgeous thing with a lot of sentimental value. If your listeners know the name Billy Strayhorn, it was one of the last things that he did. He had a lot of physical problems, he spent a lot of time in the hospital, and he put titles on his scores that he wrote while he was in the hospital. He put titles on his scores that he knew wouldn't matter because Ellington would change them anyway. But this time, Ellington left the titles the same. And this particular one was called "Blood Count." Now it sounds a little drastic but it's a lovely thing. And Strayhorn used to write a lot of things for Johnny Hodges to play on the alto sax. So he and Hodges were very good buddies. So he wrote this and it was pretty much of a Hodges solo on the saxophone. And Hodges, who is a very competent musician as far as a player is concerned, and he would never have any problems. He tries to play this solo, and toward the end, he can't hardly breathe.He's so caught up in that he thinks of his little buddy Strayhorn who was a little teeny fellow, they used to call him "Sweet Pea." And he thinks of Strayhorn there in the hospital, and Strayhorn just died. And here they rush the band into a studio and say, "You must record any non-recorded Strayhorn things that you have." And here Hodges has got to stand up and play this and he's thinking about his little buddy and he almost can't get through it. And so they couldn't even make another tape because he'd never make it, Hodges couldn't make it. And if you think about that, now I would tell that to a bunch of college students, five hundred of them sitting out in front, and you couldn't hear a whisper, some would start to cry. It was really a touching thing and I've never forgotten it. It's beautiful.[3]

Duke Ellington's ❸ **"Blood Count"** *featuring Johnny Hodges*

ML Billy Strayhorn's "Blood Count." You mentioned before we listened to that, Paul, Tommy Dorsey and Jack Teagarden, a bit silly to say which is your favorite, but do you have a favorite record of one of those that you particularly like?

PT Well, if I were going to pick out one record of those two artists, I would say Teagarden's "I Gotta Right To Sing The Blues." It's kind of the epitome of Teagarden's playing. I worked with the Spivak Band. And Charlie had just had a band with Teagarden and it wasn't successful. It was kind of hard to keep Teagarden sober enough somehow. But he was a very relaxed fellow and everybody loved him, even as he was driving down the highway with his Stanley Steamer as he was wont to do. He was a very relaxed fellow and he told Charlie, "If I fall off the stage, just grab my horn, because nothing happens to a drunk if he falls off a stage. But you take care of my horn." So Charlie had to do that.

But everybody loved Jack, he was just a marvelous fellow and, so relaxed, and it all comes out with that great big sound of his.[4]

4 *Jack Teagarden* **"I've Got a Right To Sing the Blues"**

ML Jack Teagarden, "I've Got a Right To Sing the Blues." Just finally, before I thank you very much for talking so briefly to me, Paul, we could have talked all evening, I think. It's often said by some people that Glenn's Band didn't swing. You're not really the right person to ask because you never heard it properly, you never got out front, you're always sitting right there in the middle of it, not the best place to judge it perhaps, from a musician's point of view. I think you would disagree, wouldn't you? It does swing.

PT Absolutely. Of course you can't out-swing Basie. If you say the Glenn Miller Band didn't swing, listen to Count Basie. Well, nobody swung like Count Basie. The band did swing, very, very well. The longer the band went on, the more relaxed it kind of got, so it swung better. It always swung a little better in person than on records, because it's a little tight in the studio. You're playing for posterity when you make a record.

ML They come out rather dry some of them, don't they?

PT Absolutely. You know that if you make a mistake, you live with it the rest of your life. So you hear some of the things that we did even on the radio that were much more relaxed than the studio records. So I would suggest a thing that we did on "Swing Low Sweet Chariot." It got going so well I don't think Glenn wanted to stop it, and here we were on the air, you've got to stop.

ML You are in the thick of this one, Paul Tanner. Thank you very much for talking with me. We will swing out with Glenn.[5]

5 *Glenn Miller* **"Swing Low Sweet Chariot"**

ML Glenn Miller's swinging "Swing Low, Sweet Chariot" from a radio broadcast in 1940. And with it, I thank Paul Tanner for letting me put a microphone in front of him. And send our best wishes to him for his eightieth birthday on Wednesday.

17 Plagiarism

Now here is a strange one. This fellow has evidently hired a lawyer to prove that his tune has been copied (plagiarized). Now the lawyer had hired two "experts" whom he hopes will tell him that his client has been wronged. I am one of the "experts" and I honestly don't know the other chap. It seems there was also another fellow. I have no idea who he was, maybe the injured composer, I don't know. The sad thing is that I don't think either of us gave him the satisfaction he was hoping for. But at any rate, the lawyer is setting up a conference call; evidently that's a difficult thing to establish as you'll see.

In this sue-happy era, it only seems prudent for me to leave out names (especially the lawyer's). And frankly, I have no idea at all what "the story" was. Too bad, sounds like it would make for a nice novel. You could invent your own, that could be fun. This all happened July 16, 1992.

I never heard how the case came out or if it even got to court. I know I was never paid. Plagiarism is a tough way to go unless the perpetrator was both obvious and foolish.

PT Are you picking this up off this speaker, or what?

Operator Not so well.

PT Well then, that's the way it goes. We'll have to go back to square one. Think that's enough?

Operator I think that's enough.

PT OK, bye.

Operator Bye.

Expert Hello.

Lawyer Record Company?

Expert Yes, yes, how are you, Lawyer?

Lawyer Fine, how are you doing?

Expert Fine.

Lawyer I'm setting up a conference call, so if you'll get off the line and stay off it for a few minutes, we should be contacting you.

Expert OK, I'll do that right now.

Lawyer All right, thank you.

Expert I forgot I had the speaker on. Hello.

Operator Hello, this is the conference operator, we have a conference call with Paul Tanner.

OK.

Operator I'll connect you with the conference, sir. We have Paul Tanner in conference.

PT This is Paul Tanner.

Lawyer Hi, Paul?

PT Yeah.

Lawyer Hi, Lawyer.

PT Hi Lawyer.

Lawyer We have Expert in place also.

PT Who is it?

Lawyer Expert.

PT Expert.

Expert Yes.

PT OK, good afternoon, Expert.

Expert Hi, how are you?

PT I'm fine, thank you.

Expert Good.

Lawyer We have Composer.

PT Who else do we have?

Lawyer We're getting Composer.

Expert While we're waiting, Paul, do you have the two charts in front of you?

PT Yes. Well, I have the sheet music to two tunes.

Expert OK, do you have them both in C?

PT Well, I put them in C.

Expert So you didn't get them already transposed?

PT No, but I did that. What do you do, Expert?

Operator Excuse me, we have Composer in conference. If you need further operator assistance, press zero on your touch tone phone. Thank you. You may begin.

PT OK.

Lawyer Hi Composer.

Composer Yes, hello.

PT Hi Composer.

Composer Hello.

PT This is Paul Tanner.

Composer Hello, Paul.

PT Hi.

Lawyer Go ahead.

Expert Let me. I'm going to start with what I told Lawyer. There are several similarities in the songs which I feel are essentially trivial, OK?

They are so common to so many songs that they don't count for establishing similarities between two songs.

PT Now, Expert, which tunes are you talking about?

Expert I'm talking about "Never…" and "Like…"

PT OK.

Expert Those are the only two tunes I'm going to talk about today.

PT OK.

Expert So, the fact that each of the songs has a four line verse and a four line chorus is not significant.

PT Right.

Expert There are thousands of songs that have that.

PT Right.

Expert Both songs are diatonic, so are thousands of songs, doesn't mean a whole lot.

PT Right.

Expert Harmonies of both of them are diatonic but they are both the same but they are different *(Editor's note–WOW!)* so that is immaterial. They substituted F for D minor, E minor, chords are very simple in both.

PT Yes.

Expert The similarities that I found are primarily melodic. They don't write up line for line necessarily.

PT Well, Expert, in a plagiarism case, we've got to talk about melodies. That's all they'll talk about.

Expert Right, that's what I'm talking about.

PT Yeah.

Expert So we talk about the melody of "Never...," and we go line by line; the first line of "Like..." is different. But the first line of "Never...," this line—

(Expert plays the line on the piano)

is similar to the second line of the other tune,

(Expert plays the line on the piano)

PT Well, it's partially similar. OK, go ahead.

Expert The first and second lines of "Never..." are similar to the second and third lines of "Like...," so if we were to play the first two lines of "Never..."

(Expert plays the line on the piano)

and

(Expert plays the line on the piano)

and then play

(Expert plays the line on the piano)

So, as I told Lawyer, if I were asked if either of those lines were independently composed, the answer is "Of course, yes." They are both very common kinds of step-wise motion.

PT That's right.

Expert Then in the chorus, we have again similar kinds of similarities. The first line of the chorus of "Never..." has a very common kind of progression of chords

(Expert plays chords on the piano)

"Like..." has

(Expert plays chords on the piano)

has the same way as very common kinds of movements. The same movement that we have in the other song.

PT OK.

Expert The sub dominant with the third in the melody. But in the chorus, both in the first and the last lines, have the same kind of look to them. So, Lawyer, Composer, I think I told you this as well, my testimony and my opinion is a little bias because I heard the story first.

Lawyer Paul hasn't heard any of the story.

Expert Should he hear it?

PT No, I probably shouldn't.

Expert No, you probably shouldn't. That's why you have someone look at them who hasn't heard.

PT That's right.

Expert Heard any of the details. So, my conclusion if I had seen these two lines in either the verse or the chorus, I would have said, well look, both of these songs are essentially so banal that it is hard to say that one comes from the other. If either of the songs had an odd measure, you know one accidental would be enough here, anything at all, you might be able to say there is something unusual about either of these songs. But both songs are absolutely four square, two plus two plus two. *(Editor's note–If Composer is listening, he probably gave up this particular career.)*

PT Yeah.

Expert However, the similarities in both the verse and the chorus in this case seem to me more than coincidence given the rest of the information. If it were just in the verse or just in the chorus, I would say, well that's just coincidence. But the fact that both the verse and the chorus have half of their lines similar, I'm only talking about two out of four. I conclude that there is enough similarity to make me think that the two songs might be related. And that's my opinion. *(Editor's note–Now, dear readers, you are following all this with a written word to stare at. Imagine if you were just listening to it over the telephone. And I promise you, this is all verbatim, syllable by syllable.)*

PT Expert, have you done a case on something like this?

Expert I've done similar work, but as I've said, I'm not–, I told Lawyer, what I tell a jury, what I think they're going to believe. *(HUH?)* The first thing I want, I'd rather hear what you have to say.

PT Well, in the first place, I don't think similarity will make it. They've got to be very close note for note. I've done cases where there are only two notes different in the choruses, and the jury couldn't believe it. They lost the case, and there were only two notes different. And so therefore, similarity and not being at the same spot in the chorus or the verse, either one, the other lawyers would shoot you down.

Expert I agree. And I've heard of four the same *(HUH?)* and they won. So it all depends on each case.

Lawyer The bottom line is that no one knows exactly what a trial of fact would do; and obviously, you're on a spectrum from here. What I need to know from Expert and Paul is on a spectrum from identical to no similarity, how do these compare?

PT Well, there are measures that are similar, but similar doesn't make it in the court.

Lawyer The legal test is "substantially similar."

PT Yes, because there is no concise law about what you can take from another tune.

Lawyer That's true.

PT It's up to the jury and up to the judge.

Expert On this point, I agree with Paul, but I do think I would use the term "substantially similar" between the tunes. But that doesn't mean you're going to win the case. That means that I might say that in court. But as I told Lawyer, if I would testify, I would not play these two songs in their entirety for the jury. I'm going to play what I did, I'm going to play this line and then that one on the piano and not play the harmonies.

PT Right. But remember, the opposition is not going to stick to your rules.

Expert Exactly. The opposition is going to immediately get up and then they're going to play the songs from beginning to end and they're going to overlay line A with line A and say line A doesn't look at all like line A in this song.

PT That's right.

Expert So, I—

Lawyer Let me ask a couple of questions of Expert and Paul. Are the *differences* between lines, the way they do *not* match up, is there anything that is suspicious about the way the differences appear?

PT Oh boy, I don't know about *suspicious*, I really don't know.

Expert Yeah, that's a hard one.

Lawyer I know, it's a very hard question. But if I don't have enough similarities, then I have to say is there something about the differences that would cause either one of you to suspect some plagiarism?

PT Well, like Expert said, the tunes aren't unusual tunes to start with. So there is a lot similarity between a lot of tunes. And yet there's a lot of differences between a lot of tunes. So I can't pin it down like that.

Expert Differences sometimes arrive from different word settings and–yeah, that's a hard one, I don't, you know, you might look at these for a couple of hours and make a case for it, but I think it would be easy enough to shoot down. Somebody else could say that's ridiculous. I mean that's—

PT As Expert says, the lawyer for the other side is going to get somebody in there to put bar one with bar one, and so forth.

Expert All the way through.

PT Yeah,

Expert I mean, in the chorus, you know, we don't mind that so much, in the chorus, the first line lines up with the first line.

PT Yes.

Expert The problem is that having a four line chorus that has lots of notes, lots of notes, long notes, is fairly common.

PT *(HUH?)* Well yes, I guess.

Expert So that it's not, you know, if the fingerprints are on the house and the person lives there, it doesn't do as much.

PT Right.

Expert You've got fingerprints, but they were there every day, so that's sort of what you have. Most of the similarities are because the tunes are very similar because they are both very common.

PT Just let me give you a little example, the chorus, bar one of the chorus, on beat two in "Never…," you've got a couple of notes. Well now, they don't care that the other four notes in that bar are the same, you've got a couple of notes in one tune that you don't have in the other tune. And they'll convince the jury that that makes them different.

Expert I understand. As I told Lawyer before, the music alone is not going to make this case. That if you can establish the connection the other way, the music could be circumstantial, it could be supporting evidence.

PT You mean use the lyrics?

Expert No, I mean if you've got other information, if you've got—

PT The "story," you mean.

Expert The story.

PT OK, all right.

Expert You can establish the right people were at the right place at the right time, that's circumstantial evidence. Then you can say OK, you know, this is the right caliber gun even though we don't have a bullet. You know, we're missing this piece of evidence, but at least we don't have contradictory evidence here. We have enough evidence to support something else. I think Paul is right though, I think the biggest question mark is how you're going to try it. And I think that, even if we are at our most positive in pointing out the similarities, the other side is going to be able to point to just as many–well, there are two notes here and two notes there.

PT OK, I got cha.

If we can use the other circumstantial evidence, would that help?

Lawyer That's Composer. I mean, it's somewhat rhetorical. I mean, it always helps, but is it enough?

Expert I'm sorry, but I think it's the best we can do. Paul and I might use a different word in how we describe the similarities in the final analysis, but I think we agree as to how it's going to set up in court and how effective it's going to be on its own.

Lawyer I understand. OK, I'll call you right back, Composer, right after we get off.

Composer OK, sure, about ten minutes, fine.

Lawyer Is that it with everybody?

PT Fine and dandy. You're going to call back, is that it?

Lawyer Yeah, I'm going to call Composer back.

PT OK, then how about me?

Lawyer No, I think we're about done with the conversation right now.

PT OK, well, it's nice to have met Expert and Composer.

Expert Thank you.

Composer Thank you.

Lawyer I appreciate it Paul and Expert. Thanks a lot.

And folks, those are the last words I ever heard from any of them. Seriously, could you make up a novel from that?

Three Young Ladies 18

The following interview is quite different from the others. This one was done over the telephone with three very young ladies. I suspect that the father of two of them set up the whole situation for them so that they were able to complete a class project for school. The conversation took place on March 21, 1989, and it was quite a pleasure for me.

PT Hello.

Shawn Doctor Tanner?

PT Yes.

Shawn Shawn Edwards, Jennifer Peterson, and Melissa Peterson.

PT Shawn Edwards?

Shawn Yes.

PT How do you spell that?

Shawn S-H-A-W-N.

PT Shawn, what was the last name?

Shawn Edwards, E-D-W-A-R-D-S.

PT All right.

Shawn And Jennifer Peterson.

PT Jennifer Peterson, any relation to Mark Peterson?

Shawn And Melissa Peterson.

PT Are they related to Mark Peterson?

Shawn Yes, he is their brother.

PT OK?

Shawn OK.

PT And how old are you?

Shawn I'm eleven.

PT You're eleven?

Shawn And Jennifer is fourteen, and Melissa is eleven.

PT OK, all right.

Shawn OK. We're glad that we are able to talk to you, OK?

PT Good, I'm glad.

Shawn Yeah, all right. We need to ask you some specific questions about Glenn Miller.

PT All rightie.

Shawn We have been studying Glenn Miller for about two months. We are going to do a history book project on him.

PT Oh.

Shawn And it's going to be a media presentation, and so, if you don't have any objections, we'd like to use your conversation on a little bit of our media.

PT That's OK.

Shawn OK.

PT Are you taping this now, Shawn?

Shawn Yes.

PT OK.

Shawn OK, here's our first question: Would tell us about your association with Glenn Miller?

PT That's a broad question. What do you mean my association with Glenn?

Shawn Like your relationship?

PT Well, Glenn was my boss. He was a friend as well, but actually, he was my boss, he was actually the guy who paid me.

Shawn Was it like a friend relationship?

PT A friend relationship?

Shawn Uh huh.

PT Yes, he was very nice to me. Very nice. You know, As long as I did what I was supposed to do, everything was just fine and dandy. If I did anything wrong, he'd let me know in a hurry.

Shawn OK. What did you do before you played in his band?

PT Well, I played trombone. I started playing when I was, oh, let me see, about your age. And I kept practicing and practicing. I played in a family band. When that broke up, I went with other people who had bands, and eventually, Glenn found me. So I was a trombone player all the way down the line.

Shawn Oh, that's interesting.

PT Well I'm glad.

Shawn How long did you play with him?

PT I played with Glenn all the time he had a civilian band. Now people think he had a band for ten or fifteen years, but Glenn only had his civilian band for four and a half years, and I was with him all the time. And then Glenn went in the service.

Shawn Now let's see, how good a player do you have to be to play in his band?

PT Now, are you asking me to say I was a real good player?

Shawn Yes. I mean, well, if somebody wanted to play in the band, would they have to be especially good?

PT Well, as far as Glenn's band was concerned, you have to realize, Shawn, Glenn's band was the highest paying band.

Shawn It was?

PT What that meant was that Glenn could hire anybody he wanted to hire. So he wasn't going to hire somebody that he didn't think was a good player.

Shawn Oh, that's neat. Was Glenn strict with his band?

PT Was he strict?

Shawn Yeah, like really tight and wouldn't let you goof off that much?

PT I like that. Well, you're absolutely right. We didn't goof off. Actually, with Glenn, the music came first, that's true. He figured it was like a business and you had to give one hundred per cent all the time you were there or someone else was going to be there tomorrow in your place. So you did have to be on your toes all the time, there's no question about it. And he was a real good musician, therefore he knew exactly what you were doing and what you weren't doing. So you had to play well and you had to look nice, and you had to act nice.

Shawn OK. Now we're going to have Melissa Peterson ask you some questions about Glenn.

PT OK, hi Melissa.

Melissa Hi.

PT Would you say hello to your dad for me?

Melissa OK.

PT OK.

Melissa Benny Goodman said that Glenn Miller's greatest contribution to music was as an arranger. Do you agree with him?

PT Well, not exactly. He certainly was a fine arranger, and the things that he contributed musically did stem an awful lot from his arranging. But then, you see, he also had a band that would play his arrangements as he wanted to hear them. So you've got to consider that as a contribution too. So his arranging was a big thing, especially for a fellow like Benny Goodman who actually didn't arrange. So, therefore he would look upon arranging as a big deal. Glenn was a fine arranger. But like I said, he had to rehearse the band and get the band to play his arrangements the way he wanted to hear them, and that was a big thing too.

Melissa How have arrangers copied or learned from Glenn Miller?

PT Well, Glenn had a knack of doing good musical things and pleasing the public at the same time. And I think a lot of arrangers picked up on that. Glenn didn't write far out things. Do you know what I mean by that, Melissa?

Melissa Yes.

PT OK, well, he didn't write far out things because he didn't figure that they were either good musically or that they would please the public. And he did want to please the public, and arrangers have understood that. Now he invented a couple of sounds that arrangers have used since then, like the clarinet lead over the saxophone section. But if you don't have the people that Glenn had, then it really doesn't come off very well. It comes off like an imitation instead of a real nice thing. But he did make that saxophone section blend as he wanted them to blend, so that was a big thing too.

Melissa Yes. How long did it take Glenn Miller to arrange music?

PT Oh, he was a very fast arranger. But then you see, Melissa, after Glenn got very busy, when the band started to get very popular, then Glenn got very busy, and he didn't have time to arrange. But the thing that he would do, he had a staff of arrangers, mainly Bill Finegan and Jerry Gray. And he had those fellows, he could talk to them about a given tune with some idea that Glenn had, and he would tell them, "Look, write something around this idea." And he would show them the idea and maybe even show them how to start and stop it, that kind of thing. And then they would carry on from there. And then Glenn would oversee the arrangement after it got in. But after the band got popular, he didn't have time to arrange anymore. Before the band got popular, he did all the arranging and he was a good fast arranger.

Melissa Were his arrangements difficult to play?

PT No, they truly weren't, because he was a player himself, so he understood exactly what was involved as a player. So he didn't write things that the fellows couldn't handle very, very well. In fact, if we would play someone else's arrangement and the ending was very hard or something, he would say to the first trumpet player, "Is that going to be a problem?" And if the first trumpet player would say yes, that it would be a problem to play it very consistently, then Glenn would change it. So actually, Glenn didn't write things to be hard, he wanted them to come off well musically and appealing to the public.

Melissa How long did it take to get the arrangements together in the band?

PT Well, the thing that happens is that you start out with a library of things that Glenn has written. And then you keep adding things to it. And as the book got very big, then you start taking out things that you're not using any more. So, Melissa, it was kind of an on-going thing. You're always putting things in and taking them out the whole life of the band.

Melissa Well, I'm going to have my sister Jennifer ask you some questions.

PT OK, fine.

Jennifer Hi.

PT Hi, Jennifer, how are you?

Jennifer I'm fine.

PT Good.

Jennifer Were you still in the band after he died?

PT When Glenn passed away, he was in the service, he was in the Air Force. Now that was during the war, during World War II. Now, I was in the service, but I wasn't in Glenn's band during the service. He didn't have a civilian band at that time, I was with his civilian band, not with the service band.

Jennifer OK. Who directed the band after he died?

PT After Glenn passed away in the service, for the dances, Ray McKinley, the drummer, conducted the band. For the radio programs and the records, the V Discs as they were called at that time, Jerry Gray did most of the conducting. Jerry was an arranger.

Jennifer How do you think music would be different if Glenn Miller were still alive?

PT Well, that's awfully hard to say because you're just guessing. I think the influence that his music has had on people would still have an influence. But Glenn himself was a forward looking fellow, and he was advancing his band as witnessed by that fact that when he went in the service, he had a larger band than he had as a civilian band. So he would possibly have gone that way after he came out, and if he were successful, then other people would have done that too.

Jennifer Do you have a favorite story about Glenn Miller?

PT A favorite story?

Jennifer Uh huh.

PT Oh golly, I don't know, there are just too many of them to refer to in order to nail down one special story. I was thrilled when he found me. He found me in a little joint, and I was in there with kind of a jam session band. Someone told him that if he was looking for a trombone player that he ought to come down and hear this young kid. So he did, and I was a terrible stammerer. I asked him if I could say that he liked my playing so I could use it as a recommendation. And he said, "Well, how soon can you come with me?" I pulled my toothbrush out of my pocket and said, "I'm packed, I can come right now." So he said, "OK, come now." And I was such a stammerer then that his wife said that it took me a half an hour to say all that. I was a terrible stammerer, I couldn't really talk much until I was about eighteen.

Jennifer We really appreciate your letting us interview you. Thank you. Bye.

PT Oh Jennifer.

Jennifer Yes?

PT This is on audio tape, isn't it?

Jennifer Uh huh.

PT Well, you know, I never know what it was that I said. So it would be awfully nice if you'd send me a copy of the tape.

Jennifer OK.

PT That's very nice. Now would you tell your dad I said hello?

Jennifer OK.

PT All right.

Jennifer Bye.

PT Bye.

19 Polly Haynes

This next is an interview with dear Polly Haynes by Jim Berger of KGIL in Los Angeles. This was done in 1982 in the studio. Polly ran the Glenn Miller office in New York City and was married to Don Haynes, Glenn Miller's personal manager both as a civilian and in the service. Polly was undoubtedly Helen Miller's closest friend, the same relationship which her husband savored with Glenn. She enlightens us with approaches we don't often consider as she looks at Glenn, his history, his tunes, and his personnel in the band.

JB This is Jim Bergen, manager of KGIL Radio, and for those of you who enjoy our format, Ballads, Blues, and Big Bands too, you know that music is very much a part of our life and it's a labor of love for many of us here at KGIL and we share it with you and are proud to do so. One of the most exhilarating things that I think I've ever done is to stand before a big band that is really wailing, whether it's Count Basie or Duke Ellington, Harry James, Woody Herman, Les Brown, many great bands that are still working today and have been working for thirty or forty years. One of the bands that I never had the opportunity to stand next to was the Glenn Miller Band. But the lady that I'm about to introduce to you did on many occasions. Her name is Mrs. Polly Haynes, she is the wife of the late Don Haynes. Don was the personal manager, business confidant, close personal friend of Glenn Miller. And Polly, as you reminisce about the great legend of Glenn Miller, I suspect that you may even remember the first time that you ever met Glenn.

PH Yes, I think the first time I ever met Glenn Miller and his wife Helen, I believe it was with the Ray Noble days. At that time, I was married to Claude Thornhill. Claude Thornhill and Glenn Miller helped Ray Noble get musicians from New York when he came over with his personal manager to have a band to play at the Rainbow Room.

JB Did Glenn Miller, in the impressions of the first time meeting and in the weeks to come, and now literally forty plus years later, did you see something special in the man when you first met him?

PH He seemed so serious. The other boys in the band and the musicians we knew, they were fun fellows. Glenn had his side of good times and all, but he was always very serious. He was always studying. Studied the entire time he was with the Ray Noble Band.

JB The articles I read about the early Glenn Miller said that he was a very intense, dedicated young man who wanted to think he knew where he was going, even in the days as an arranger and the struggling days of the early '30s in New York.

PH I think that was very true. I think the only one that really knew Glenn Miller and knew his ideals and the things he wanted to attain was Helen at that particular time. It came out with me as we became closer and more of a family. He was very serious minded, and Helen was a perfect wife because she was that way as well.

JB And our guest Polly Haynes says that I guess you met Glenn on or around the time that he was formulating a band and spinning off from Ray Noble, was he not?

PH I think it was just a short time after he had left Ray Noble. Glenn decided to try his own ideas. He went out and I would say at least, he tried out four or five different bands, each one seemed to fail until he was fortunate enough to have many people who were interested in what he was doing. And several people came to his help. I guess it must have been either the fourth or fifth try that in Boston it happened that the sound came about that he was always looking for.

JB You told me that you had come to California, he was in New York. One day you get a phone call, he said,"Polly, I want you to join me." And you said, "I like it in California." and what did he say, he must have been a pretty good salesman.

PH I had a phone call from Glenn and Helen one Sunday saying, "Well, it looks like something's starting to happen, and we want you to come back."

JB And that was a difficult decision, right?

PH Yes, because at that time, I had a lovely apartment, and I was very happy, and I said, "Well, what do you think you can pay me?" So he said, "I think we can make it around fifty dollars." So I said, "Oh." He said, "Get yourself on the plane, the ticket will be coming in the next two days." And I went back to New York.

JB Polly, close friend of the Miller family and Glenn Miller over the years. And Polly, you were telling me a cute story about in the '39 or '40 period when the band really hit, it was becoming so famous because they were in demand on radio, in concerts, in ballrooms. The Glenn Miller sound had well been established. The sound was somewhat of an accident as you mentioned earlier, had begun in Boston and was toned and refined, and to this day, when you hear that clarinet and the four saxes, that is something that Glenn had and then the public picked it up after a period of time, did it not?

PH Yes, it seemed to mushroom. I guess the main reason for it was because of being on the radio so much. I think it was every night at Glen Island. And it just seemed that after that, he would, say, have a job of a one-nighter in Hershey, Pennsylvania, and Glenn always seemed to think that the crowd came after the people would go to someplace else like a country fair at the time the band was there. Until finally, he realized they were coming to see the Glenn Miller Band. And they wouldn't dance but they would stand. And it seemed to be the sound, and it just, everything just seemed to mushroom in what appeared in such a short time. And naturally, the busier Glenn was, the more my duties were heavier, and everyone else in the office. I started out with one girl, a receptionist, and wound up with thirty people.

JB And he was so busy that he would delegate the authorization of the checks and ask you to write Glenn Miller and you simulated his signature, did you not?

PH Oh yes, in fact, we did a publicity folder and I learned at that time how to duplicate his signature.

JB You told a cute story about going to or him going to the bank, that he was at lunch or whatever the reason, and he needed some money, so you might tell the story to our listeners.

PH Glenn never carried money. He would carry maybe enough for a cab, and this one day he went into the bank that we used and he went up to the teller and wanted a hundred dollars. He signed Glenn Miller and the teller told him he would have to see the manager, she didn't recognize him. He had never been in the bank before. And he went to the manager and the manager didn't recognize him. He said, "Well this isn't the account of Glenn Miller. I don't recognize the signature." So he had to call me at the office and I had to OK the check before he could get his hundred dollars.

JB And Polly, if I may, I know in reading about Glenn Miller, the fact that he was very human, a man of good quality, great sensitivity. He made decisions quickly and rationally. He was also strong willed, maybe a little stubborn at times, but always extremely fair. He might have been a success in most any business that he would have attempted, would you say?

PH He had drive that I have seen in very few people, maybe one or two others.

JB I would like to play a little game for just a moment. Many of the fine musicians who joined the band later went on to become rather successful and famous in their own rights. But at the time they joined the Miller Band, they were musicians that were struggling up the same ladder that Glenn had climbed. I'll give you a few names and you just give me some impression if you will. Hal McIntyre.

PH Hal McIntyre was a lovely young man. Glenn liked him. He was a personable charming young person. A lovely wife and he was a very intricate part of the Glenn Miller organization.

JB As we progress through the weekend, we'll be talking about other people that were a part of the Glenn Miller era.

And in our conversation, Polly, we mentioned some of the people. Tex Beneke.

PH Tex Beneke was a charmer, one of my very favorite people. Glenn had a special feeling for Tex because he was a gentle man.

JB Ray Eberle.

PH Ray Eberle was also a charmer. Bob, of course, was singing with Jimmy Dorsey. And I think it's been in many books throughout the years that have been written about Glenn that Glenn went to Bob and asked if he had a brother. Well, he hired him, I think in about twenty-four hours.

JB A little nepotism there, he recommended his brother. How about Marion Huton who sang with the band so beautifully?

PH Well, Marion had a sister Betty who was doing very well, and it was almost an identical situation; Betty was a very vibrant girl. When Glenn saw Marion, he made it a point to interview her. And she was the down home type that he liked. That was his style. He seemed to like the low key people in his band. It was sort of a family, he liked the good feeling about it. Of course, I'm sure there are people at times that didn't agree with Glenn, because the busier he became, I think that was mentioned in one of George Simon's books, one of my quotes that people thought he was stubborn and had to have his way. He didn't have time to be as close to his organization of people in the beginning. Because he relied on his boys in the band to do the way he wanted things to be done.

JB Polly, what about Billy May? A good friend of KGIL and I know, a good friend of yours.

PH Yes, I love Billy May. Billy started arranging and playing, was a marvelous musician; not only on his instrument, but on arranging. I would say Bobby Hackett was one of the greatest additions Glenn made. There was only one Bobby Hackett on the cornet.

JB A man that many people may not be that familiar with, but in his own right, has contributed a great deal to education. Paul Tanner.

PH Paul Tanner is one of my very favorites. He was very young. He was slower in walking and his attitude; and his slowness caused Glenn to nickname him "Lightnin'." Paul was a great technical musician. And in later years, he finished his education, got his Master's and he taught at UCLA, "Professor of Jazz;" in fact, he was just made Professor Emeritus at UCLA. It will probably go down the way he was received and when he left just last year, I think there was more publicity when Paul Tanner retired of any professor at any college I've ever known.

JB Our special guest over this Glenn Miller weekend on KGIL is Polly Haynes, long time friend of the Miller family and personal friend of Glenn Miller. And we've been talking about many subjects that I hope you have enjoyed. Polly, in talking about word association of music, the wonderful music of Miller, I'll pick one at random and you give me a comment about it. "String of Pearls."

PH "String of Pearls" was an immediate hit. It just caught on, so different, and the youngsters loved it.

JB "Chattanooga Choo Choo."

PH "Chattanooga Choo Choo" was a favorite of Glenn's. I think it was a Harry Warren tune with Johnny Mercer *(Editor's note–actually with Mack Gordon)*. I think a lot of that was due of course to the way Tex

Beneke performed and the Modernaires. It was a great favorite, it is today, I believe.

JB Great, one more. I know that Erskine Hawkins made famous "Tuxedo Junction." And then Glenn picked it up and made it more famous.

PH Yes, well that was Glenn's style. It seemed he never was afraid to do another version of a very famous tune by a very famous performer, instrumentalist or composer.

JB Polly, what about "In the Mood"?

PH Well, I think "In the Mood" was really the stopper of them all. The kids just kept looking and looking and they never would dance after the pause. They kept waiting for the band to go lower and softer. Then Glenn had a way of working the hats which most people thought was commercial, and no doubt it was, but it's what the kids liked. And he always wanted to give them what the kids would enjoy.

JB There was a lot of showmanship in the band. The band was very visual, wasn't it?

PH Yes, it was. In fact, I think a lot of people thought that it was too visual. But apparently the youngsters didn't seem to think so. They enjoyed it; they got a big kick out of it. And I might add that I believe that "In the Mood" has been done in these past few years by many performers. There's been jazz versions, there's been electrical sound versions, it's been copied many, many times.

JB And all the songs that Glenn Miller has recorded, the one that I think most of us relate to "oohs" and "ahs" and goose bumps would be the lovely theme song of "Moonlight Serenade." As you and I were chatting prior to taping, you told me that the song was once called "Now I Lay Me Down To Weep." I wonder how it ever got from that title to "Moonlight Serenade."

PH Well, this goes into a whole different way of speaking what I feel like I need to say. No one liked it; now it is as "Moonlight Serenade."

JB Was it originally just a melody and had no lyrics? Was it just a melody that someone called "Now I Lay Me Down To Weep"?

PH Everyone thought it was too sad. And I think my analogy to it is that the tune itself was beautiful, but I always related it to the first set of lyrics, and I think that's why I never hear it unless it brings tears to my eyes. Because it represents to me, it was always his theme song, he never used any other. So I can only see the struggle and the final degree, the mastering that was done with the instruments of the band. And Glenn's softness, his dedication, his love for his children, his wife, his family. And he was never able to come back and enjoy it. And I think that I am the one and only one left to have those memories–and I do weep as the original lyrics were.

JB It is our pleasure to be talking with Polly Haynes, personal friend of the Miller family for so many years. And I know that in my retrospect of the Miller family and reading about them, he and his wife Helen were married in 1928, and the busy thirties came about and the success and the heartache of the band that became so successful in 1939, 1940, and '41. And Polly, Helen Miller passed away a few years ago. I know that you and she were very good friends. And a lot of people don't know that there are two Miller children.

PH Yes, Helen and Glenn were blessed with having a son Steven, Steven Davis Miller and Jonnie Dee Miller. And I'm glad to say that we remained friends. We've been close, in fact, the children growing up with my son, Peter. I see Steven and Jonnie, and I love them and they have a place in my heart along with my son, Peter.

JB In reading of Glenn Miller, George Simon, Lee Walker, Leonard Feather, so many of the people that have written always talked about the dedication between Helen and Glenn. It seemed like somewhat of a perennial honeymoon in the years that they were married, did it not?

PH It was a fairy tale marriage from the beginning to the end. And while they had their ups and downs, they were happy. They would discuss the band, Glenn always discussed everything with Helen. And she was a very wise woman, and of course, a tragedy by his not coming back. So all in all, I would say they were blessed. They had many blessings, and I'm sure they're both watching over all of us that are left.

JB We have been spending some outstanding memories with Polly Haynes, friend of the Glenn Miller family and confidant of Glenn Miller. And now, all these years later, you reflect on what might have been in the arts. You talk about Picasso or Norman Rockwell, the world of jazz, Louis Armstrong, Duke Ellington. And maybe in that of big band leaders that really arrested the world and provided love and entertainment for millions of people. It originated from America but went all over the world. There were Benny Goodmans, the Tommy Dorseys, the Artie Shaws, but honestly not as big a giant anywhere in the field of commercial success in the very short life of the Glenn Miller Band from 1938 through 1942. And Polly, would Glenn, in his own way, put himself in with the Goodmans, and the Dorseys, and the Shaws?

PH Oh yes, indeed, I think he would have. While Glenn never considered himself strictly a musician, he took in other aspects of a business. The band, the big band era, was the big band business. There were others that he admired–Benny Goodman, and he liked his presentation. He thought Artie Shaw's tone on the clarinet could never be duplicated. Tommy Dorsey–in fact, he would hesitate to do solos; in fact, he did very few solos on the trombone. He had an organization, and he was a giant.

JB We have been spending some outstanding memories. Did he ever talk to you about any of the things he would do after the war?

PH He had everything planned. All the things that he would do when he returned. Of course, none of us ever even thought that he would not return. He never had a vacation as I think back now. I think we spent two days at Pinehurst out of all the years he struggled. Helen and Glenn, Don and myself, we sat in a room and knitted and made afghans and Glenn and Don went on the golf course at five o'clock in the morning and Glenn had a hole-in-one one day, and that was one of the happiest days of his life. So he would have continued in music, but I do think that he had a feeling that he didn't want to rest. He wanted to come out to the ranch that he built in California, and relax say three or four months of the year. And study what he wanted to do.

JB Polly, on behalf of the station and our listeners, we want to thank you. You've been a most gracious, warm, and lovely lady. We thank you for joining us and sharing with us, from the heart, all the memories of Glenn Miller.

PH I want to thank you, Jim, for the invitation. I might say that publicly, this is my first appearance. I hope that someway I could get across the warmness that I felt for the Millers and I hope it is returned, and I feel it is.

20 Interviews in South Africa

These interviews were down in Johannesburg, South Africa, in 1983. They sort of shared me with each other in what is called the Springbok Network. The first is with the gentleman who was sort of in charge of me, his name is Henry Holloway.

HH It's eleven minutes past six. One of the members of the original Glenn Miller Band, trombonist Paul Tanner, who also went on to other big bands such as Sonny Burke's, is now Professor Paul Tanner. And is on a holiday visit to this country at the invitation of the Glenn Miller Appreciation Society. The professorial title is because of his association with the University of California, Los Angeles.

PT Actually I enrolled in UCLA as a freshman. I had never had any college and I was the oldest freshman in captivity.

HH How old were you?

PT Oh, I must have been about eighty-nine. Well, I was well in my thirties, I was older than some of my teachers. They'd call roll, it would be like Sam, Frank, Mr. Tanner, Jim, Fred. But I went on through and I finally graduated in 1958. And when I was about to graduate, they asked me to come on the faculty. But all this time, I was also on the staff of the American Broadcasting Company as their lead trombone player. So I was still playing. In fact, I was so busy I didn't have time to eat some times. It's very nice though when people want what it is you can do. So I went on the faculty at UCLA and stayed there twenty-three years, I enjoyed it thoroughly. I just retired in 1981.

HH You were teaching jazz?

PT I was teaching performance, I was teaching theory, I was teaching music education, musicology, everything. Then gradually my history of jazz classes got so big that I had to give up teaching all other courses.

Because I ended up teaching the history of jazz classes to seventy-five thousand students.

HH Not all at once.

PT No, but I've worked cities that were smaller than that. The class would meet four times a week, and I would have eleven hundred in a class. There for a while I had sixteen hundred and I went to the office and said, "That's too many." Because I corrected all the exams and everything myself, so they cut it back to eleven. But about three times that many would try to enroll in it, but I could only handle so many because of space. I taught it in an auditorium, so I would just handle eleven hundred a day, four days a week.

HH Did you find it unusual that so many people, so many students, were interested in jazz?

PT Well now, I realize I had a hot subject. And besides that, they figured, "Well, he's been into this and so he didn't get this out of a book somewhere, that this fellow was truly involved in it." Now, we had a couple of faculty members who taught Bach that were alive in those days, but I wasn't. So I would tell the students an awful lot of the stories and happenings, and I would give them all the facts they had to know, but when I would interject these stories and all, I would tell them that I was sorry that I got sidetracked. They'd say, "Please don't stop with those because we feel like we're being 'let in' on what was going on." It gave us a whole extra seventy-five thousand listeners to jazz music.

HH What did it do as far as the curriculum was concerned? How did it figure in the final mark on graduation?

PT Oh, it was a four unit course, this is as high as it gets. The exams were very hard. The lectures weren't hard because I was very relaxed. And we had a lot of fun during the lectures. In fact, I'd look out there some day and there would be Stan Kenton sitting out there; and I'd say, "Come on up and talk to them." So he would. We'd have an open conversation, things like that. So the kids never missed classes because they never knew what was going to happen. One day we even had a flasher and I didn't know what was going to happen. And that was a surprise too. I won't go into that on the air. Some of the music faculty at first may have looked down a little bit on jazz, they would think nothing has happened since Bach died. But they got over it in a hurry. Because the money allotted to the department comes from ADA, the average daily attendance, so how many students are taking how many units–this gives the department that much money. So it ended up that the jazz classes were supporting the department.

HH Presumably, to get your own professorship, you had to write a thesis of your own?

PT You have to do a doctoral dissertation to get your doctorate, you do a thesis to get your Master's.

HH What was yours on?

PT Actually, on composing. I also have composed a whole stack of things, so I did it on that. It would have been too easy to do it on jazz. Besides that, I have a textbook on it, and they don't want you to do a dissertation on something that you have published. So I wrote a rather involved concerto for trombone and symphony orchestra and also for concert band. Then I wrote a real long explanation of every note and that ended up being my doctoral dissertation.

Sonny Burke's Band 1
"Just One Of Those Things"

(He played "Just One Of Those Things" by Sonny Burke's Band.)[1]

HH Oh, I love that kind of music, I really do, the big band stuff, really tremendous stuff indeed. Now Paul Tanner speaks with Peter Bumfield.

PB Springbok Tonight. Jazz is still a major musical form around the world. And in South Africa right now, is the former professor of jazz history at the University of California Los Angeles, Professor Paul Tanner. Well, it's often been said that the roots of jazz lie in Africa.

PT That's actually a little bit of a myth. The main impact from Africa is the emphasis on rhythm, and of course, that great call and response pattern that they have. But from Europe, you get melody, harmony, and the instrumentation. So actually, it came from both continents. Everything in America must usually come from someplace else. So it came together in America. But the roots of it did come from both Europe and Africa.

PB And as far as the roots in America are concerned, I would imagine, starting from the blues, the Black American.

PT Well, it goes even further back than that. You'd have to go all the way back to the religious meetings. There were lots of secret religious meetings among the slaves. Then eventually, you do get into blues which was a secular way of expressing themselves. The blues goes all the way through jazz. Some of the most contemporary things done today are done off the blues chord progression.

PB Is there some kind of line of progression, say from blues to such and such to hard bop to mainstream? Can you outline that for me?

PT Definitely. It does definitely go from one style to another style to another style, and they play today exactly because of the way they played yesterday.

PB What are those styles, can you outline them?

PT Well, you have to start with Ragtime and Dixieland, and the first Dixieland was what they called Early New Orleans Dixieland.

PB When was that?

PT That was before the 1920s, like from 1900 up to about 1918 or 1920. Then the next thing you get is Chicago Style Dixieland, which was the Roaring Twenties. And along with all that, Boogie Woogie is going on; you can't just capture that and say that was happening during a certain year. And after Chicago Style Dixieland, you get into Swing Music, and that would take you from the early thirties on into the early forties. After that you have Bop, and that'll take you up to 1949 or so. Then you have Cool jazz. Then about 1955, you get what is called Funky. After Funky, you start to have so many different things branching out, so many different styles, that you have to look back eventually and say, well this is really what was happening in 1970. But that's done with hindsight which is much easier.

PB It seems that the fine old female jazz vocalists are dying out.

PT There aren't as many communicative records made that there have been in the past. Ella Fitzgerald made so many records that you can't even collect them all and they were all just excellent. And, of course, Dinah Washington died, but Sarah Vaughan is doing very well. There are others coming on all the time, Edie Gorme and people like that. As far as out and out jazz female singers, Mildred Bailey is no longer with us. Even if you want to talk about Janis Joplin, she's no longer with us. So there isn't the training area that there used to be for female jazz singers, or men either I guess. I think that's probably why there aren't as many good singers as there have been in the past. But with the style of popular music changing so much, it doesn't lend itself to singing well. If you put the microphone inside your mouth, you can't even understand the words. And I mean that as a criticism, and I don't criticize too often.

(Next is a long conversation in German. No, I didn't enter it. Back to English.)

PB Paul, the Doctor, the Doctor Paul Tanner, is that a Doctor of Music of some sort?

PT No, actually a Doctor of Music would be DM. This is a Doctor of Philosophy. But you can get it in many different subjects in the universities in America anyway. And I got mine in music composition. You can get a Doctor of Music in music composition, a Doctor of Philosophy is more broad, it covers a lot more area. You have to get deeply into philosophy and everything.

PB Now how does this tie up with Glenn Miller? Did you do a thesis on Glenn Miller or something?

(I'll omit a reiteration of a previous interview about my doctoral work.)

Tell me something. You were talking about classical music. And yet, you are here as a guest of Henry Holloway who is just crazy about jazz music. Do you find that most jazz musicians have a classical or serious background? *(Editor's note–What a temptation it was for me to explain how most all musicians I know are quite "serious" about what they play. But I realized it would make him apologize, so I skipped it.)*

PT No, but they certainly have a good understanding about it, certainly admire it a great deal. Most jazz musicians who have done any studying at all; if they are Cool jazz musicians, they are deeply into Debussy and Ravel. Otherwise, if they are very contemporary, they are into Scriabin, Shostakovich, and so forth. So, they pick up harmonies and everything else from the classical musicians.

PB I'd like you to recollect the early days with the Glenn Miller Orchestra. Henry said something about the late 30s and the early 40s of course. Glenn Miller died in the early 40s. You were near him fairly near his death.

PT Well, Glenn broke up his band in September of 1942 and then went on in the service. He disappeared in December of 1944. Glenn previously had a band before the band that was successful, and he broke that band up. He organized a new band in 1938 in about the summer, and I joined him then and stayed with him until he disbanded his orchestra in order to go into the service himself in 1942.

PB What was he like to play with? He always came across well in his music and his films, tell us the true Glenn Miller.

PT He was a very complex man, truthfully. I did a paper fairly recently on just that; and I did one entire page on Glenn as a great musician. Glenn was a fine businessman, Glenn was this, Glenn was that, and then I did the rest of the paper explaining each phrase. So he was a very complex man. He loved precision, and he loved attention to what you were doing, and so forth and so on. He didn't ask you to do anything that he didn't demand of himself. So, I thoroughly enjoyed working for him, he was very, very good to me. I have no complaints at all, I enjoyed it.

PB Do you think he would have changed and kept up with the pace if he had been alive?

PT He would have changed some, because he certainly had his eye on what the public was going to buy. And Glenn was a smart businessman, as long as he didn't have to sacrifice the music. You can tell by the band he had in the service that he would have gone for a larger orchestra and the harmonies would have been richer because of having strings and french horns and so forth and so on. But he still would have kept it so the average fan would have appreciated it. He would have gotten more depth in the harmonies, but not as far out in the 40s as say, Kenton, for example or Boyd Raeburn, someone like that.

PB You think of Artie Shaw and other people in that area who were going away slightly.

PT Well, Shaw didn't get too far out.

PB Not too. There have been cover versions of Glenn Miller music. Lots of people got together members of the orchestra after the war, didn't they? But the sound was never quite the same.

PT Well, Glenn's office put together a band that had Tex Beneke in front of it, and after I got out of the service, I worked for Tex for six years. And gradually, Tex wanted it to be his own personal situation. So, he started to get away from it a little bit. But you have to understand that there was only one Glenn Miller. So any orchestra that says Glenn Miller and His Orchestra, it's still only going to be Glenn who really had the final say over every note you played. His office also handles other bands that are Glenn Miller's Orchestra, there's one now with a very fine trombone player named Larry O'Brien. That is, the office owns the orchestra and Larry O'Brien is in front of it. Pardon me if I'm using hand gestures on the radio.

PB That's all right, it still comes across for our guests here on Springbok. Do you think the name of Glenn Miller will live on for a long, long time?

PT There are people who didn't think it would live on at all after Glenn disappeared, and they're very surprised. We are all surprised that it has lived on so well, but that's due to efforts from people like Henry Holloway and also the people in England and so forth. And it does keep on, but there is a tremendous push now all over the world for nostalgia. And so, as I said before, people seem to think that band went on for fifteen or twenty years.

PB That was a time when recordings were being made with decent quality, the start of decent quality. And you can still play the original stuff quite well.

PT Well, if you are going to play the 78 RPMs, you'd better have pretty good equipment, the 33⅓s of course have a lot better quality.

PB I'm going to say thank you very much for coming to the studio, Paul Tanner, for a chat with us.

Sonny Burke's ❷ **"Just One of Those Things"**

PT My pleasure.[2]

(New theme song, new interviewer, Marilyn Verster.)

MV Doctor Paul Tanner, may I say to you, big welcome to the studio.

PT Thank you very, very much. Thank you, Marilyn.

MV Paul Tanner, trombonist, also teacher of many kinds of music, but Paul, I think we must start right at the beginning and talk about your association with the Glenn Miller Band. How did that come about?

(I'll take a detour here as I have told this lots of times on earlier interviews.)

PT After seventeen years on the road, I stopped traveling.

MV Well, we're going to talk about the stopping of the traveling a little later. Did you have any classical background, did you have lessons as a child?

PT No, actually, my dad was the head of a state reformatory, so the reform school kids taught me how to start on the trombone. Then after that, it was just a lot of practicing, a lot of listening. Later on, when I settled in California, I did study an awful lot of classical music. But at first, I just learned from listening to people and taking advice.

MV That always helps, doesn't it?

PT Sure does.

MV But you've got to have that desire to want to play.

PT I practiced so much that I was practicing way past what was doing me any good.

MV I don't believe it. Anyway, we're going to listen to you. Can you tell me anything about your first choice of music this evening?

PT All right. This first tune is "Without a Song," and the arrangement was by Hank Mancini. Hank was the piano player in Tex's band at that time. So, he wrote this thing so that one trombone player, that's the part I'm playing, plays the melody nice and straight, nice and pretty, and the other trombone player, Bobby Pring, kind of noodles around. And this was taken off the air up in Oregon somewhere. And when I was teaching at UCLA, I walked into a record store, and some students said, "Doctor Tanner, you've got to buy this record, your picture's on it."

MV You didn't know about it.

PT No, I didn't know about it; futhermore, I never got paid for it. So, it was never meant to be a record; it was only meant to be a radio broadcast up in Oregon. But it's a nice record.[3]

3 *Tex Beneke's Band* **"Without a Song"**

MV Thank you very much, Paul Tanner, that was lovely. How do you feel about listening to yourself?

PT Well, even up to the time that I stopped taking the horn out of the case, I had never played anything that I was happy with. That caused a little frustration, but I lived with it. I always thought I could do it much better. I've never played anything in my life that I didn't think I could play better.

MV You say you've stopped taking the horn out of the case.

PT Yes. When you played at a certain level, you couldn't stand to play at less than that level. So, you have to play all the time. That's just a set of muscles around your lips, so you have to keep them in trim just like an athlete would.

MV Do you take your horn out occasionally?

PT No.

MV No, never. I'm sure it would be so frustrating.

PT It would be terrible. I wouldn't know which end of the horn to hold.

MV Unlike very many people who start off as classical musicians, then take a separate path, classical or jazz or some other over to jazz music, you started with jazz and went to classical music as well. How does that work?

PT Well, I realized that I had an awful lot to learn. I knew a great deal about some aspects of music, I knew nothing about other aspects. And

I thought those terrible holes should be filled up. So, I started to study very hard when I got to California and settled down and I wanted to learn about as much music as I could. Sometimes if a person is a classically trained musician and goes into jazz, he has nice technique, a good sound, and so forth. And he can apply that. Sometimes a jazz musician going into classical has a lot of speed on the instrument, a lot more range than is demanded in classical music. And he can apply that. So it works both ways; it's good.

MV But you didn't just do it half way. You didn't just get one degree, you got your doctorate. And you became a teacher at UCLA.

PT When I graduated, or just before I graduated, they asked me to come on the faculty which was a nice compliment because they never hire their own. They call that "inbreeding" which sounds sexy to me, I don't know why. I went ahead and started to teach right away. They had me teach in every field that they offer: musicology, theory, performance, music education and everything. I kept on teaching in those fields until my history of jazz classes got so big that I had to drop everything else and just teach history of jazz.

MV And how big did you say those classes became?

PT Well, I would have eleven hundred students a day in the history of jazz, four days a week. There for a while, I had sixteen hundred a day. Then I complained that it was getting too much to handle because I did all the exams myself.

MV I was going to say papers to mark.

PT Yes, I did them myself. So, then they cut back to eleven hundred because they felt that I was going to quit. And I've had seventy-five thousand students in the history of jazz. Which was a lot of fun especially if you're the fellow who wrote the textbook.

MV And what is the textbook called?

PT *A Study of Jazz*, of course.

MV Well, Paul, I think we must get back to some more music, it's still Tex Beneke's group which was the Glenn Miller Orchestra, the year 1949.

PT That's right.

MV And what is the song?

PT It's called "Blue Is the Night." It's a very pretty tune and this was never meant to be a record, it was a radio broadcast. I don't exactly come in on this with a solo until the very end. But being the ham that I was, I shot on up to the upper register at the end of the thing. And I probably wouldn't have done that on a record. I'm not sure it's musically feasible or even in good taste. But I was an awful ham, so I went ahead and did it anyway. Also, I was young.[4]

4 **"Blue Is the Night"**

MV And that was Paul Tanner playing very cool trombone with the Tex Beneke Orchestra. My guest in *Just Jazz* tonight, American Doctor Paul Tanner. Paul, do you listen to a lot of jazz?

PT Oh, I listen to a great deal of jazz. In fact, while I was teaching, I had to listen in order to keep abreast of what was happening. Because you can't go in and talk to students about just things in the past. You have to be aware of what they are hearing. So, I constantly listen to jazz.

MV Did they often come in and say, "Have you heard this, or have you heard that? What do you think of it?"

PT That's right, they sure did. But the thing is, I never tried to con them, I never tried to kid with them. If it were something that I hadn't heard, I would say, "Is it something that I should hear?" And they would often bring me the record so I would hear it. And if I liked it, I would buy it. They helped to keep me abreast, there's no question about it.

MV So you've been extending your collection all the time.

PT Constantly. I have ten thousand now.

MV Who do you listen to when you're listening?

PT If I'm doing other work, I can listen to some nice, easy listening type of thing. If the jazz is more complicated, more complex, then I can't do anything else and listen at the same time because I listen too closely. So I can't do anything else. Cool jazz things are very easy for listening and work. I can listen to Paul Horn, I can listen to Urbie Green play trombone. But if I get into complex harmonies and so forth, I have to stop everything and just listen. And I don't mind that at all, I love it.

MV You talk about complex jazz, can you give any names?

PT You have to start with Kenton and keep on going up to date. You get to some nice complex things by fellows like Don Sebesky, Don Costa, Bob James, and people like this. They like nice complex things.

MV I like Bob James.

PT He's a very talented player, also a very good writer. There are people who have other piano players on the record session and still hire Bob

James to come on in and just sit in the booth and listen and give suggestions. They've got that much respect for this young fellow.

MV Do you get to any Jazz Festivals?

PT I don't now because of the fact that I've been just too busy.

MV Do you approve of the direction that jazz seems to be taking now?

PT Well, it's taking several directions at once, that's the problem. The directions that are a little more classically oriented are very easy to approve of. The things that are a little more rock oriented are just fine too because they'll often have a big band playing good jazz things and put a rock beat behind it. That's fine with me because the music moves. But if you get into some of the *avant garde* things, Marilyn, where fellows are just making funny sounds on their instruments and things like that, I can't go along with them. Because I like any kind of music that's played well. And I don't consider those fellows are playing well if they are just making strange sounds on the instrument. They may be expressing themselves individually, I don't really know about that. But if they are just squealing and swawking on the instrument just for the sound's sake, well, I don't approve of that at all.

MV Do you think there is an overlap between the direction that some jazz is taking with contemporary music?

PT Do the people on the radio know that you use your hands for descriptions?

Contemporary jazz and contemporary classical music? Oh yes, I think so, especially harmonically. But I think the jazz players are borrowing more from classical than otherwise, as far as the harmonies are concerned. As far as the movement of the music in the way of rhythm, of course, the classical players are borrowing from the jazz players.

MV When you were playing with Warren Baker, I'm sure you weren't making funny sounds.

PT Well, I wasn't doing it intentionally. I should set this up just a little for you, Marilyn. I was in Los Angeles. You do an awful lot of freelance work there. And this particular fellow was an old friend, and he put together an orchestra called Warren Baker and the Baker's Dozen. Now, of course, that means that there are thirteen players in the orchestra. But I felt very chintzy because I was the only fellow there playing one instrument. Between the other twelve fellows, they played forty or fifty instruments, and I'm sitting there just playing the trombone. But they wanted me there because I played high pretty solos for them. And that's what this tune is, "Love Your Magic Spell Is Everywhere." 5

⑤ **"Love Your Magic Spell Is Everywhere"** *featuring Paul Tanner on trombone*

MV And that was Paul Tanner playing with the Warren Baker Band, "Love Your Magic Spell Is Everywhere." What a fantastic title. Paul, I want to thank you so much for your visit.

PT It's a pleasure.

MV I hope you're going to have a good stay here in South Africa.

PT I'm enjoying myself thoroughly due to the Glenn Miller Society and the Big Band Society.

MV That's great, and I hope you'll be back soon.

PT I will.

(Their theme song. Another program's theme song, evidently this next program is called Back To the Big Bands *and is featuring Henry Holloway)*

Announcer: It's Saturday night, it's *Back To the Big Bands*, and here to give you the downbeat is Henry Holloway.

HH Good evening. Last week I promised you a surprise for tonight and I'm keeping my word. I have sitting opposite me here in Studio P5, a living legend. I'm referring to Professor Doctor Paul Tanner who has just retired as professor of music at the University of California Los Angeles. But in his young days, a stalwart member of the fabulous Glenn Miller Orchestra.

PT But these are my young days, Henry, these are my young days. How old do you have to be to be a "living legend"?

HH I don't think it really has to do with age, Paul, I think it has to do with what you've achieved.

PT I thought you were going to say it's how you look.

HH Just as well we're not on television.

PT Right.

HH Paul, it's lovely to have you here.

PT I'm having a great time.

HH You like South Africa, I believe.

PT I love it. I've already decided to come back as soon as I can.

HH And you've only been here two days.

PT That's right.

HH It just shows what South Africa and South African people do to you.

PT They're just lovely.

HH Wonderful. Paul, we're going to talk about music, about big bands, and a little bit about universities, tutors, lecturers, and things like that.

PT I know all about that sort of thing.

HH So it won't be too difficult. Let's start at the beginning. How did you meet Glenn Miller? I know that's an interesting story, and I'm sure the people would like to hear it.

(All this is covered in detail in earlier interviews, so I won't reiterate here.)

HH That was '38.

PT 1938.

HH 1938.

PT Not 1838.

HH Not 1838. And that was the start of a wonderful career ending in September '42.

PT Yes, Glenn only had a band about four and a half years. People think because the band had so much impact that he had a band for fifteen or twenty years. But the band was really only in existence about four and a half years.

HH That orchestra was collectively a legend.

PT Well, it was surely the most popular orchestra that there was. The people saw to that, and Glenn saw to it that he pleased the people.

HH I think we should get into some music quickly.

PT All right.

"Just One Of Those Things" 6

(A reiteration of my getting with Sonny Burke's Orchestra, leading to an introduction to his record "Just One Of Those Things.")[6]

HH "Just One Of Those Things," the Sonny Burke Orchestra in 1951, with my guest Paul Tanner. Blowing some pretty high notes there, Paul?

PT Yes, that was pretty high, especially to be so loud. Usually, you get that high, you back off a little. But I was young and ambitious and straight ahead.

HH That was a great band. You had marvelous players, Conrad Gozzo, Pete Condoli, Ollie Mitchell in the trumpet section.

PT Well, that just gives you a sample of what was going on all through the rest of the band, like Paul Smith was playing piano.

HH What a band.

PT Oh, it was a great band.

HH Paul, let's talk about the other bands. When you left Glenn and he went into the service, I know that the Miller trombone section went as a unit to Charlie Spivak.

PT That's right. I was offered a couple of other things, Henry, but it was a very comfortable thing to do, to go on over with Spivak's Band with the other trombone players. Nelson Riddle was already there, so that made four trombones. Furthermore, I knew I was going to go into the service pretty soon. So there was no reason to be involved with, even for more money, people like Horace Heidt and those kinds of bands. Besides that, Davey Tough was playing drums, Willie Smith was playing alto, Neal Hefti was playing trumpet, so the band was a lot of fun.

HH I guess that Hefti and Nelson Riddle did arrangements for Spivak.

PT Oh yes, in fact, they were a big help to me after I settled down in California because we were already friends. They were doing well out there then.

HH Paul, how about another number? [7]

(A reiteration of the story about meeting Warren Baker, so I won't repeat this here. It led to an introduction to "Love Your Magic Spell Is Everywhere.")

7 **"Love Your Magic Spell Is Everywhere"**
featuring Paul Tanner

HH "Love Your magic Spell Is Everywhere," Warren Baker and the Baker's Dozen. That was 'round about '52, '53, Paul?

PT That's just about right.

HH You joined the resuscitated, reorganized Glenn Miller Orchestra after the War.

PT That's right. I had signed a contract with Glenn to play for him for at least a year after the War. And when he told me what he had going after the War, I just couldn't wait to get started on it. But then, of course, he didn't come back. Well, Glenn's office held some of us to that contract.

HH So you went with Tex and that lasted quite a few years.

PT I stayed with Tex for six years. I kept trying to leave, but he kept giving me more money. Actually, I was telling him that I had to get off the road. I had been out there so long. I ended up being on the road seventeen years. Each time I told him, "Tex, I've got to leave." Then he would give me more money.

HH You know, I've been thinking of something. Time just flits by so quickly, and we must play one more record. But I don't think we can end on this note, because there's still your academic career to talk about. So how about us playing one more record, ending this program, and you coming back next week for another program?

PT I'd love to. That would be a lot of fun.

Tex Beneke's 8 **"Without a Song"**

HH That would be lovely. So let's swing into the third record.[8]

(A repeat of the explanation of Tex Beneke's of "Without a Song.")

(Henry's theme song.)

HH Paul, I'm afraid Old Father Time's caught up with us. But I'm delighted that you'll be coming back next Saturday. So, until then, goodbye.

PT This is Paul Tanner, goodbye.

HH And goodbye from yours truly, Henry Holloway.

(Henry's theme song.)

Announcer: It's Saturday night, *Back To the Big Bands*, and here to give you the downbeat is Henry Holloway.

(Actually it is only a few minutes after the last interview.)

HH Hello again. As I promised last week, I have in the studio with me once more, my good friend, Paul Tanner. How are you doing tonight, Paul?

PT Fine. You see, I didn't leave for America yet.

HH I'm so glad they held the plane back a bit. I think tonight we must step forward and talk about your academic career. Obviously, we're going to play some records as well. While playing first trombone for the American Broadcasting Company, you entered the academic field.

(No sense going over the details of my faculty career again.)

"Love For Sale" 9 *featuring Paul Tanner*

HH How about some music?[9]

(Explanation and introduction of Memo Bernabei's Band.)

HH "Love For Sale," recorded in the '50s. Paul, that last note you hit there, I believe up to that time, I believe was probably the highest note that anybody had the audacity to hit on the trombone.

PT I did it loudly. If there is a trumpet out there, that would be your A above high C.

HH It was loud and it was clear and it was good.

PT Cole Porter would have loved it.

HH Yes, Cole wrote that didn't he?

PT Yes.

HH Well, played beautifully. Tell us about your doctorate.

(More details about academia previously covered.)

HH I'm sure your students enjoyed your classes. I've seen articles about it. And after twenty-three years, you eventually retired and they just didn't want you to.

PT Well, the students were very nice, they gave me "a day." In fact, the first part of that day, they came into the class; now you look out into an auditorium of people and you see eleven hundred people out there, each one has a balloon with your face on it. It's frightening, I'm telling you. Then they hired Tex Beneke's Band to come down and play. Les Brown came down, an awful lot of the musicians out of Los Angeles, including Willie Schwartz and Johnny Best. I told them, I said, "I don't really understand. You have Pulitzer Prize people here." And they said, "The funny thing is we don't get to know them and we feel that we know you." Which is nice.

HH But what professor would put personal notes on seventy-five thousand students' report cards or exam papers?

PT Well, the larger the class, the more I felt obligated to make them feel that I was personally identified with them, so I always put little notes on their grade cards. Sometimes it's pretty hard if a fellow has flunked, I didn't know what to say to him.

HH Paul, some more music. What will it be?

PT This one is from *The Glenn Miller Story*.

HH "Too Little Time," a beautiful ballad played by the Tex Beneke Orchestra live at Disneyland with a gorgeous trombone solo by my guest, Paul Tanner. [10]

(10) **"Too Little Time"**
Paul Tanner's trombone solo

PT It was a lot of fun, it really was.

HH Paul, we're on the home stretch now and I'm afraid we're going to leave it to you to wrap it up.

PT Well, let me talk a little more about *The Glenn Miller Story*. Jimmy Stewart was, of course, the star with June Allyson. But Stewart was so ambitious, so anxious to do a good job that, would you believe, he learned the slide positions for every one of Glenn's solos. Now nobody but another trombone player is going to know what slide positions he was using. He stuffed up the mouthpiece and tried to blow so it would look like he was working very hard with his embouchure. He was a very conscientious actor.

HH Of course, you appeared in the *"Glenn Miller Story,"* and I have the movie where you, as they come down the stairs, you play "Pennsylvania 6-5000."

PT Now, the solos are divided between two or three different people: Murray McEachern, Joe Yukl, and I did some.

HH Paul, we have time for just one more number.

PT Well, last week we mentioned Sonny Burke's Orchestra. So why don't we take a piece of that and go on out with that? It was a very exciting band and we're playing "Samba Americana."

HH Any notable solos on that by a certain trombone player?

PT Oh yes, he works pretty hard.

HH Paul, you know I could go on talking with you for six more programs, but I think I'd be fired from my position doing this program, so I'm afraid that we'll have to say goodbye. I'm dreadfully sorry but it was an absolute delight to have you on the program. And I just hope that when you come back again, and I know you'll come back to South Africa, we're going to have more sessions.

PT Well, could I say what a pleasure it's been to get to know the folks in the Glenn Miller Society here and the Big Band Society. It's just a real pleasure.

HH That's wonderful. Well friends, that's it. Our great thanks for coming in and talking to us, and we are going to corner him when he comes back again. So for now, goodbye for Paul Tanner.

PT Thank you very, very much, it's been a real pleasure.

more of the Sonny Burke record 11

HH And goodbye for me, Henry Holloway. [11]

Interview with Neville Dawson 21

More from South Africa, February 6, 1983

ND It's *Springbok Spotlight*—with words and music and me, Neville Dawson. Welcome to another line up for the very latest in news, interviews, and music from that glittering world of show business, and with the accent this week from big band music. Our distinguished American guest will be Doctor Paul Tanner, who was trombonist with the great Glenn Miller Orchestra. So stay with us, you're right on the beam, *Springbok Spotlight.*

(Theme for yet another program.)

ND The big band music of today–Swingtime's Greatest Hits with a disco beat...

(A medley of Miller hits all played in disco. How's that to wake up to! Evidently I had arrived in town the night before and was shuttled to the studio early in the morning for more contact with the folks in South Africa. This interview was done February 6, 1983. The gentleman's name is Neville Dawson.)

ND One of my friends recently said to me that they just don't write them like that any more, but they do still play them.[1]

1 "Moonlight Serenade"

(Now I hear "Moonlight Serenade" as we know it, not as a disco.)

ND Our program today began with modern arrangements of Swingtime's Biggest Hits. But right now, we are listening to the original Glenn Miller Orchestra playing Glenn's famous signature tune, "Moonlight Serenade," recorded in April 1939. One of the musicians on this record is Paul Tanner, trombonist with the Miller Band during the late '30s and the early '40s. Today, a Doctor of Music from the University of California. Paul is on a short visit to South Africa to meet members of the Glenn Miller Appreciation Society and to talk about that wonderful heyday of the big bands. Paul, you must have played on most of those gigantic hits.

PT Well, I'm on everything that Glenn did with the band that he kept. He had a band before and he broke that band up. But this band he started around the summer of 1938 and kept until he broke up the band in September 1942. So, I was on everything that he recorded. But like I said, he did some before with the band that he had to disband. It just didn't make out financially.

ND How old would you have been, if I may ask, in 1938 when you joined the band?

PT Oh, I must have been about 18, somewhere around there, an old man really for the job.

ND And Paul, you talk about those four very important years, '38 to '42, when you were with the Glenn Miller civilian band. That certainly was the time when most of those big ones were recorded, I mean numbers like "In the Mood."

PT That was the time when all of his big ones were recorded. You know, Neville, people think that the band kept going for ten or fifteen years, the band only existed about four and a half years. But when you look back at the impact that he made and everything, the people think he must have been going for ten or fifteen years. Some say, "Well, I used to dance to the band," "My parents used to take me to the band." But it was only four and a half years, and in that time, he made all of those records that were hits.

ND The list was virtually endless, wasn't it?

PT Well, I just did some fairly recent research work, and I had to find out who had million-seller records. Of course, Glenn had many more than anyone else. They are usually surprised that Goodman didn't have any, Tommy Dorsey had about four or five, Jimmy Dorsey had about seven or eight because of the things with Bob Eberly and Helen O'Connell. The guy who had more than any of them except for Glenn was Harry James. But Glenn had many more million-selling records than anybody else.

ND He had such a charisma.

PT That's right.

ND Did he always take the solo when the trombone was featured in the arrangement?

PT Yes. Now, I have home movies of me playing a solo, but it was rare. He said to me, "Go on down and play a solo." So I did. But Glenn played all the solos and he played all the lead trombone. So, he was a much underrated trombone player, really a fine trombone player. But he didn't feature himself playing ballads because he knew he'd be compared to Tommy Dorsey and come out second. He didn't feature himself playing improvisations, he knew he'd be compared to Teagarden and some other people, and come out second. So he played mainly lead over the section. And he was strong, a good sound, in tune, you can't ask much more than that. He was a good player.

ND When the famous clarinet player, Peanuts Hucko, was with us last year, he told me at the time that Glenn was a disciplinarian, but a very fine person. Paul, what were your own impressions of Miller the man?

PT As far as being a disciplinarian was concerned, he certainly was. You had to look good on the stand. He wouldn't have you sit up there and have your navel showing or something like that. But you had to have your hair cut, you had to have the right tie on, and the right socks, and so forth. But as far as the playing was concerned, you also had to stop notes on the right beat and so forth. But he also said that you must enjoy yourself; otherwise the people won't enjoy themselves, and that's what they pay you for, to come in and enjoy themselves. So, he didn't ask you to do anything that he wouldn't do himself. But you had to do what he wanted you to do, and you had to do it with pleasure, and of course, the pay check helped.

ND Glenn enlisted, didn't he, in 1942? And from what you have told me already, I gather that the band virtually broke up at that stage.

PT It actually did. It disbanded entirely.

ND That's the civilian band.

PT Yes, that was September of '42.

ND In the meantime of course, Glenn was across in Europe and he had his Air Force Band, didn't he?

PT Afterward, yes. He had only told us about a month before that he was going to do that. So we all had to see to it that we had places to go work when he broke up. But there was no problem. We didn't know that there was going to be no problem, but there wasn't any problem. And he went on into the service. But there was quite a lot between then and the time he went overseas. He had to go though basic training, and he had to do an awful lot of work for the service in America before he could even talk his way into going overseas. They wanted him to stay there and train bands. But what Glenn wanted to do was to go overseas; and he felt that the one thing he could give the fellows who were drafted and taken away from their homes and their careers, their jobs, and so forth, the one thing he could do for them was to take them a little piece of home. And the only way he could do that was to go over and play for them. So that was exactly what he wanted to do. And sometimes he had to fight the army brass in order to do that; but he was very stubborn and he hung in there.

ND But Paul, you were to get back to the Glenn Miller Band because it was reorganized after the War, under the direction of Tex Beneke, a very capable musician himself.

PT Oh yes, I got out of the service before Tex got it started. So I went with Les Brown, and I stayed with Les until Tex got going. Then I went over with Tex and stayed with him for six years. Then I quit and went to California, and I was on the American Broadcasting Company staff as lead trombone player for sixteen years, then I taught at UCLA for twenty-three, I was on the road for seventeen years. That makes me a hundred and five. I look good, don't I?

ND You do indeed. Especially for a guy who has flown all the way from Los Angeles and come to South Africa for the first time. Paul, we were talking about the Miller Band being reorganized under Tex Beneke, a great musician as we agree, but to what extent do you feel he was able to retain that very distinctive sound?

PT Now, he had the library, and he had quite a few of the musicians who had played the music. Tex is a good musician and he is a very fine fellow and a very dear friend of mine. There was only one Glenn. So, when you get right down to the perfection of it, Tex wouldn't be able to handle what Glenn could handle. Besides that, Tex was also interested in building up his own musical personality. So, he gradually got away from it a little bit. But even today, Tex is doing very, very well incidentally. He plays "In the Mood" and "Chattanooga Choo Choo" and "String of Pearls" and so on. The people demand it of him.

ND Still plays tenor sax?

"Chattanooga Choo Choo" ❷

PT Oh yeah, and he plays well. And still sings the same, whether you like it or not, that's it. I enjoyed Tex's singing, I thought that it was very friendly. Well, Bob Eberly he wasn't, but he was very friendly.[2]

(Played a bit of "Chattanooga Choo Choo.")

ND Tex Beneke and one of his most famous recordings, recorded in July 1941. In a few moments, we'll be back with Glenn Miller's trombonist.

(Break)

ND Our Spotlight guest is Doctor Paul Tanner, he was trombonist with the famous Glenn Miller Orchestra during the big band era. Paul, in the early 1950s, you began something of a new career, studying at the University of California.

(A reiteration about my coming into UCLA and my faculty work there.)

ND I understand that you will be showing some interesting private films to members of the Glenn Miller Appreciation Society.

PT Well, that's true. But they have to understand that these are little amateur eight millimeter home movies. Like, if the band were on stage, the lights continually change, sometimes you get no lights, sometimes too much light. But they are very homey type movies, like you say to Tex, "Wave at the camera, Tex." So Tex waves at the camera.

ND In other words, you're telling us that the private films that you brought do go back to the great days of the Glenn Miller Band and they were about the band?

PT Yes, absolutely. I think what you see more in these is what the band did to relax, because that's usually when I could take the pictures. What we did between shows, what we did in between engagements and things like that.

ND Well, I don't care if they are simple amateur eight millimeter films, I can assure you there are many, many Glenn Miller fans in South Africa who'd give the world just to see them.

PT Well, that's just fine; that's why I brought them.

ND Paul, you have been described, and I say this very sincerely, as something of a living legend.

PT Well, I don't know about either one of those words, but OK.

ND I use the expression, and I mean it sincerely, let me say, Paul, it's a great honor indeed for us to have you visiting South Africa. Now a recording featuring Paul Tanner in Cole Porter's "Just One Of Those Things."[3]

3 *Sonny Burke's* **"Just One Of Those Things"**

22 Interview with Alan Dell

"Moonlight Serenade" 1

Alan Dell was probably one of the most respected disc jockeys in London. He considered himself more of a master of ceremonies than anything else. He was most pleasant as well as knowledgeable. This British Broadcasting Company interview was in 1983. I was whisked away from my hotel over to the BBC studios in one of those huge London taxicabs, and we got right into the interview.[1]

"Sold American" 2

AD After last week's edition in which you heard a number of Glenn Miller's successors, tonight, the man himself. And joining me on the program, someone who can talk first hand about Glenn Miller and his music, trombonist Paul Tanner, who served for the duration in Miller's famous civilian band. And as far as the musical content of this program is concerned, for the most part, and for a change, a few of the more infrequently played Miller records, studio and broadcast performances. Let's begin with an instrumental from June 1939, composed and arranged by Miller who also plays a tidy trombone. Also featured are Tex Beneke and Clyde Hurley on tenor and trumpet in "Sold American."[2]

"The Starlit Hour" 3

It's no problem, of course, to sort out half a dozen well-known ballads that Ray Eberle sang during his years with the Miller Orchestra. Less often played, and I don't know why, is this also earlier recording, another Glenn Miller arrangement of "The Starlit Hour."[3]

AD Pretty song that, "Starlit Hour," and the Miller ballad sound in all its finery. While we're about it, we might listen to another routine that became a style and a feature with the band, and two of the other vocalists. This is extracted from a Chesterfield show of July 1940, played at the Chicago Civic Theater. Glenn Miller makes the introductions.

"The Gentleman Needs a Shave" 4
with Marion Hutton and Tex Beneke

Glenn Miller ... *Tex may have what it takes with most of the gals, but he's a dead pigeon with Marion 'cause the gentleman needs a shave.*[4]

AD Marion Hutton, Tex Beneke and "The Gentleman Needs a Shave." Those of you who have been to the recent Syd Lawrence concerts and have enjoyed his tribute to Glenn Miller will have had the chance to see and hear Mr. Paul Tanner who had been in Britain on a vacation. But we've taken advantage of his time somewhat. I must say he seems to have enjoyed it very much. After the disaster of Glenn Miller's first band in 1937, he began forming what became the famous and successful orchestra during the summer of 1938. And he chose for his trombone section, it was only a three man section, one of them being Paul Tanner. Paul was to stay with the orchestra until that famous last concert in September 1942 before Miller enlisted in the Army Air Force. I haven't checked exactly, but Paul was on all the record dates as far as I can remember, and in the two films. And if anyone should know what it was like to be in the band, it must be him. I asked Paul the question when he sat in on one of those programs during the last few weeks.

PT Well, to tell you the truth, Alan, I was sitting in the middle of the band, and I never really got the impact as much as people who stood out front. Now, I came across that when I catalogued my Miller records to give to the university back in California. I really had forgotten, or maybe I never realized, how good the band really was 'cause I never heard the whole thing. I'm sitting in the middle and trumpet players are bending my ears forward, and I could hear a lot of drums and a lot of amplifier from vocals and things like that. It really was a good band. Now, we knew that the band was big 'cause we sold out every night. And the kids were just screaming at the band, and we knew the band was going over really well. But we had no idea of the impact it was making to still be going on today. In fact, if we had, I would have done some things differently.

AD Really?

PT Sure, I would have taken more pictures for one thing. No, it was a good job and a lot of fun, it truly was.[5]

5 *Miller's* **"Boulder Buff"**

AD I know that Glenn struggled for a little while at the Paradise Restaurant and so forth; then he got the Glen Island Casino booking. Glenn must have been fairly despondent because he wasn't getting the success at that time that he thought perhaps he should get. And it really clicked off at the Glen Island Casino, didn't it?

PT Well, you know, Alan, at one time, he was going to break the band up. He didn't have any bookings at all. He called us into a hotel room in Boston, and told us, he said, "Now if you've got anything, any offers from anybody, go to them." And you know, most of the fellows were very young like I was, and the best band I had ever worked with. So I said, "Let's rehearse, let's do something." So he said, "Well, if you fellows feel that way, we'll hang in there." And so, then pretty soon he came to us and said, "We've got the Meadowbrook, then we've got the Glen Island all Summer, then we're back at the Meadowbrook." And we knew all about the air time you got from both of those places. So, we knew we had it made then. But it must have been frustrating for him to realize that he wasn't really appreciated very much up until then. But he knew the business very well and he knew he had to get air time.

AD Yes, that was the crunch, wasn't it? That was the thing.

PT You know how important radio is, Alan.

AD I've heard that it's quite important.

Miller's 6 **"So You're the One"** *with the Modernaires*

AD "So You're the One," a song featuring the Modernaires, an excerpt from a Chesterfield broadcast of January 1941. The tune before that was "Boulder Buff," the studio recording of May 1941. From which you will gather that I'm not trying to match music to time and locations as mentioned by Paul. I'm just trying to represent as many facets of the Glenn Miller Orchestra and its personnel as I can. On that subject, inevitably, we must ask, "What was the boss like?" One has heard many conflicting stories. Well, if anyone should know, it's surely Paul Tanner.[6]

PT I had to write a piece about Glenn not too long ago. And I started the first page with what kind of a fellow Glenn Miller was. I wrote a whole page on he was this, he was that, he was this. He was an excellent musician, he was an excellent businessman, he was very patriotic, he was an athlete, he was very stern, he never asked you to do anything that he wouldn't do, and on and on and on. And I spent the rest of the essay explaining each one of those. He really was very complex. And he thought that playing for the people was a business, and you do it properly or you don't do it at all. But the music came first, it really did.

AD He was a fine arranger.

PT Excellent arranger. And also had a very fine ear. Also, he was an excellent trombone player, very underrated trombone player. He played all the lead trombone in that band. And you could tell he had a good firm sound, played in tune, good interpretation; who needs anything more than that.

AD Well, he had worked with the best, hadn't he? Like Tommy.

PT Tommy Dorsey, Jack Teagarden, everybody who was a good trombone player. And Glenn was a good listener, so he learned from them.[7]

AD Obviously, in a band which is on the road all the time and you're touring and you're in a bus and you live with somebody in a room. Who did you live with?

PT Most of the time I lived with Jimmy Priddy.

AD Your trombone side-kick.

PT That's right. Of course, my wife and I drove a great deal of the time. There was no space on the bus for wives, so we drove a great deal. But when I rode on the bus, I roomed with Jimmy. In fact, Alan, we used to have a deal going. You know, sometimes you get into a hotel early in the morning after riding all night, and there's a shortage of rooms with twin beds and a shower. So Jimmy and I had a deal. I was so slow that Glenn called me "Lightnin'." Jimmy would get up toward the front of the bus as we were getting in to the hotel, and I would get in the aisle and just clobber things up terribly so nobody could get around me. And everybody would say, "OK, Lightnin', let's go." Meanwhile, Jimmy's gone in the hotel and gotten the room with twin beds and a shower. It was a matter of survival.

AD Did they kill you? The one-night stands?

PT Oh no, I was very young, I didn't mind the slightest, not really, no.

AD Jimmy Priddy, you roomed with him. Other personalities in the band, and there must have been a lot of personalities. I mean, I know Johnny Best, Billy May. Any anecdotes, any stories?

PT One thing you have to remember, Alan, and that is when you're with a band like that, and you're traveling all the time, your friends are chosen for you. You have no choice about with whom you are going to live and work and play. So, your friends are chosen for you. So, Glenn was very careful. He would look into a fellow's personality before he'd hire him. First, he had to be the musician Glenn wanted. But then, if there was a personality problem, then Glenn didn't want him on the band. In fact, if there was a problem with the wife, a trouble-maker or something like that, then Glenn stayed clear of the fellow. And I've known several musicians who had that problem and had trouble getting hired by a road band. They can be hired to do studio work because you go home, but with a road band, you can't have a person like that. So, your friends are chosen for you, you have to wear well, and you have to be quite flexible.

Miller's 8 **"Papa Nicolini"**

Glenn Miller ... *Now a tune about a happy little cobbler who is never so busy about all the events that he can't take on a job that has nothing to do with shoe repairing. Ray first, then Marion, Tex, and the Modernaires, tell you how he goes about them. Here's "Papa Nicolini."* [8]

AD Glenn broke records wherever he went. He played everything and the attendance records were colossal.

PT Sometimes that's pretty amazing, especially in theaters, because you have to figure very often the audiences wouldn't leave. And Glenn would even send Ray Eberle out for milk shakes for some of the kids who were sitting down front who hadn't been home to eat all day. But they would still break the record. And do you know who's record was the hardest to break? Kay Kyser. Now at the Savoy Ballroom in Harlem, do you know who had the record before Glenn? Guy Lombardo. That's amazing, isn't it? You would have thought Basie, Chick Webb, somebody.

AD Chick was a resident, wasn't he?

PT For a while, but the guy who had the record up there was Guy Lombardo, isn't that amazing. "The home of happy feet." But Glenn did break the record. And I'll tell you, they had three bands. There was always a name band, a semi name band, and then the house band, the Savoy Sultans. And you hoped you didn't follow the house band, because they just out-swung everybody, seven fellows. But we would stand over on the side of the ballroom and watch the stand and watch the people dance when it wasn't our turn to play. And we could see the piano going up and down. The ballroom was on the second floor; we were sure that some day it was going to be on the first floor.

AD Or even the basement.

PT Right.

AD Yes, I've been into places like that myself.

PT Scary, isn't it?

AD Really, it is true. So there you were in the Miller Band from 1938 to '42. Played a lot of good records.

PT We made a lot of records in that band. Some of them, except for folks like you, a lot of people haven't heard them.

AD It was a super band.

PT It was, and it was a lot of fun to play in it too.

AD You liked it?

PT Oh yeah, yes, I liked it. You did have to be careful though, you couldn't relax too much even though Glenn wanted you to, you knew that mistakes weren't allowed. The funny thing about mistakes, Alan, is that a brass player could miss a note, OK, Glenn was a brass player, he thought that was human. But if you came in wrong, that was carelessness, and he wouldn't stand for that, absolutely not.

AD I remember you once saying that you didn't quit, the job went away.

PT I have a tendency to stay on jobs until the jobs go away. But who is going to quit that job anyway. I stayed there until Glenn decided to break it up to go into the service. And that was a pretty weepy time. The last show in the theater in New Jersey.

AD Passaic.

PT Marion Hutton couldn't finish her tunes, the Modernaires couldn't finish theirs. Glenn looked out and there were just a lot of kids crying as if they had lost something very precious. So, he just had them bring down the curtain. And everyone was choked up pretty much. Even though it was a little exciting thinking you'll be going on to a new job and so forth, and yet, it was a very sad thing. It was like a family breaking up, Alan, we had been together a long time. We had lived and worked with people and all of a sudden, you're going to break up. So everyone, as I said, was pretty well choked up.

AD Yes, I can imagine.[9]

Glenn Miller ... *That was "Juke Box Saturday Night" and that lad that imitated Harry James really did a job. The reason, 'cause it was Harry James himself. You know, folks, it makes me feel sad to leave Marion and Tex, Skip, the Modernaires, this wonderful gang of boys in the band, and all our friends listening. But there's a lot of swell guys in the outfit I'm going in, and maybe all of us can get together again after this thing is over. In the meantime, I'll see you all in the army, and we'll say goodbye in the best way we know how.*[10]

AD Well, that was the end of the nation's number one band, Glenn Miller's civilian orchestra. Paul Tanner and the others went their separate ways. And Glenn became Captain Miller and formed his never to be repeated Army Air Force Orchestra which is remembered with so much affection here in Britain. Which we recall all too briefly with one of their most famous arrangements.[11]

9 *Miller's* **"Juke Box Saturday Night"** *including Harry James*

10 **"Moonlight Serenade"**

11 *Miller's AAF Band* **"Oranges and Lemons"**

(Plays Miller's AAF Band playing "Oranges and Lemons.")

"Moonlight Serenade" ⓬ AD Jerry Gray's arrangement for the Army Air Force Orchestra of "Oranges and Lemons." My very sincere thanks to Paul Tanner for his reminisces. And maybe, we can, some other time, have a "What happened to him?" when the civilian orchestra broke up. Meanwhile, 'til we meet again next Sunday or Monday, Alan Dell saying "good night" and leaving you in the only possible way. [12]

Interview with Chris Nielsen 23

The next interview is with an ambitious sounding gentleman from WUKY which is located at the University of Kentucky in Lexington, Kentucky. It was sometime in the 1990s, and the disc jockey's name is Chris Nielsen. He made it sound like two different interviews, a week apart. However, as you can imagine, contacting me long enough to do one of these is a pretty good maneuver. So what he did was to hold me on the phone while he had me, without any risk of not being able to contact me again. This way he was able, with plenty of records, to make our conversations into two interviews, good for him, I'd say.

(His theme song, a pretty good record, whatever it was.)

CN Hi everybody, Chris Nielsen here and the show is *One Night Stand*, and featuring the sounds of the great bands. And this week, I'm honored to have another veteran of the big band era to share some information about his career, Doctor Paul Tanner. We'll hear from Paul shortly, let's get some music. One of those budget albums that came out of the sixties, seventies, and eighties which we feature a lot of the musicians out of the big band era including our special guest, Paul Tanner. An unknown band as far as the title, but some pretty good sounds, here is "Swinging at the Ritz."[1]

1 "Swinging at the Ritz"

CN "Swinging at the Ritz," by an all-star band recorded on the west coast. That's one of those budget albums called the *Stereophonic Sounds of Glenn Miller, Volume 2*, by members of the Glenn Miller Orchestra. The tune "Swinging at the Ritz;" and it does give a lot of the personnel that played with Glenn Miller. Who is to say that this is exactly true because I've heard some of these albums and they switch them around a lot. But anyway, our very special guest this week is Mr. Paul Tanner, trombone man and a lot more as you'll learn. Paul, born in Skunk Hollow, Kentucky, on October 15, 1917. Paul, where did your career start and take it up to say 1938?

(Instead of repeating all this data about my getting started, we'll skip right over it here. We'll also skip over my meeting and joining Glenn Miller as it's all been covered in previous interviews.)

"By the Waters of the Minnetonka" 2

CN Our special guest, Mr. Paul Tanner, and now with Glenn Miller and the Orchestra in 1938. Let's go back to the early recordings of that Glenn Miller Orchestra. One of those extended play type of things recorded on September 26, 1938. Like I say, an early recording, here's "By the Waters of the Minnetonka."[2]

CN One of the early records by Glenn Miller and His Orchestra from 1938, "By the Waters of the Minnetonka." And in that band, our very special guest, Doctor Paul Tanner. Paul, getting back to the career, you spent four years with Glenn Miller until he went into the service. What was he like as a boss and as a musician and as a band leader and possibly even as a friend?

PT As a boss, Glenn was just fine, you did your job and you had no problem at all. As a musician, he was excellent, of course, everybody knows that. As a band leader, he knew what he wanted and he knew how to get it. As a friend, he was busy, so socializing was at a minimum, but he sure treated me OK. *(Editor's note–listening to this tape, I can't believe how slowly I used to talk, especially compared to a fellow like this Chris Nielsen.)*

"Shut Eye" 3
vocal by Marion Hutton

CN Getting back to the career again of Paul Tanner with Glenn Miller, let's bring another one of the old tunes on, this one from 1939, featuring Marion Hutton on the vocal. Here's a tune called "Shut Eye."[3]

CN Recorded on February 6, 1939, Glenn Miller and the Orchestra, Marion Hutton on the vocal, the tune was called "Shut Eye." And with that band, our very special guest, Doctor Paul Tanner. Paul, four years with one band was a long time. Were you the longest serving member of the Glenn Miller organization?

PT I joined the band after it had been going about a week or so. The only other fellow who is still around today who has as much longevity is Tex Beneke. He was there when I joined the band, and we both stayed with Glenn until the band broke up.

CN Four years is a long time to stay with a band and let's get into the old transcriptions and bring up a couple of tunes by the Glenn Miller Orchestra again with our very special guest, Doctor Paul Tanner, and also featuring Tex Beneke. The first one is a nice easy swinging thing that I happened to like; no commercial recording ever made of this and you've heard it before on *One Night Stand*, here's the Miller Orchestra with "Sarong."[4 & 5]

4 **"Sarong"**

5 **"Dig It"**
Marion Hutton and Tex Beneke on vocals

CN From the 1940 to 1941 period, a couple of live recordings by Glenn Miller and the Orchestra, starting out with "Sarong," a very pretty instrumental. And after that, "Dig It," featuring Tex Beneke and Marion Hutton. The great sounds of Glenn Miller and His Band, and our very special guest, Paul Tanner, Miller music. Paul, did you ever have any favorite charts when you were with the band?

PT Well, some of the up-tempo pieces were of course exciting, but as I listen to the records now, I seem to favor the really pretty things, tunes like "Rhapsody In Blue," "Serenade In Blue," "I Know Why," "Perfidia," "You Stepped Out Of a Dream," and so on.

CN Let's bring on one of those very pretty tunes from back then, here's "Perfidia."[6]

6 **"Perfidia"**
with Dorothy Claire and The Modernaires

CN Recorded on February 4, 1941, one of Paul Tanner's favorite charts with the Glenn Miller Orchestra featuring Dorothy Claire and The Modernaires, "Perfidia." Paul, the Glenn Miller Band as a whole, what would be your capsule review of the band?

PT My capsule review of the band as a whole would be that it was really a fine band, It played pretty tunes exquisitely, and some of the later things like "Johnny Comes Marching Home" and "Jingle Bells" and "The Volga Boatmen" and things like that proved that the band could also swing. That the band was very versatile and very precise.

CN Back in the vintage pile for more Glenn Miller music, here's "The Volga Boatmen."[7]

7 **"The Volga Boatmen"**

CN More of the classic sounds of Glenn Miller on *One Night Stand*, the song of "The Volga Boatmen," recorded back in 1941. Paul, getting back to the career, September 1942, Glenn went into the service. I believe that the late Jimmy Priddy told me that the whole Miller trombone section moved over to the Charlie Spivak Orchestra. Was that true?

PT *(Editor's note–Of course, it was true, why else would Jimmy say that?)* Yes, the trombone section did go over to Charlie Spivak's Band. And adding Nelson Riddle who was already there, we had four trombones. Charlie had a good band, including Willie Smith on alto sax, Davey Tough was playing drums, Neal Hefti was on trumpet and so on.

Spivak's 8
"It Ain't Necessarily So"

CN From that period with the Charlie Spivak Band, here's that great orchestra with "It Ain't Necessarily So."[8]

CN Back to 1942, that time for the Charlie Spivak Orchestra, "It Ain't Necessarily So." In that band, transferring from the Glenn Miller Orchestra, our special guest, Paul Tanner. Paul, I really haven't asked yet, was Paul Tanner really featured on any solos, with either Glenn Miller or Charlie Spivak?

PT No, no trombone player except Glenn played solos in that band. Although I do have a whole movie shot of me playing a jazz solo at the microphone in the New York Paramount Theater. But that was rare. Also, I should say, that was as it should be. Glenn was by far the best trombone player on his stage. When we went over to Charlie Spivak's Band, and from then on, we all had a lot more to do as soloists.

CN I don't really have any solos by Paul with the Charlie Spivak Orchestra. *(Editor's note–There was a strike at that time, a recording ban–he should have known that–and no bands were making any records at all. So that trombone section from Glenn's band never made any records for Spivak; hence no recorded solos at that time.)*

Spivak's 9
"Come Close To Me"

CN But we'll bring back another tune from that period that I happen to think is a very pretty tune. Here's Charlie Spivak and the Orchestra with "Come Close To Me."[9]

CN Charlie Spivak and the Orchestra, "Come Close To Me," recorded back in the early 1940s, and in the trombone section our special guest, Paul Tanner. Paul, a thought comes up here, you didn't stay with Glenn when he went in the service, where did your career take you?

PT In the years 1943 to 1945, I wasn't with Glenn's Service Band, but I surely was in the army. I had asked Glenn not to request me because I thought I had a nice situation set up. Of course, it fouled up in the army.

Miller's 10
"Boulder Buff"

CN The old snafu, I guess you could call it. Before we get away from Charlie Spivak and Glenn Miller, let's get back to one more tune from the Glenn Miller Orchestra. A lesser known instrumental I happen to like, in this band of course, our special guest, Paul Tanner. Here's "Boulder Buff."[10]

CN A 1941 era instrumental by Glenn Miller and His Orchestra, a tune called "Boulder Buff." Paul, the World War II years are passed. Wasn't your next stop a brief one with Les Brown? How did that come about, I believe in 1945?

PT Well, it was time for me to get out of the army, and I went to my old friend Frank Dailey who owned the Meadowbrook Ballroom in Cedar grove, New Jersey. And as a consequence, he cashed salary checks for all the bands. So I asked him who I should go with and he suggested Les Brown. So I got out of the army on a Saturday in New York City, and I joined Les Brown on Sunday at the Sherman Hotel in Chicago.

CN Out special guest, Paul Tanner, now with Les Brown and the Band of Renown. From that period, here's Les and the Band with "Ready To Go Steady."[11]

11 *Brown's* **"Ready To Go Steady"**

CN The middle part of the 1940s, Les Brown and the Band of Renown on "Ready To Go Steady." Paul, getting back to the career now, 1946, the Miller sound was once again very prominent with the Miller Orchestra under the direction of Tex Beneke and later of course, the Tex Beneke Orchestra. How did you come to join Tex?

PT When Glenn disbanded, he asked me to sign a contract to work for him for at least a year after the War. Of course, Glenn didn't come back, but his office held me to the contract. So, I had to leave Les Brown and join my old buddy Tex. Now that wasn't a bad thing, that was a nice thing. I stayed with Tex for six years.

CN Our special guest, Paul Tanner, now with the Tex Beneke Orchestra, or actually the Miller Orchestra under the direction of Tex Beneke. Let's go to the Hollywood Palladium, September 1946, an old broadcast by Tex Beneke and the Orchestra. And we'll start that with "My Melancholy Baby."[12]

12 *Beneke's* **"My Melancholy Baby"** **"These Foolish Things"**

Announcer: *That was our maestro, Tex Beneke, singing "My Melancholy Baby." Also a very fine saxophone chorus by Tex Beneke. And now here's another oldie; however quite a different tempo, a very beautiful tune called "These Foolish Things."*

CN From a 1946 broadcast from the Hollywood Palladium, Tex Beneke and the Orchestra with a medley of "My Melancholy Baby" and "These Foolish Things." And in the band, our special guest, Mr. Paul Tanner. Paul, your tenure with Tex lasted until the early 1950s. Was this a good band to play with and was Tex a good man to work for?

PT I enjoyed working for Tex. It was relaxed and it was good music at the same time. Tex was extremely nice to me.

CN Let's go back to the Tex Beneke Orchestra for another live recording. This time a very pretty thing called "All the Things You Are."[13]

13 *Beneke's* **"All the Things You Are"**

CN The great sound of Tex Beneke and His Orchestra, and in that band, our very special guest, Mr. Paul Tanner, "All the Things You Are." Chris Nielsen here, thanks for joining me this week on *One Night Stand*. Please join me again next week when Paul Tanner will be with us again to finish out Part 2 of his career. And until then, have a good week, take care when out and about, support the bands in your area, and don't forget to keep on dancing whenever the opportunity comes up. Let's finish out the hour in a musical mood with the Glenn Miller Orchestra. This is Chris Nielsen again saying so long.

(A new program, same theme.)

CN Hi dance band fans, Chris Nielsen coming on board with another edition of *One Night Stand*. And this week, with the great dance bands, our very special guest, Paul Tanner, as we look at Part 2 of Paul's career, going back into the middle 1940s. Paul Tanner, trombone man born October 15,1917, in Skunk Hollow, Kentucky. Let's get right back to Paul now. He's with the Tex Beneke Orchestra and let's see, Paul, were you a featured soloist with Tex and do you have some favorite charts with this band?

PT I had some solos in Tex's Band, but the only real feature was Tex, of course, and that's the way it should have been. As far as favorite charts, I guess "Swing Low Sweet Chariot" comes to mind. But I loved hearing Tex play pretty tunes like "Georgia On My Mind," things like that.

Beneke's 14 **"Swing Low, Sweet Chariot"**

"Georgia On My Mind' 15

"Tenderly" 16

CN Let's get into some of the music of Tex Beneke here, and start out with a nice long medley of three, two of the ones mentioned by Paul Tanner, "Swing Low, Sweet Chariot" and "Georgia On My Mind" and also a very pretty rendition of "Tenderly." And in "Tenderly," you'll hear the trombone of our special guest, Mr. Paul Tanner. In the meantime, here's "Swing Low." [14-16]

CN From the vintage pile, the sounds of Tex Beneke and His Orchestra. In the trombone section of that band, our special guest, Mr. Paul Tanner. We started out with "Swing Low Sweet Chariot," after that, kind of a scratchy version of "Georgia On My Mind," But that happens when you have to use some of the 78s, and finally, from a broadcast a pretty rendition of "Tenderly." In the tune "Tenderly," you heard the trombone on a solo by Mr. Paul Tanner. Paul, getting back to the career now, I believe you joined the ABC staff in 1951 and stayed for sixteen or seventeen years, something like that. Give us some insight into the scope of the work, the places, shows, the kind of things you played for.

PT Well, it takes six months to get your local union card. I joined the American Broadcasting Company staff two days after I got my union card here in Los Angeles and stayed there for sixteen years. One of the best things about the staff job is that you had to do so darned many different kinds of music. You had to play everything from classical music to dixieland to the latest in jazz and big bands and so on. You never knew from one day to the next what was going to be asked of you.

CN I guess I'd have to say there'd be no boredom involved when you're playing all kinds of music. Something different each day. And when we get back to the musical career *(Editor's note– Chris, that's a musical career I'm talking about.)* of our special guest, Paul Tanner. We're going back to April 17, 1954, at the Shrine Auditorium in Los Angeles. This was a concert by "The Original Reunion of the Glenn Miller Band." It was narrated by Gene Norman, Billy May conducted the band. And in the band was our very special guest, Mr. Paul Tanner, lots of others from the Glenn Miller Band also included people like Willie Schwartz, Chuck Gentry, Clyde Hurley, John Best, Zeke Zarchy, Billy May and so forth. And we have a couple of numbers from that concert, and let's get right to it now, without further intro, "The Original Reunion of the Glenn Miller Band." [17 & 18]

17 **"Too Little Time"**

18 **"American Patrol"**

Gene Norman ... *Story recently of Universal's outstanding picture. A fine story not only of Glenn Miller's wonderful success as a band leader, but also Glenn and Helen Miller's warm personal story of devotion ...*

CN Recorded on April 17, 1954 at the Shrine Auditorium in Los Angeles. The concert was called "The Original Reunion of the Glenn Miller Orchestra," and in that band, our special guest, Paul Tanner. OK, Paul, getting back to the career again. On top of the ABC work, I understand you were quite busy as a section man on recordings with other bands. How about some insight into this part of your career?

PT I was really busy. Lots of my friends had migrated to the studio work in Los Angeles and were doing well. Henry Mancini had been a piano player with Tex, Billy May had played trumpet with Glenn, Nelson Riddle had played trombone with Spivak, and so on. And gratefully, they really kept me busy. Sometimes there were solos, especially high register things, but mainly just playing the best I could.

Gray's 19
"Off the Wall"

Burke's 20
"Stomping at the Savoy"

CN Let's get into some of the music now of the Paul Tanner career in the early 1950s. We'll start out with a number by Jerry Gray, and after that, one by Sonny Burke. With Jerry Gray, here's a swinger called "Off the Wall." [19 & 20]

CN The swinging sounds of the dance bands from the early 1950s on *One Night Stand.* We started out with Jerry Gray and the Orchestra and "Off the Wall." And after that, the Sonny Burke Orchestra, "Stomping at the Savoy." In the trombone section of that band, our special guest, Mr. Paul Tanner. Paul, getting back to the career. We've covered your music career pretty well. How about your career as a teacher at UCLA? Give us some background on that aspect of your career.

PT My deadline for leaving Tex, getting off the road, was that I wanted to get in on the G.I. Bill for college. So, at thirty-five years of age, I enrolled at UCLA as a freshman. That was 1951. Because of working so much and ABC staff and in the other studios, it took me until 1958 to graduate. As soon as I graduated, they put me on the faculty and I stayed there for twenty-three years.

Burke's 21
"What Where and When"

CN Let's get back to a little more music of Paul Tanner's career, going back to the Sonny Burke Band again. We heard the band swing, a little less swing this time, here's Sonny Burke and the Orchestra in "What Where and When." [21]

CN I guess I dropped a clinker when I said that wasn't as swinging as the last one. That was a good swinging rendition of a tune by Sonny Burke, "What Where and When." And in the trombone section, our special guest, Mr. Paul Tanner. Paul, we're up to the 1980s now and I believe you retired in 1981 from UCLA. What keeps Paul Tanner busy today?

PT Since I retired in 1981, I've never been busier. My wife and I travel almost incessantly. I lecture all over the world at universities in London, Paris, Tokyo, and so on, and I lecture on cruises. Usually on the history of jazz, but on cruises, they mainly like to hear stories and anecdotes about the big swing bands. And of course, that's fun for me. Besides the lecturing and traveling, I do an awful lot of writing, mainly textbooks.

Tex and the band 22
"S' Wonderful"

CN I would like to say that I would like to hear one of those lectures, especially on the big band days. And speaking of the big band days, let's go back to another tune from Paul's career with Tex Beneke. This was the closing number on a show in the late 1940s. Here is Tex and the band with "S' Wonderful." [22]

CN The end of a 1949 broadcast by Tex Beneke and His Orchestra with "S' Wonderful," and, of course, "Moonlight Serenade" to close down the show. And in the trombone section is our special guest, Paul Tanner. Very much the Miller sound as we close down that show with "Moonlight Serenade." Paul, by the way, do you keep in touch with any of the Miller alumni now?[23]

23 **"Moonlight Serenade"**

PT I don't see Miller alumni nearly like I would like. I just came back from Tokyo where I was with Johnny Best and Zeke Zarchy. I talk on the phone every now and then to Tex. We all sort have our own paths that we go. We still love each other but just seldom have time to get together.

CN While we're speaking about the Glenn Miller sound, one thing we have not done yet is have one of the old, new, borrowed, and blue medleys. So, from an old broadcast, let's do it.[24]

24 *Medley*
"Who"
"Ooh What You Said"
Marion Hutton on the vocal
"Dipsy Doodle"
"The Birth of the Blues"

CN Something old, new, borrowed, and blue by Glenn Miller and the Orchestra. And again, our featured guest, Paul Tanner in the trombone section. The great sounds of Miller and Beneke very prevalent on this show. And Paul,we're getting to the music of today. What do you think of the music of today?

PT Today's music scene is in an entirely different world. I'm glad I don't play trombone now. They don't use as many as they used to. I wish there were more good tunes. There are some like "Moon River," "If," Jobim songs and so forth. But today, the emphasis is a bit lopsided toward rhythm. I'd like to see a better balance with melody and harmony used a little more.

CN I would have to agree with that. We've got about fifteen minutes left on *One Night Stand*, so instead of the music of today, let's go back to the 1940s again and bring on a nice long dancing medley by Glenn Miller and Tex Beneke. Let's start out with Glenn Miller and the Orchestra and "Gabby Goose."[25 & 26]

25 *Miller's*
"Gabby Goose"

26 *Beneke's*
"Loose Like"

CN Some swinging sounds from the career of our special guest, Paul Tanner. Starting out with Glenn Miller recorded live with "Gabby Goose," and after that, an opus called "Loose Like," Tex Beneke and the Orchestra giving the guys in the band a chance to shine. And Paul, let's get back to one more swinger from your career. This happens to be one I like, from the pen of Jerry Gray, Glenn Miller and the Orchestra with "Solid as a Stone Wall Jackson."[27]

27 **"Solid as a Stone Wall Jackson"**

"Walking By the River" 28 *with Ray Eberle and the Modernaires*

Glenn Miller ... *"Now Ray sings one of today's top tunes, "Walking By the River" with some fancy harmonizing on the side by the Modernaires."* [28]

Beneke's 29 **"Moonlight Serenade"**

Announcer ... *"It's the music of the young man with the big smile, the man with the easy to listen to mode of music, our spotlight turns to Tex Beneke and His Orchestra."* [29]

Beneke's 30 **"Rainbow Rhapsody"**

Tex Beneke ... *"First, an all-time favorite of our band."* [30]

CN Well, once again it's time to shut down the bandstand for another week here on *One Night Stand*. Chris Nielsen here. Thanks so much for joining me here this week. In the background, Tex Beneke and the Orchestra with "Rainbow Rhapsody." Before that, we heard "Walking By the River," Glenn Miller and the Orchestra. And to start out our last medley, "Solid As a Stone Wall Jackson," again Glenn Miller. I must express my appreciation here also to Paul Tanner for joining me this week. And also last week on *One Night Stand*. It's been very interesting learning about his career and, Paul, thank you very much.

PT Chris, this has surely been a pleasure for me to be on your program. Maybe, if you like, we can do it again sometime.

Beneke's 31 **"Rainbow Rhapsody"**

CN I think I would like to do it again. I'm sure there's lots of other things I can bring up as far as questions. And until next week, have a good week, take care when out and about, and again *One Night Stand* comes to you from WUKY, the University of Kentucky in Lexington. Until we meet again, I'll be seeing you. This is Chris Nielsen saying so long, and here's Tex Beneke. [31]

Interview with Doug Best **24**

Doug Best is a regular staple in our neighborhood, you automatically tune in to his program every Saturday morning. He is a good friend too and that doesn't hurt. When he did this program, he was at a station in Oceanside, then moved to Escondido, now he is in Carlsbad, all within a good golf shot of each other here in Southern California. He and his partner Chuck Strutton have plenty of records and it was fun to go talk with them as they did a program which they called A Salute to Paul Tanner.

(Les Brown's "Leap Frog" is his theme.)

Announcer: *You're enjoying* Doug Best Swings *on KGMG, Oceanside, 1320 AM.*

DB Well, Paul Tanner has arrived and so we can get everything in order. We're going to have a record with Les Brown and Doris Day, then we'll get into our salute to this good guy, Paul Tanner. So, you don't mind Doris Day, do you; you wouldn't mind listening to Doris Day?

PT Did you know I was on Les Brown's Band when she was the girl singer?

DB Really?

PT In fact, every time you play your theme song, I kind of play it in my mind. She was a nice girl. Pardon me, is a nice girl.

DB You know what, I had somebody tell me you should not call people that age girls. And I said, "Anybody under sixty-five is a girl to me."

PT And anybody who looks like that can be called whatever she likes.

DB That's right.

DB OK. There we have the Les Brown Band with Doris Day with a little bit of "Moon Mist." Now we're going to get into whatever amount of time it takes to have a good chat with our good friend, Paul Tanner. Here we go, this will bring memories.[1]

(1) *Les Brown's* **"Moon Mist"** *with Doris Day*

"Moonlight Serenade" 2

DB Well, certainly, for a guy who spent all of those years with the Miller Band, that's got to bring back a lot of memories, Paul, "Moonlight Serenade."[2]

PT Do you know, Doug, I have ten or twelve different records on "Moonlight Serenade," so a lot of people recorded it. It's a good tune.

DB Yes, indeed it is. Paul, you have been a man who has been very, very blessed over the years. The good Lord has been very, very kind to you. The experience of being with the Miller Band, Les Brown, Spivak, why don't you give us a little laundry list of all the things you did?

PT Oh now, I've lived a long life. How much time have you got, Doug?

DB Well, you sent us a list and —

PT Oh, you mean of tunes?

DB Yeah, but we want to get into, as we play these, we want to get into why you picked these particular songs out of the multitude of recordings that you did with the Miller Band.

PT Well, now, "Moonlight Serenade" is–I don't know how many people know, but Glenn was studying, he was studying legit composition with a fellow named Dr. Joseph Schillinger. And this "Moonlight Serenade" was an exercise that he wrote for Schillinger. And I have a picture of it and it's called "Miller's Tune." And later on, it was called "Now I Lay Me Down To Weep" and something else, and then he got the fellow who wrote the lyrics for "Stardust," Mitchell Parrish, to go ahead and write lyrics to it, then they called it "Moonlight Serenade."

DB Well, we're going to tune this up a little bit; get the next record ready, and then we'll continue on with Dr. Paul.

(More of Miller's record of "Moonlight Serenade.")

DB Well, anybody who ever knew anything about music has heard that song.

PT Well now, just a couple of things about it, Doug. There's a clarinet solo on there by fellow named Willie Schwartz, and he was a little heavyset fellow from New Jersey that no one ever heard of. And when the record came out, all the people who wrote about it in the trade magazines swore up and down that Glenn was going to have a terrible time convincing people that he didn't get his friend Benny Goodman or Artie Shaw to come and play that. It was that good; Willie plays so well. And yet, a couple of years ago, I was over in Japan, and there was a little girl who was so little when she stood up, she couldn't see over the music stand. And she stood up and played that gorgeous solo, just note for note, like Willie. I listened to her and she was really great. I was really thrilled to hear it.

DB You know what, we need to do something.

(A commercial, then Les Brown's "Leap Frog" as a theme, then Miller's "Little Brown Jug.")[3]

3 Miller's **"Little Brown Jug"**

DB Wow, we're still in the year 1939, and we're talking to Paul Tanner. First of all, I want to ask you about your book; by the way, it's fascinating reading, all you ever wanted to know about Glenn Miller and Paul Tanner.

PT Thank you.

DB It's a great book. It's entitled *Every Night Was New Year's Eve,* and we want to help you promote the book.

PT Oh good, I'm sure the publisher will be thrilled.

DB But everybody would assume that being nicknamed Lightnin' that you were one of those fast guys. That isn't how you got that name at all.

PT Just the opposite. I stammered so badly that until I was about 18 or so, I couldn't talk at all. And I always moved just about that same way. I was the slowest guy Glenn ever saw in his life, and he said, "Lightnin'" and it stuck.

DB Even to this day, I remember the first time you visited us and Chuck called you Lightnin', your eyes sort of lit up. Well, there was an incident in there also about the chairs that you...

(I reckon there is no need to reiterate the story about falling off a chair that had been "fixed" by my new friends.)

DB OK, you wanted to talk about "Little Brown Jug."

(Story about Jackie Cooper playing our mistake in the earlier interviews.)

DB All right, we're going to continue on. What do we have tuned up now? "Stairway To the Stars," is that it? We're talking to Paul Tanner, Doctor Paul. And you can see what a marvelous, marvelous life that he's led, time with the Miller Band, and the things that happened thereafter, his years at UCLA.[4]

4 Miller's **"Stairway To the Stars"** *with Ray Eberle*

PT And it's all in *Every Night Was New Year's Eve.*

DB Fascinating book, I couldn't put it down, and I'm a slow reader and I fall asleep early too, but what the heck.

DB Now Paul, let's talk about the record we just had.

PT Well, I had to put "Stairway To the Stars" on that list because that's my wife's favorite. I get real flashbacks of the Glen Island Casino whenever I hear it. Because we used to sit there on the bandstand and we'd look out over the dance floor. They had those big glass doors open and we could look right out on to the Sound. And people were lying out there on their boats, listening to the band. And when the band wasn't playing, they were also taking a break, and we used to watch them, and get excited, and so on and so on. Also, a lot of people don't realize that that's from "Park Avenue Fantasy," a theme from that. Ray Eberle sounds a little high pitched there but he sounds very sweet, very pure, very nice. And in the criticism he's had, comparing him to his brother Bob who is a fine, fine singer, is that Ray didn't have the sound. Well, Ray did exactly what Glenn told him to do, he surely did.

DB And I understand that he was one very nice person.

PT Absolutely, and as strong as an ox, but a charming fellow, he really was, and a good singer.

DB Paul, you mentioned in your book that the audiences were anywhere from five thousand people on up in some of the various places you appeared. That's hard to believe back in those days with the limited sound systems that they had in comparison to now.

PT Well, the only electronics you had on a band like that was for someone to walk out and sing or someone to walk out and play a solo at a microphone. I remember a time, in Kansas City, where we were doing a Chesterfield from there in a big auditorium in the middle of town. And they got fifteen thousand people in there and we played a fifteen minute program. Then they cleared those fifteen thousand out, and got in another fifteen thousand, and we pretended we were playing the fifteen minute program.

"In the Mood" ⑤

DB OK, what do we have coming up? Oh, "In the Mood." Do you want to talk about it now or after?[5]

(Reiteration of getting Joe Garland's arrangement of "In the Mood," including Glenn's gag on me with this tune.)

DB What marvelous memories you have. We want to mention Johnny Best here too because Johnny is such a good friend of ours.

PT And a good player.

DB Paul, just so everybody knows, what is a rim shot?

PT That's when the drummer puts his stick across the head of the drum and the rim and then hits it with the other stick. If you are good enough, you can hit the rim and the head at the same time. That's about as loud as you can get.

DB OK, I knew, of course. I'm informed.

PT Of course.

DB But a lot of people might not know. Well, we need to do a little bit of selling right now.

PT Go right ahead.

DB We had "In the Mood." What do we have coming up next, Charles? "Danny Boy"? So we'll have Paul talk about that after we're back.[6]

6 **"Danny Boy"**

PT "Danny Boy" was an arrangement of Glenn's. And he had it set up to where he played for a while, the saxes played for a while alone, and the brass played for a while alone. That made a good stage number. We would all go out front, and Glenn would be in the middle, saxes on one side and the brass on the other. The problem is that you'd get into a theater and the people working the lights didn't quite understand all that. So, they'd put the spotlight on saxes when the brass are playing and on the brass when Glenn was playing, and so forth. That happened one night in Providence up in Rhode Island, and I remember, they had the spotlight on Glenn and he wasn't playing. So, of all things, Glenn went into a soft shoe number. And you know, some people would be shocked if they saw Glenn go into a soft shoe number, but he did.

DB Oh, he was very staid and proper, wasn't he?

PT Yeah, but he had a good sense of humor.

DB Well, for those of you who may have just tuned in, we're talking to Paul Tanner, who from the age of nineteen back in 1939, played trombone with the Miller Band until Glenn went into the Army Air Corps, right?

PT Those people will start to figure up how old I am if you say things like that.

DB We did that quickly, we're going to let you talk about that. At any rate, that's who we're talking to, and it's really a fascinating situation to be able to sit here and talk to Paul; and, of course, we want to mention his book that was just released in the last couple of months.

PT Yes, actually, they haven't gotten it to a distributor as yet, so it still isn't in the stores. But it can be purchased. I have an address on that, but it's called *Every Night Was New Year's Eve*. And you know, it's a nice "class" book, very well done. Mr Aoki over in Tokyo had an expert artist do the front cover, and it's a high compliment, it's a beautiful thing. And the whole book is done very nice, it's a coffee table type of book, *Every Night Was New Year's Eve*. And I put in a lot of pictures that hadn't been used in any other book. And I told about some of the unusual things that happen to you on the road with a big band and so forth. I had a lot of fun doing it.

DB Some of those vehicles that you talk about in there must have been a real challenge. Well, you know what, Paul, I fouled up a few minutes earlier, and I played these commercials over one another. People pay good money, so I'm going to redo this and then we'll be back.

PT I think you should.

"The Volga Boatmen" 7

DB There we go. Talk to me about it. You picked it, I want you to talk to me about it.[7]

PT Well, in the first place, it was a Finegan work. And Bill is really talented. The canon that we played in there where the trombones play a line, trombones in unison, four of them, then four trumpets in unison come in and play the same line after we do. That's called a canon. And I mean to say that was hard to get four guys to play that all the way through without any mistakes or any intonation problems. It was a real union test. But it was a good thing. The mumbling that went on in the first part of the record is another one of the things that Legh Knowles got started. Here these fellows in the Volga, they're rowing, so he thought there should be some groaning in there, and Glenn liked it and left it in.

DB Paul, talk to me a little bit more about some of the road trips. You mentioned about some of the busses. You finally got a bus with air conditioning but no windows that could be opened.

PT You've been reading *Every Night Was New Year's Eve*. The thing that happens, Doug, is if you get an air conditioned bus, that means the windows are sealed. And so, if it gets pretty strong in there, the windows are still sealed. And if you get about 25 healthy people on a summer's day in there, air conditioning doesn't make it. And if anybody gets sick, then you're really in trouble.

DB I didn't know that they had vehicle air conditioning back in those days.

PT Oh yeah, on buses. The cars, you just wound down the windows.

DB And we'll give a free plug to Buick. You had a thing about a Buick.

PT I thought it was a good car, Doug. I tell you the truth, you bought cars in those days for the size of the trunk. You had to carry your life with you. You didn't have a home. So if a Buick had a good size trunk, then that was it. Eventually other cars did have good size trunks. And then they started making station wagons, but you could see what you were carrying, so you were subject to a lot of vandalism.

DB Once again, we're talking to Paul Tanner who went through life playing with the Glenn Miller Orchestra, played with various other orchestras, went to UCLA, graduated, a doctor's degree in music, and you instructed for 23 years there.

PT It's a long time, but I really enjoyed it.

DB It had to be fun.

PT Right, but I'm having fun now. I really am. Some guy just handed me a thing and told me that I'm on his cruise.

DB Oh, that has to be Gil Oftedal.

PT Gil Oftedal and Fan-To-Sea Cruise Club. Do you know that he's got me in February going up the Mississippi River? And the Glenn Miller Band will be there and Les Elgart and another band, the Four Lads, and I'm to talk and all, like that on this cruise, isn't that nice?

DB Nice. And I must compliment you. You are one of the easiest interviews that I've ever done. I just pop you a question and you run with it. There's nothing worse than trying to interview somebody and they say "yes," "no," "yes." It's terrible. What do we need to do here, Charles? We're doing fine. What's on our list, Charles, "Spring Will Be So Sad." Do you want to talk about this now or after?

PT No, I'll talk about it after, I'll just let people sit around and dream a bit while they hear it.[8]

8 *Miller's* **"Spring Will Be So Sad"**

DB Now I see what you mean. Of course, I've heard that before, but it is beautiful.

PT Jerry Gray wrote that arrangement. It's pretty hard to tell sometimes the difference between Finegan and Gray because Glenn had them writing just as he wanted them to write. This is Jerry Gray's, but you have to admire what Bill Conway did with the Modernaires because he wrote everything the Modernaires sang. Then he would turn over his stuff to the arranger who would write the accompaniment behind him. He taught the other fellows what to sing by rote, except of course Ralph Brewster could read music, but the other two fellows couldn't. And Conway was talented. But I always thought that that one, "Spring Will Be So Sad," that if you don't get goose bumps from that, then you just don't have any goose bumps.

DB All right, Paul, I'm going to talk about you and I'm going to talk about Fan-To-Sea Travel. And we're going to plug you all the way down the Mississippi.

PT Mr. Wonderful, Gil Oftedal.

DB There's loveable Doug and Mr. Wonderful.

(Long, long commercial about our previously mentioned Mississippi River cruise. Then he plays Miller's record of "I Know Why" with Paula Kelly) [9]

DB Well, we're into the year of 1941, Paul, that was Paula Kelly.

PT Well, you know, Paula didn't get enough credit. She was a fine singer. And the funny thing about it is that they usually say that she came in as a substitute for Marion Hutton. Well, Marion was the prettiest thing that there was, but so was Paula, and Paula could sing so well. She was married to one of the Modernaires, Hal Dickinson, and some people thought that was a political thing getting her to sing, and you know Glenn would never stand for that. Either she could sing or she couldn't. But this record shows her off well.

DB I understand that Marion Hutton was so full of bubbles that she didn't hardly have to sing at all.

PT All she had to do was walk out there and she'd jump start all the guys in the front row.

DB She was healthy in other words.

PT Yes, very.

Miller's 10
"Jingle Bells"

(More commercials, then the Miller record of "Jingle Bells.") [10]

DB Well, we're still in the year of 1941, and we're talking to Paul Tanner, trombonist of the Miller Band.

PT Does that "Jingle Bells" give you the Christmas spirit, Doug? It's a good record and the band swings well; the band was getting a little looser.

DB Why don't we talk about "When Johnny Comes Marching Home," 1942, this one.

PT Well, this is a Finegan arrangement. You know, the band used to win so many awards for being a sweet band that some people would even think that the band didn't swing. Well, this record, "When Johnny Comes Marching Home," is one of the things that shows that the band could and did swing very well. One thing to remember about this is that the War was active and Glenn was a super patriot.

DB It was a major sacrifice for him to go in the service from a dollar and cents point of view.

PT Well, he had been living country club type of living except that he was working hard. But when I saw the airport over in England where he took off from, I cried. It was really bad looking, but it was that way for millions of people. He did sacrifice a lot, but he was patriotic.

DB Nothing wrong with that; I love a little bit of flag waving. We're talking to Paul Tanner, trombonist with the Miller Band.[11]

11 "When Johnny Comes Marching Home"

DB In the book, *Every Night Was New Year's Eve*, you mentioned what an astute businessman Glenn was.

PT He was. Just to give you a clue. He had a choice of whether to stay on thirty-five cent Bluebird records or to go over on to the seventy-five cent Victor records. He figured he'd sell three Bluebirds before he'd sell one Victor, so he stayed on the cheaper record. He walked in there and he knew he had a product, and he ended up with five cents on every thirty-five cent record. Now nobody was getting that kind of a deal.

DB Did you know Johnny Best had dinner with Glenn the night before Glenn took off from that airport?

PT Glenn was very fond of John, and why not? It's not so easy for John to get around now, but he's playing very well, and a good guy.

(Commercials, then Miller's record of "Serenade In Blue" with Ray Eberle and the Modernaires. A reiteration about the introduction to "Serenade In Blue" followed.)[12]

12 "Serenade In Blue"

(An introduction to "Caribbean Clipper," then plays Miller's record of the same.)[13]

13 "Caribbean Clipper"

DB "Rhapsody In Blue" is coming up. But I wanted to ask you about Billy May, certainly a man of enormous talent, not only from an arranging point of view and writing and so forth, but as a trumpet player. Then you had Johnny Best. How in the world can you put two such talented guys together and have them work together without a little friction, does that happen?

"Rhapsody In Blue" 14

PT You know, Doug, I remember hearing these two fellows talking, and Billy complimenting John on sounding so much like Armstrong, and Johnny complimenting Billy on sounding so much like Cootie Williams. And that's just the way it was. That's like when Bobby Hackett joined the band; you're going to hear him now on "Rhapsody In Blue." When Bobby joined the band, he told me he would give his right arm to play like McMickle who was playing lead. And McMickle said he'd give his right arm to play like Bobby. I told Bobby that we were so thrilled to have him in the band. He told me he was so thrilled to be in the band.[14]

Dorsey Brothers' **"Annie's Cousin Fanny"** 15

PT "Annie's Cousin Fanny." Glenn wrote it but we would never play it with Glenn's band. I think Helen, his wife, was a little embarrassed by it because of the line "You've never seen a fanny as pretty as mine." This is a Dorsey Brothers record, about 1934, you'll hear Glenn actually sing on it.[15]

PT Isn't that a riot? Can you imagine putting that out as a commercial record?

DB Now, what do you have in your hand?

PT Well, it's the address of where people can buy *Every Night Was New Year's Eve. (Gives the address of the Glenn Miller Birthplace Society, P.O. Box 61, Clarinda, Iowa 51632)*

Beneke's' **"Swing Low Sweet Chariot"** 16

(Commercial about Mississippi River Cruise. Plays Beneke's record of "Swing Low Sweet Chariot.")[16]

PT That was the Beneke Band. It was a lot of fun. I was supposed to go with that band for a year, Doug, and I stayed with him for six years.

(A reiteration about my going into UCLA)

DB It's been a pleasure for all of us here to have you, Paul. The only requirement is that you have to come visit us more frequently.

PT Well, I'd be very happy doing that.

"Slumber Song" 17

DB Why don't you comment about our next selection, "Slumber Song"?[17]

(A reiteration about the ASCAP strike.)

DB Paul, our sincere thanks once again for joining us here.

PT It's been a lot of fun, I enjoyed it.

DB What a neat experience having Paul Tanner in for the last hour and a half …

Interview with Dr. Douglas Darnall 25

Dr. Douglas C. Darnall (pronounced Darnell) is one of my two charming stepsons. Dr. Darnall is an extremely successful psychologist, and he was contracted to do a series of talk radio shows. He decided that he would open up said series with an interview with me. Dr. Darnall has written a fine book entitled Divorce Casualties. *I know the book is doing very well because he appears often as a guest on popular TV talk shows. I must admit that I do not relate at all to the contents of his book, as he doesn't relate to any book publishings I have on the subject of jazz.*

The date on the tape Dr. Darnall gave me lists our conversation as December 21, 1998. Now you must picture that I am sitting at the dining table at our home about 25 miles north of San Diego, California, Dr. Darnall is at his home in Mineral Ridge, Ohio (a suburb of Youngstown). A radio station in Phoenix, Arizona, picks us up and whisks our voices away to Providence, Rhode Island. It would surely take an accomplished psychologist to pull all of that together, I personally would not even ask how.

DD Welcome to *People Talk*, this your host, Douglas Darnall. I think we are going to have a very exciting show. As you know, we have talked about having future shows dealing with families and conflicts, divorce courts, and a lot of other issues. And one of the things I've been trying to do is to let people know about my book, *Divorce Casualties*. But since this is a holiday season, I thought I would bring someone special to you. His name is Doctor Paul Tanner, and I'm also proud to state that he is my stepfather. Paul was a member of the original Glenn Miller Orchestra. And we're going to devote this hour learning about the Glenn Miller Orchestra, and we're going to encourage your phone calls to think back on days when Glenn Miller was around. Maybe some of the older listeners would have some questions they would like to know about the orchestra, and you can call if you live in the immediate–Anyway, Paul, welcome to our show, *People Talk*.

PT Hi, Doug. How you doing?

DD I'm doing fine, and like I said, it's very exciting to have you here and I want to encourage the listeners to give us a call and ask some questions about the Glenn Miller Orchestra. Let us begin a little bit. Why don't you talk about when you were involved with the Glenn Miller Orchestra and how did you initially get involved with the orchestra?

PT Well, of course, I was a trombone player for many, many years. Glenn had a band that really didn't work out very well for him, so he disbanded it. And he organized one in 1938 and that did become successful. Now there are four of us who joined Glenn when he started this band. *(Editor's note–it was not a quartet, it was a big band.)* We four played every one-nighter, every broadcast, every record, made the movies, everything, until Glenn went in the service in September of 1942. There are still two of us around, Tex Beneke and me.

DD OK, but back then, were you just like four guys and Glenn Miller who kind of . . . ? Like nowadays you think of a band starting in a garage of someone's house. Was it that kind of thing?

PT Oh no, the bands were big bands then, Doug. This was a full band that he was organizing. He was a very fine arranger, so he would have none other than a excellent full band–trumpet section, trombone section, saxophone section, rhythm section, singers. You know, a whole big band.

DD Well, did you feel confident when he was putting it all together that you were going to get paid? Or was that not an issue?

PT No, that was an issue to start with, otherwise he couldn't have gotten guys to come with him. So, you had to talk money. So, he put this band together in 1938, and there were four of us who stayed with him until he broke the band up in September of 1942.

DD The only thing I know about the history of the Glenn Miller Orchestra is what I remember seeing in the Glenn Miller movie.

PT Well, that was about 1954. That was made with Jimmy Stewart.

DD And the image was that there were two central themes going back in those days. One was that he at times would go broke and have to hock everything to make the payroll and to get to the next city. And then the other central theme was his looking for the sound. Was that real?

PT No, that was kind of Hollywood. He did have to borrow money. He borrowed twenty-five thousand dollars from Tommy Dorsey in order to keep going. Then as far as the sound was concerned, he had that in mind before he started this band, he invented that sound long before, and kept it to himself.

DD OK, so, it wasn't any big revelation as it was sort of characterized in the movie?

PT No, that was Hollywood for you.

DD OK, so anyway, what was life like back in those days, I mean in terms of going from city to city and all that?

PT Well, you know, we worked very hard. There were lots of one-night stands, especially when he was getting started. But we did spend our winters in the Hotel Pennsylvania in New York City, and we made a couple of movies, that was in Hollywood; that's easy, you know. But I'll give you an example, one time in New York, we were booked at the Hotel Pennsylvania and at the Paramount Theater at the same time. Now, when you add on our commercial programs for the Chesterfield people, we played 140 different playing sessions in two weeks.

DD Oh, my goodness.

PT Now, that takes a lot of effort, but when you're out on the road, the band was your family. Your car or the bus was your home. But we didn't know anything different. It was exciting and it was a good paying job, and we all loved playing music, we all loved to entertain. But I tell you, it was not a job for a fellow with a family.

DD Well, how did Glenn actually find you?

PT Aha, that's one of the first questions I get when people look at me. About that time …

(A reiteration about my getting with Glenn.)

DD It's good you were willing to take that kind of risk.

PT Well, he was taking a risk on me too, you know.

DD So, you just got in your car and followed him, I guess.

PT Well, I didn't have a car, so I got in his car.

(A reiteration about Glenn's cars.)

DD Well, what kind of person, how would you characterize Glenn?

PT Well, I get asked that an awful lot. He was an exceptional musician, no question about it. He was also an astute businessman, he was truly a hard working fellow, he was very fair all the way down the line, he was quite athletic which allowed him to work hard, and he was an extremely patriotic fellow. When the time came that this country went into the War, he gave up country club type of living to go ahead and serve; he didn't have to, his eyes weren't good enough, and he was above age for the draft, but he was really patriotic.

DD So, he kind of came from money?

PT Glenn, oh no, his family came from a little town in Iowa, and in Nebraska, they lived under a sod roof. No, he just worked very, very hard and studied hard.

DD Well, how did the other members of the band receive you, you know, this young kid that all of a sudden is kind of joining?

PT Well, from what I'm told now, and I had no idea at that time, but from what I'm told now is that he came back to the guys and said, "Wow, have I found a trombone player!" Which thrills me, and it would have thrilled me then had I known this. There was never any problem. I did what I was supposed to do, so I was well accepted in spite of the fact that I was younger.

DD So, anyway, you just started going on this tour from city to city?

PT That's right. That's all he had at that time. In fact, he didn't have every night booked, it was pretty tough going at first. He had a tough time meeting salaries and the salaries were as low as you could get then. But eventually, with some help, the salaries got bigger and bigger and as I said, 140 playing situations in two weeks. Now that's making his wallet fat too.

DD Later on, I've got your book here entitled *Every Night Was New Year's Eve*. And in the back of the book, you have listed some of the places that you have played, and toward the end of the show, I will mention some of these places.

(Commercials)

DD Welcome back to *People Talk* and this is your host, Doctor Doug Darnall, and today we have Paul Tanner who was a member of the original Glenn Miller Orchestra, and we're kind of reminiscing and talking about the old days of the Glenn Miller Orchestra. And also, talking a little bit about the movie and how real life contrasted with what they showed us with James Stewart on *The Glenn Miller Story*.

At first, it was "Miller's Tune."
1939

Then, eventually, it became "Moonlight Serenade." *1939*

O.K., you'll all get in somehow. *1942*

There he is, kids, in the doorway. *1942*

Glenn never did mind autographs. *1942*

1942

Husky Raul Hildalgo helps Glenn with the throngs. *1942*

1942

Is it really lonely at the top? *1942*

Sure, we played at shipyards. *1942*

The "wheels" are turning–
Si Schribman, Don Haynes, and PR man George Evans. *1942*

Come on in out of the cold, folks. *1942*

Atlantic City. *1942*

On the road with a bit of class. *1942*

Bobby Hackett says, "No beards in Glenn's band."
1940

For crying out loud, Marion, play the 2 of diamonds, then the 3, the 6 of hearts on the 7 of clubs, the 5 of spades on the 6 of hearts, the 9 of hearts out of your hand on that 10 of clubs, the 8 of spades on that, and on and on. My goodness! *1942*

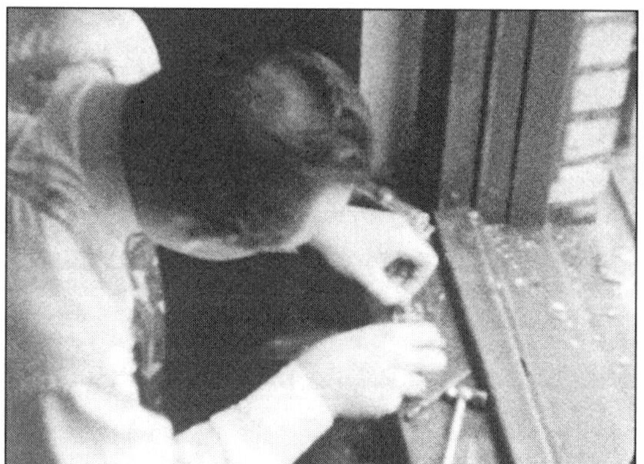
Billy May made HO gauge trains. *1940*

Yep, Billy May made HO gauge trains. *1940*

War bond rally on a cold day in front of the Treasury Building in Washington D.C. *1942*

Glenn at the recruiting office.
September 1942

Singers plus one. *1942*

Hurry, you know how Glenn is, they'll leave without us if we are late. Ray Eberle and Marion Hutton. *1942*

"Did I do that?"
"You sure did, Marion." *1942*

Glenn, Ray Eberle, Marion Hutton, Tex Beneke *1942*

Orchestra Wives set–Marion, Ray, and The Modernaires. The attentive piano player is Cesar Romero. *1942*

Orchestra Wives–Ann Rutherford and Harry Morgan. *1942*

The ***real*** Orchestra Wives with George Montgomery, Cesar Romero, and Jackie Gleason. *1942*

By golly, they did it again–Nicholas Brothers. *1942*

Sad news. *January 8, 1945*

MILESTONES

Born. To Erskine Caldwell, 41, novelist, (*see* U.S. AT WAR) and June Johnson Caldwell, 22, his third wife: their first (his fourth) child, a son; in Tucson, Ariz. Name: Jay Erskine. Weight: 6 lbs. 12 oz.

Married. Thomas Austin Yawkey, 41, Detroit-born millionaire-owner of the Boston Red Sox; and Jean Hiller, 34, onetime Saks Fifth Avenue model; six weeks after he was divorced by Elise Sparrow Yawkey, ex-cover girl; both for the second time; in Georgetown, S.C.

Marriage Revealed. Ted Husing, 42, high-domed, fast-talking sportscaster; and Iris Lemerise, 27, onetime Columbia Broadcasting System receptionist; in a secret ceremony last April; he for the third time, she for the first; in Louisville.

Reported Missing. Major Glenn Miller, 39, begoggled, popular trombonist and bandsman, leader of the Army Air Forces Band currently entertaining in Paris; while a passenger on a flight from England to Paris. Born in Clarinda, Iowa, Miller played with Ben Pollack, the Dorsey Bros., Ray Noble; in 1939 he became king of the juke boxes.

Died. Rear Admiral Ernest Gregor ("Shorty") Small, 56, modest, soft-spoken onetime commander of the heavy cruiser

Tex Beneke and His Orchestra. *1945*

Tex Beneke and the Glenn Miller Orchestra plus wives. Can you recognize anyone? *1945*

Charlie Spivak's Band. Trombones are: P.T., Jim Priddy, Frankie D'Anolfo, and Nelson Riddle. Note Willie Smith on alto sax.
1945

Hank Mancini relaxes away from the piano.
1948

TROMBONE COMPOSITIONS

by

PAUL TANNER

1967 Publication

P.T. on his Theremin. *1959*

UCLA students threw a huge block party for me. Here I am with Les Brown and Tex Beneke. *May 5, 1981*

Billy May tells it like it is.

With Bobby Gibbons and Jim Priddy. *May 5, 1981*

Once again, Tex, thanks for coming and bringing a great band. *May 5, 1981*

Tex throws a party: L to R: Paula Kelly, P.T., Johnny Best, Tex, Ray Anthony, Billy May, Rolly Bundock, and a rear view of Chuck Gentry. *1985*

Mrs. Hostess, Sandi Beneke. *1985*

There's a character I remember–the bashful one, Ray Anthony. *1985*

P.T., Tex, Ginny and Hank Mancini. *1985*

Rolly Bundock was an absolute gem, with a million stories, most of them true. *1985*

Buddies from 'way back: Billy May, Will Schwartz, and P.T. *1985*

With Jim Priddy. *1985*

Tex with Paula Kelly. *1985*

It was good to see busy Ginny and Hank relaxing. *1985*

The group. *1985*

The Glenn Miller birthplace. *1983*

Herb Miller, brother of Glenn, dies

BANDLEADER Herb Miller, brother of the late great Glenn, died at his London home yesterday aged 74.

He got up with a headache, collapsed and never recovered. His son John, 46, will take over the 16-piece band which leaves for a Scandinavian tour next week.

Herb was his brother's road manager for three months in the 1930s. He played trumpet, taught music, later switched to Trombone and, after his family grew up, set out to get as near to Glenn's sound as he could.

London Daily Mail.
October 1, 1987

Street sign in Clarinda, Iowa. *1983*

P.T. in the parade in Clarinda. *1983*

Jonnie Miller (Glenn's daughter) and her grandniece. *1983*

P.T. with Mr. Hideomi Aoki, #1 publisher. *1992*

Larry O'Brien and the Band. *1992*

Norman Leyden, Tommy Shiels, and P.T. *1992*

Loveable Stan Aronson. *1997*

The Panel: L to R: Tommy Shiels, Norm Leyden, P.T., Stan Aronson, Whitey Thomas, Garry Stevens, Pat Friday. *1998*

Bring on the coffee: L to R: Steve Miller, P.T., Whitey Thomas, Tommy Shiels, Norman Leyden. *1998*

Parade in Clarinda, Iowa. *1998*

Norm and his clarinet. *1998*

Steve Miller, Glenn's son. *1998*

Barnes and Noble book signing. *1998*

Straight off the internet. *1998*

It's Hep! It's Hilarious! It's Hot!
WHEN THE KING OF SWING
STARTS SWINGING!
Songs!
GEORGE MONTGOMERY
ANN RUTHERFORD
Glenn MILLER
AND HIS BAND
in
Orchestra Wives
with Lynn Bari
Carole Landis
Mary Beth Hughes
Cesar Romero
Nicholas Brothers
DIRECTED BY ARCHIE MAYO
PRODUCED BY WILLIAM LEBARON
Screen Play by Karl Tunberg and Darrell Ware
FOR GENERAL EXHIBITION
20th CENTURY-FOX PICTURE

Sonja HENIE ★ John PAYNE
in
SUN VALLEY SERENADE
with
GLENN MILLER
AND HIS ORCHESTRA
Milton BERLE - Lynn BARI - Joan DAVIS - NICHOLAS Brothers
Milton Sperling - H. BRUCE HUMBERSTONE
A 20th CENTURY-FOX Encore Hit!

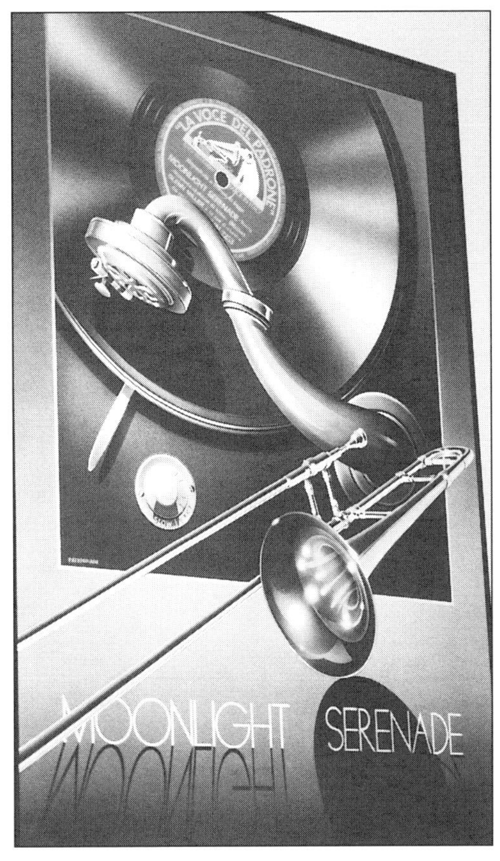
LA VOCE DEL PADRONE
MOONLIGHT SERENADE
MOONLIGHT SERENADE

Their Love Made Such Wonderful Music!
Universal International presents
"The GLENN MILLER STORY"
COLOR BY Technicolor
FOR GENERAL EXHIBITION
JAMES STEWART
JUNE ALLYSON
CHARLES DRAKE·GEORGE TOBIAS·HENRY MORGAN
and these Great Musical Stars! FRANCES LANGFORD·LOUIS ARMSTRONG·GENE KRUPA·BEN POLLACK·THE MODERNAIRES
DIRECTED BY ANTHONY MANN

JAMES STEWART
JUNE ALLYSON
See it and Hear it as Never Before.
IT WAS A TIME THAT CHANGED THE WORLD
AND ONE MAN PUT IT TO MUSIC.
The GLENN MILLER Story
For The First Time in Dolby Stereo
HENRY MORGAN FRANCES LANGFORD LOUIS ARMSTRONG GENE KRUPA

John Miller enjoys dressing in the uniform of his famous uncle. *1998*

Toasting to Glenn. Dick March of London's Glenn Miller Society took me to the famous Glenn Miller's Bar at the Mount Royale Hotel. *1998*

The cover of the activities of the Glenn Miller Birthplace Society-Japan Branch. *1993*

A tribute to Japan where they give a tribute to Glenn Miller. *1993*

Matsue and Hideomi Aoki are ready for dinner. *1993*

An elementary school group plays–would you believe it–"Little Brown Jug." *1993*

The Tamana girls High School treat us well and they also play really well. *1993*

P.T. signs a few books. *1993*

Johnny Best decides to play a Louis Armstrong cadenza in the Tokyo train station. Mary Lou seems to enjoy it too. *1998*

Hideomi Aoki, #1 publisher, makes a lucky wish, about this book, I suppose. *1998*

Erin Kiernan/Register

Peter Cofrancesco, 38, of Hamden, kneels by the monument he erected to the late band leader Glenn Miller.

GLENN MILLER

SWINGING *on Grove Street*

Fan remembers the great band leader

By Jim Shelton
Register Staff

NEW HAVEN — At Grove Street Cemetery, swing is king again.

Yes, the revival's going on just down the path from the caretaker's office. Older folks are reliving their youth and college kids are asking questions about jump and jive.

It's all because Peter Cofrancesco, a 38-year-old Hamden man, has erected a monument to the late bandleader Glenn Miller, who disappeared while flying over the English Channel in 1944.

Cofrancesco has spent more than $5,000 of his own money on the project, including a cemetery plot and a black granite marker with an engraving of Miller in his World War II military uniform.

"I just quietly put it up about three weeks ago. I didn't ask anybody for any help," Cofrancesco said during a recent visit to the cemetery.

The monument has started to attract attention. Grove Street superintendent Bill Cameron said he's fielding questions nearly every day about Miller's music, his military career and his connection to New Haven.

Glenn took off on December 15, 1944 from this airstrip at Twinwood Farm near Bedford, England. *1998*

The tower at Twinwood Farm. *1998*

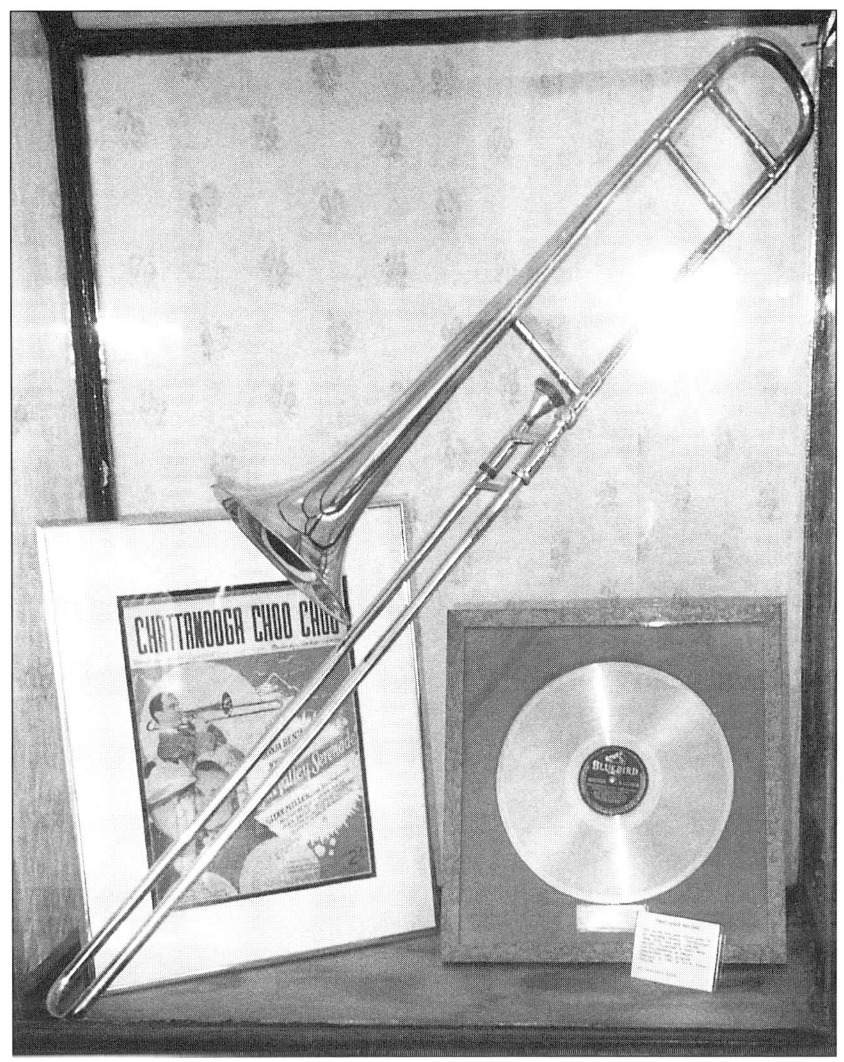

At the museum in Clarinda, Iowa.

Glenn Miller's trombone. *1939*

No wonder I enjoy traveling–look at Jan, my traveling partner. *1998*

DD Anyway, Paul, let's kind of get back into talking a little bit about Glenn Miller. Give us a little bit about your background in terms of how you were drawn towards music and how you came about learning the trombone.

PT Well, I don't know how much you want to get back into my early life. But it was fairly normal except for a couple of things. For one thing, my folks had six sons, and we were all highly stimulated musically. Also, at one time, my dad was the superintendent of the state reformatory back in Delaware. The reform school kids actually showed me how to hold the trombone and got me started, showed me the trombone positions and all that sort of thing. So when I tell people I learned to play trombone in a reformatory, they're a little bit shocked. I don't tell them that my dad ran the place.

DD Well, did you get formal lessons at some point or is this something that you were able to learn from the kids at the reformatory?

PT I had one lesson later on. There was a guy named Will Bradley who was a tremendous trombone player. I was in New York City after the War and I was playing lead trombone with Les Brown, and Tex Beneke was getting started with the Glenn Miller Orchestra at the same time and I was playing lead in that band. So here I am playing lead with two bands at the same time because their hours didn't conflict. So, I called Will Bradley and said I'm leaving town and I'm not coming back. I would really appreciate one lesson. So he said to come down to the studio, and he spent three or four hours with me. And that was my trombone lesson.

DD And other than that, you were self taught?

PT Well, that's right, but I did a lot of listening.

DD You must have a tremendous ear.

PT Well, as I said, a lot of listening and a lot of imitating and it all worked out nicely for me.

DD Did you have any sense, at any point, that you were going to be involved with an orchestra that was going to have such fame? I mean the people that you were associated with were phenomenal. I mean when did you get that sense that you were into something big?

PT Well, Doug, you know, I always thought that hard work would pay off. So I worked very hard thinking some day I would do OK on the thing. Not to be a big name about it, but successful and earn a nice living playing trombone. I had that in mind all the time.

DD One of the things that impressed me looking at your book, again it's called *Every Night Was New Year's Eve*.

PT You don't have the new book?

DD No, tell us what the new book is, and also give a phone number or tell people how they can get it.

PT Well, the new book is called *Conversations with a Musician*. They just had a big book signing party for me up here at Barnes and Noble in Encinitas, California. So, I know that the Barnes and Noble people across the country can get it, if they have any trouble at all, tell them to look under books in print. They can get it there, also they can get it on the internet in Amazon books, *Conversations with a Musician*.

DD Actually, this book, *Every Night Was New Year's Eve* has fantastic pictures. One of the reasons is because my mother's picture is in there, I think that's kind of neat.

PT Well, there are lots of pictures of your mother in *Conversations with a Musician*. There's a whole lot back there that says, "Always on a honeymoon." That's us.

DD I remember seeing that, I think that's fantastic. What are some of the big name people that you have worked with?

PT Well, by the time I settled down in California, some people who had played with either Tex Beneke and the Glenn Miller Orchestra or the Glenn Miller Orchestra itself were by that time quite successful. For example, Hank Mancini was a piano player with Tex. So, by the time I settled in California, he was doing pretty well. Nelson Riddle was playing fourth trombone with Charlie Spivak's Band when I played with him. So, Nelson and I were very good friends. So, you add all these people together, my freelance playing was so occupied. It kept me doing records with Frank Sinatra, Ella Fitzgerald, Nat Cole and other people like that. But you see I was on the American Broadcasting Company staff for 16 years.

DD Hold that thought, we've got to take another break here, Paul.

(Commercials)

DD I understand that we have a caller. Jane, are you on the line?

Jane Yes.

DD Yes, what would you like to ask Paul?

Jane Yes, hello Doctor Tanner.

PT Jane, is it?

Jane Yes.

PT Now does this make you a call girl?

Jane I don't think so.

PT Good.

Jane OK. What I'd like to ask you is what is your favorite Glenn Miller tune?

PT Well, it surprises a lot of people I know, I have been asked that before. I have a tendency, Jane, to like the pretty tunes more than the up tempo things. And yet of the ten most popular records that Glenn made, there are only a couple of the pretty tunes in there. One is "Moonlight Serenade" of course, the theme. Then another would be "Serenade In Blue" from the second movie. I think I prefer "Rhapsody In Blue" as much as any of them, it's a gorgeous thing. Wasn't that pretty?

Jane Oh, yes. And "Elmer's Tune"?

PT Well, that was a kind of cute little novelty.

Jane Yes, you played that one?

PT I played every record the band played.

Jane Oh, wonderful. I was wondering also what song got the most requests?

PT Well, when you add them all together, you can't include "Moonlight Serenade" because that was the theme song and we played it a couple of times every time we played. But outside of that, probably "In the Mood" or "Chattanooga Choo Choo," they were both requested a lot. In fact, "Chattanooga Choo Choo" was the first record that started the whole trend of gold records. But after "Chattanooga Choo Choo," they started doing that. You had to sell a million copies before you had a gold record.

Jane I see, thank you.

DD Thanks a lot for your call.

Jane Thank you.

DD When you were doing the different concerts and all that, did you feel you were part of a celebrity thing? Much like what we think of today?

PT Well, in the first place, Doug, we didn't play many concerts. We played an awful lot of music for dancing. It was primarily a dance band. But you looked out there and you saw thousands of people every night, so you knew somebody was doing well. And if you're in a ballroom, nobody could get close to the band. About the first hundred or so people would just stand there packed up to the bandstand. They'd just watch you and the people behind them were doing the dancing, So you knew it was a very popular thing and you were thrilled and very happy to be part of it.

DD Did the girls squeal and scream?

PT Only for the singers, not for the trombone players.

DD You missed out on that one, huh?

PT Sure did.

DD Anyway, what impact did the movie, *The Glenn Miller Story*, have on your life? This obviously came about after Glenn had passed away. We're going to talk about that in a few minutes. But did *The Glenn Miller Story* help or hurt the legacy?

PT Actually, it helped, Doug. It's a funny thing, when Mancini recorded the music for *The Glenn Miller Story*, he used as many of the ex Glenn Miller fellows as he could get together here in California. But now here's a real ego thing, I'm the only guy they asked to be in the filming. How do you like that?

DD That's kind of neat. Now what parts of the film were you in?

PT Oh, I was in several parts, but most of it ended up on the cutting room floor where it belonged. But the spot that's easy to see me is where in the picture, he threw an anniversary party for June Allyson, his wife, and she's coming down the stairs. There we are, some members of the band underneath the stairs, playing "Pennsylvania 6-5000," a piece like that. I'm the fellow standing along side of Jimmy Stewart. Jimmy Stewart is the good-looking one.

DD Oh, is that it?

PT Yeah.

DD Well, you were both tall and thin.

PT Well, I think that's why they asked me to come in, because they needed another tall, thin trombone player.

DD OK. So that had to be a kick though.

PT Yes, it did. And then, you see, this movie was made in 1954, Glenn disappeared in '44, but in '54, the movie really took off and was a big money maker and people started to be more and more conscious of that kind of music, that particular band. So, it did help the band, and now, of course, people all around the world are imitating the Glenn Miller Band.

DD Yeah. Let me digress a bit. How did you hear about Glenn Miller's death?

PT I heard it on the radio. It was a bit of a shock because I had signed a contract to work for Glenn after the War. He called me in and asked me, he showed me what contracts he had. Oh man, he had contracts you wouldn't believe. And he said, "How about working for me for at least a year after the War?" I said, "Of course, where do I sign?"

DD Sure.

PT And so it made a real good outlook on the future, and then, of course, he didn't come back. So they gave the baton to Tex Beneke. And for a while it was Glenn Miller and the Tex Beneke Band, then Tex Beneke and the Glenn Miller Orchestra, and then the Tex Beneke Orchestra.

DD I think a lot of people don't realize that when he went into the military, he actually had to form a new band. The original band obviously wasn't with him.

PT Yeah, he had a brand new set of guys, and a much bigger band, a complete string section and so forth. It was just a great band. I wasn't in that band.

DD Yeah, I know that. How do you feel about it? There seems to be a lot of imitations out there. I guess there has to be, I guess you can't say there's really an original Glenn Miller Orchestra anywhere. But I think they all kind of say they are.

PT Yeah, they do. There's an office now, a lawyer named McKay who worked for Glenn when Glenn was around. And then when Glenn went overseas, he told McKay to take care of Helen, that's his wife, and see to it that everything goes well with the finances and everything. So ,then when Glenn didn't come back, then Helen said, "Well, gosh, I don't know anything about this business. Glenn took care of everything." So, then McKay and Helen split everything, just fifty-fifty. He took care of the band, and she took her profit. And then when she died, he took over everything himself. So, he owns the Glenn Miller name, this lawyer named McKay.

DD Is that still true today, is he still alive?

PT No, but his son owns it now. He inherited it. And now there is one band over here, and it's a very good band; it's run by a trombone player named Larry O'Brien, and it's a fine band, and they stick as close to Glenn as they possibly can. He's doing a wonderful job. Then there's one band in England that uses the Glenn Miller name; and there's a guy in Branson, Missouri, who is paying for use of the name there in his casino.

DD OK. We're going to have to take a break and we're going to be gone for about three minutes.

(Commercials)

DD Anyway, Paul, before we get involved in conversation again, why don't you tell people about the two books you have out. And let me say this first. Paul has really written a number of books. In fact, many of the books on jazz that are currently being used in universities are books that he has written. He wrote *The Study of Jazz*, and also he's in the eighth edition of a book simply entitled *Jazz*. So Paul is an expert in music that goes well beyond his experience with the Glenn Miller Orchestra. What are your two latest books?

PT Well, there's *Every Night Was New Year's Eve*, there's a sub title of that called *On the Road with Glenn Miller*. And then, *Conversations with a Musician* through Barnes and Noble books in print and also on the Amazon internet.

DD And I want to encourage people to buy his books. I've obviously got an autographed copy.

PT Well, you've got connections, Doug.

DD I've got connections, that's right. We've got it autographed and I'm very proud of it.

PT I married your charming mother.

DD Absolutely, and now you've said that over national radio.

PT I'm proud of it.

DD You know, she's a good woman.

PT Yes, she is.

DD Something that a lot of people don't realize, Glenn Miller also did two movies.

PT Yes, the first one in 1941 was called *Sun Valley Serenade*; and in 1942, we did one called *Orchestra Wives*. They were a lot of fun. You know, part of making a movie is boring because you sit around a lot while they adjust the lighting and everything. But also, it's very easy to lie around out here in California, March and April and May; that's not a bad life.

DD No, not at all; that's what you're doing now.

PT Well, sort of, yes.

DD At any rate, the movies, I don't know if they were big hits or not, I've seen them, they're a lot of fun to watch, they're black and white movies. And, of course, a lot of fun is watching you in the movies because you're there as a member of the orchestra. But you really do get a chance to kind of see how the orchestra and the music sounded in those days. You, right now, and I think a lot of people don't realize, do a lot of speaking to different fan clubs. My understanding is that Glenn Miller today is still very popular, not only in the United States but in other areas of the world.

PT That's true, Doug. In fact, your mother and I take an awful lot of cruises, and that's because they ask us to come on the cruises and talk about the swing era. So many of the people who cruise a lot remember the big bands, and they are very enthusiastic about it. But what they don't realize is that I also played some with Tommy Dorsey, Goodman, and Charlie Barnet and a half a dozen other bands. But they also want me to talk about the Glenn Miller Band. And so, he is still very popular. Now in Japan, he's a lot more popular than he is over here. And in England, he's more popular than he is here, and some other places of the world. I suppose it's one of those things where if it's your own, you're not quite as enthusiastic about it, I don't know. But they really are in those other countries. In fact, we just had a lady here from Russia who said exactly the same thing that the big wigs in Japan say. They said that when they hear this band that it gives them hope that things can be a lot better. Which is nice.

DD What are your thoughts about the music we hear today? Rap, and they have many different names, the music of today? I don't even know what all of it is called, but I guess it's sort of showing my age.

PT Actually, they miss a lot of what they could have. I would prefer much more melody and a little less emphasis on the beat; but they put a lot of emphasis on energy and so forth, and that's important. But music has to have melody, harmony, and form, and so forth. Sometimes they miss the balance of that entirely.

DD I bet a lot of the new music won't have the staying power of Glenn Miller and the whole big band era.

PT In fact, the poor rap guys were fading out as fast as they came in.

DD A lot of them have, but they've had remarkable tenacity because rock and roll still–there are so many shows that have the oldies but goodies on now. And they seem to be still very popular, and they do very well.

PT Well, a guy like Presley set up a lot of things for them. The funny thing is that the Miller Band had more big hits than Presley and the Beatles put together.

DD No kidding.

PT Yes, isn't that amazing.

DD It really is. I would venture to say that not a whole lot of people know that.

PT Yeah, that's a fact though. We got this straight from the record companies.

DD So tell me, after you got out of the big bands and all that, how did you spend your life? What did you do for yourself?

PT Well, I played with Tex, and I played for him for six years.

DD What are your plans now as far as meeting the public and doing things?

PT Well, we do an awful lot of cruises where we talk to people about their favorite bands. We tell them a lot of stories because there are a lot of stories, and it's lot of fun, very easy.

DD So you're really out and about, and as people get your books, they can learn a lot more about Glenn Miller. Do you want to tell me again the two titles?

PT *Conversations with a Musician* and *Every Night Was New Year's Eve*.

DD Very good. And Paul, I really appreciate it, and I'm sure the listeners appreciate hearing about Glenn Miller, and obviously we'll be talking more during the holidays. And say hi to my mother.

PT I sure will.

DD I think that'll be great.

Cam Miller's Article 26

MUSIC TRAVELS FAR FROM SKUNK HOLLOW

San Diego Union, May 15, 1986

La Costa. When your hometown is so small that polecats outnumber the humans by at least three to one, there's not much incentive to hang around.

So if you're Paul Tanner, you pick up your horn and head for a strip joint in Atlantic City where, with luck, you'll be picked up by a big band.

That was in 1938, and chances are it wouldn't work that way today. But for the kid from Skunk Hollow, Kentucky, it was the right route.

Because into that dingy dive, the Swing Club, walked a young bandleader named Glenn Miller, who listened to Tanner's trombone, liked what he heard and offered him a job.

"When Glenn asked me how long it would take to get packed," Tanner recalled, "I whipped a toothbrush out of my coat pocket and replied, "I'm packed, let's go."

And so began a relationship between the young Southerner and the scholarly Midwestern bandleader that was to span the entire life of the Miller Band.

That included bad times as well as good.

"Today, you remember Glenn for his successes–without a doubt his was the most popular band to come out of the big band era.

Tanner, a resident of La Costa since 1981, attributes Miller's popularity to "knowing what the public wanted and giving it to them without sacrificing musical integrity."

"Glenn was a genius at marketing his band." said the 68-year-old Tanner. "He just kept adding things like you'd add another topping to ice cream: one at a time. Ray Eberle, the Modernaires, that great trumpeter Bobby Hackett–not all at once, but one at a time–something new for Glenn's fans to get excited about."

Although Miller has been dead for more than four decades, Tanner said there still is a phenomenal interest in Miller.

"Next month I'm riding in a parade in Glenn's honor in his hometown (Clarinda, Iowa). Of course, Glenn's music is being kept alive by several leaders–Beneke, for example–and I suppose that accounts for some of the interest.

"But I think it's more than that–and I'm not sure what it is,"added Tanner, who eventually found his way to UCLA where he headed jazz studies for 23 years before retiring 5 years ago.

He considered his physical handicap: stammering, "No one ever knew what caused it, and no one ever knew why it disappeared–but I do know that while it was with me, I stammered so badly, I could barely communicate," said Tanner who today speaks without a trace of the affliction.

Tanner was asked to leave the University of Delaware. "I only made one mistake. I didn't attend classes," said Tanner, who was 16 at the time. "I don't think I would have lasted a semester except that no one else in the band could handle lead trombone and the only reason anyone ever went to the university football game was to hear the band, so it had to be good."

It was another 17 years before Tanner would touch a text again–as a 33-year-old UCLA freshman. Tanner was hired directly from the classroom–a rarity at the Westwood institution–and obtained his master's and doctorate while carrying a full teaching load.

"As I said, I've always been very lucky in that I've never had a job I didn't enjoy or one that didn't pay well." His wife, Jan, takes exception. "It's funny, but the harder Paul worked, the luckier he got," she said.

In addition to authoring a dozen musical texts, Tanner left another legacy to his alma mater: a collection of 10,000 jazz albums and 78 rpm records. The cataloging was a two-year project. "It wasn't that tough," Tanner said matter-of-factly, "I did most of it by ear, I simply knew enough about the musicians to recognize relationships. All you needed was a good ear and a good memory."

Jack Broward's Article 27

SONG IS A TRULY GREAT THING ON WHICH TO HANG MEMORIES

The Coast News, November 19, 1998

Paul Tanner acknowledges in the first paragraph of his new book, *Conversations With a Musician*, that, "The old truism was right on target–the harder I worked, the luckier I got."

There is convincing evidence in my mind that hard work and luck were strong companions contributing much to the distinctions won by Tanner in his 81 years of life.

But desire was and continues to be the La Costa man's strongest asset, along with a passion for music.

The 262-page volume relates from start to conclusion the association with the legendary Glenn Miller Band held by Tanner during the period from 1938 until Miller formed an Army Air Corps musical group in 1942.

Today, trombonist Tanner and saxophonist Tex Beneke are the only surviving members of the Glenn Miller group who hold charter membership with Miller's civilian band and remained with him until he went into the military.

As a major, Miller was presumed dead in late 1944 after his plane was reported missing during a flight from London to Paris. He had organized his musical group in the Air Corps and was scheduled to perform with his band in Paris.

Conversations, as trombonist Tanner explains, was created by way of responding to an innocent question posed by his wife Jan, "What ever happened to music?"

Tanner's response to his wife's query evolved into a manuscript that, when submitted to an agent, became the genesis of the book. It is perhaps the author's conversational style, punctuated with humor and ease of reading that appealed so strongly to me.

There are also the anecdotal references to celebrity performers about whom syndicated columnist Walter Winchell reported so regularly during those pre-television days.

The book's simplicity and raw candor is compelling in its subtle eloquence of the descriptions of the rich and famous of that era. The Tanner couple–Jan formerly owned and operated a travel agency in La Costa and today manages her husband's lecture, travel and special events schedules with constant cruises on which Doctor Tanner lectures.

Not surprisingly, the Glenn Miller music commands global appeal today, 54 years after his presumed death. So revered in Japan the band leader has inspired a Glenn Miller Birthplace Society in Tokyo that convenes yearly to pay tribute to his music. And Tanner is one of the principals each year who unites yearly in Miller's Iowa birthplace for a week-long celebration of his legacies.

At age 81, with white hair neatly parted with a mustache, six-foot three-inch Tanner presents himself as a man of great dignity. He's greeted sometimes following lectures by those who ask if he's been a musician all his life.

"Not yet, is his response.

As an expression of affection for their music professor, the UCLA band once forced his name on the football field during a game half-time.

Amazingly, Tanner successfully juggled teaching commitments with band performances, movies, recording dates, and a kaleidoscopic existence with constantly varying dynamics.

Tanner writes on with logical suggestions for rock musicians ending up with–"I say cut down a bit (big bit) on the volume, back off a little from the microphone, try singing for a change, think a little harder for lyrics, add at least a little interest in the chords, put on clothes that others can understand, brush the hair and for goodness sake–take a shower."

He ends the volume with one burning question: what in the world happened to music?

Marcia Manna's Article 28

STRING OF PEARLS

North County Times, November 1, 1998

Former trombonist with the Glenn Miller Orchestra has plenty of gems to share. When Paul Tanner of La Costa wrote *Conversations With a Musician*, he originally intended to answer a question posed by his wife Jan, that had started him thinking.

"What in the world has happened to music?" she asked, and as trombonist for the legendary Glenn Miller Orchestra and UCLA faculty member, Tanner had plenty to say on the subject.

He proceeded to write a tongue-in-cheek response to the question. When he presented the results to a literary agent, he was told that people would really be interested in reading his memoirs.

Tanner said, "I can do that." And he rewrote *Conversations With a Musician*, a humorous look at what has happened to music in his lifetime combined with his experiences playing with Big-Band era legends. *Conversations* offers a unique perspective on one of the most exciting periods in musical history. He writes about appearances on the Chesterfield radio show and performing for more than 4,000 "Lindy Hoppers" at the Savoy Ballroom in Harlem. And he recalls the great jazz and popular vocalists, Ella Fitzgerald, Frank Sinatra, and others.

A long-time North County resident, Tanner stays busy by giving lectures on cruise ships about his experiences with the Glenn Miller Orchestra.

"It was very relaxing after everything I had done," Tanner said about his cruise gig. "I wanted to get out of the rat race and I was ready to stop playing. Fan-To-Sea Cruises in Escondido keeps me busy. When people ask me where to go to hear a swing band and dance, I tell them to take a cruise."

In the last chapters of *Conversations With a Musician*, Tanner admits he's opinionated about music, but he says he enjoys writing from the perspective of an educator and composer.

"Popular music has changed so rapidly that the public may not be aware that sides have been chosen," he writes. "When one is confronted with 'if it's too loud, you're too old,' an easy response could be 'if it's too soft, you've lost your hearing.' "But I noticed in my recent travels that more and more often, younger adults are listening and dancing to the earlier version of mainstream."

Eileen Goss' Article 29

LA COSTAN SWINGS TO BIG BAND BEAT

North County Active Lifestyles, November, 1991

Glenn Miller...Tex Beneke...Les Brown...Henry Mancini...Charlie Spivak all evoke musical associations that are permanently stored in our memory banks. The music of these giants colored our senses and punctuated world events as they influenced the personal lives of those of us who survived the Great Depression and participated in bringing the Allies to victory during World War II. Later, as we re-established our lives in postwar America, we replanted our roots and raised our families to the continuing beat of the Big Bands.

When World War II broke out, Glenn Miller, who was a super-patriot according to Tanner, dissolved the civilian band and created his military orchestra to "take a piece of home" to the fighting men.

Following the end of the war, Paul Tanner resumed his musical career and played with many of the great Big Band names.

Before the advent of jet travel and MTV, bands lived and died on the road with the bus as the primary mode of transportation. The schedule was brutal. Tanner recalls that at one point he was involved with 140 appearances in two weeks. Finally, in 1951 he realized that if he did not take advantage of it, he would lose the benefit of the GI Bill so he changed direction and headed for Los Angeles and UCLA where he graduated *magna cum laude* and ultimately attained his doctoral degree. Tanner remained at UCLA for 23 years, teaching in all four fields offered: performance, theory, musicology, and music education.

In the 1980s, Tanner retired from performing and teaching and moved into the quiet community of La Costa. Not one to sit still for very long, Paul and his wife Jan travel all over the world. "American music is extremely popular in other countries," he points out. As one of the few surviving members of the original Miller orchestra, Tanner is invited to music festivals and universities, sometimes to speak and sometimes just to make an appearance. He recalls one trip to Japan where he was brought out on a stage but never uttered a word because he does not speak or understand the language.

In addition to his other activities, Paul Tanner is very active on the lecture circuit. He and Jan are about to embark on a cruise next spring where he will lecture on Glenn Miller and "A Tribute to Swing," a 12-day Royal Cruise Lines sojourn from Tahiti to Hawaii.

Brian Hanrahan's Article **30**

STILL SWINGING AFTER 23 YEARS

Music professor Paul Tanner talks about teaching and music.
Daily Bruin, June 5, 1981

BH Did you ever want to start your own band?

PT No.

BH Did you ever lead one?

PT Yeah, but I didn't like it at all. I'm just not a leader of men. Glenn Miller's wife told me that I was the next guy in line, that Glenn wanted to back me in a band. That would have been a terrible mistake. I'm highly complimented, that's really nice of him, but gosh, I'm just not a leader, that's all. I just sort of coast through life. I work hard, and I've practiced a lot, but man, I keep saying to my wife, gee, I'm really the luckiest guy in the world because really the story of my life is that I've been in the right place at the right time always, and that's how you spell having a successful career. And she says, but how about all the hours you've practiced? Suppose you're at the right place and can't cut it? It seems like–and this is her saying–the harder you practice the luckier you get, which is beautiful.

BH When you were hired to teach here, did they actually come to you or did you apply?

PT No, they came to me. I said to them you must be sure I'm going to graduate. They said, "We looked at your 3.8 grade point average, you're going to graduate."

BH Did that take a lot of time away from studio work?

PT Well, when I got very involved, then there comes a time when you have to make a choice, and to me that choice was school. At one time I was working five days a week on ABC staff, I was a student here, I was working six nights a week at the Palladium, and I was getting my share of TV and movie work. I got everything done except I didn't have time to go to sleep. I got all my studying done, but I had to stay awake so I ate constantly. In the Palladium, they were just cracking up. I'd sit there in between sets eating bananas and things like that just to stay awake. Oh, also at the same time, I was building a house. I mean with a saw and hammer. Another guy and I; he was the brains, I was the labor.

BH What do your middle initials, O.W., stand for?

PT Old Weatherbeaten.

BH Is that your given name?

PT No. That's something I adopted along the way. The given name you'll never find out.

BH Leonard Feather says he does not consider the Miller Band to be a jazz orchestra. Do you consider it to be a jazz orchestra?

PT Well, we certainly played jazz at the time. I don't say it was as good a jazz orchestra as Count Basie or Duke Ellington, but everything is relative.

BH When you started college you were in your 30s. Did this cause any problems? Did you feel like you didn't fit in with the students?

PT No, the students were just great to me. In the first place, I was here because I wanted to be, I wasn't here because dad said go here. I only remember one problem I ran into and that was in a Spanish class where the instructor–he graded on a curve–he said, if you all want to know who the average-raiser is, it's him. Boy, I called that guy aside and just read the riot act to him. Never do that to anybody, that's a terrible thing to do to somebody. What do you want me to do, miss things, things on purpose? I was older than most of my instructors.

BH Do you think there's any difference between the way you present yourself to classes and the way you act when you're with friends? Do you have a stage persona?

PT You want me to be real honest, right? OK, actually I'm a loner, except for my wife. I do get "on stage" there isn't any question about it. The adrenaline gets flowing, and so I am different on stage than when I sit and talk privately. I'm really extremely comfortable with my wife; we've been married a long time and there's not many more people I am really at ease with.

BH What are your hobbies?

PT Golf. Oh, avid golfer.

BH Do you think the transition from teaching to retirement will be difficult?

PT No. I'm looking forward to it. I have a lot to do, and so I'll never be hurting for something to do. I'm not the kind of guy who's going to drop out of the world anyway. I've been offered two jobs, one at another university and another to be a consultant to a radio station.

BH Why are you retiring?

PT There are two or three reasons. I've worked for a living for 51 years, and that's long enough.

31 David Miller's Article

THE TANNERIN

Dave's Theremin Home Page explains an interview with Dr. Paul Tanner. This interview was copied with permission from Dave Miller's home page on the Internet.

On this page will be the information on a new theremin-like instrument Tom Polk and myself are designing. It is based on Paul Tanner's late 1950s instrument, the one used in the Beach Boys' "Good Vibrations" as well as many TV themes and movie sound tracks and electronic albums.

We are calling the instrument the Tannerin to honor Dr. Tanner and to distinguish it from the traditional theremin. There has always been a bit of confusion as to what exactly Paul's instrument was. It ended up being called an electro-theremin though it is not a theremin in the traditional sense of the word. I might add that Paul himself did not name the instrument. His instrument was finished at two in the morning prior to its first recording session. The producers needed a name right away, I suppose. Paul said his friends referred to the instrument as Paul's box. So, through the years the instrument became known as the electro-theremin. An interesting point is that the first record album appeared in 1959 ("Music For Heavenly Bodies"), the liner notes set the record straight at the very beginning that this was not a traditional theremin. They even compared its sound to Sam Hoffman's RCA theremin and point out how Paul's uses a sine wave. The liner notes make it clear that the instrument is a mechanical apparatus to control pitch.

What one finds when listening to Paul's instrument is that it is a very precise instrument. Its tone is that of something out in the galaxies. Truly a unique sound all its own.

Paul's "box" soon became a hit for those needing that certain ooOOoo sound. One of the first TV show themes to use the instrument was *The D.A.'s Man*, a 1959 drama. The composer on this score was none other than Frank Comstock, a colleague from the big band era. The electro-theremin soars above the driving rhythm of drums and big band horn sections in this theme. Very effective writing to say the least.

When you play lead trombone for the ABC orchestra, the likelihood of being called on other projects is quite high, particularly if you happen to be the only one around with a theremin-like instrument. So the word got out, and Tanner was being used on more and more projects. One such project was the new TV show, *My Favorite Martian.*

Tanner recalls having to be flown in just to do that one show. He was the only one with the instrument. Not only is the instrument featured on the theme tune, it was used every time Ray Walston (the Martian) would levitate items, or extend his antenna. Tanner recounts that pitch had to be exact, because of the chord structure under him.

It operates on a slide, and those who know about electronics will guess immediately that the sound is created by a variable oscillator. The audio range covers the complete sound spectrum, from 0 to over 20,000 cycles per second. Its highs and lows can only be measured on an oscilloscope. Its sounds are pure sine waves without harmonics, making it an ideal instrument with which to test your audio equipment.

Its advantage over other types of theremins is that it enables the musician to play staccato notes because of a contact switch under a finger. Essentially, the instrument was Paul Tanner's brainchild and can convey, mood-wise, the awe-inspiring feeling of asteroids and comets.

The unusual thing is that today, Paul has no idea at all how he built it. He simply does not recall how it worked inside the box any more than I have explained. He says he is sorry because he would truly like to help us in our research. When he started hearing synthesizers, he says that he realized that they could do much more than he could, so he actually gave the instrument away. He gave it to a hospital (which one he doesn't recall) to use in testing hearing. He doubts if it is still in use. He says that playing trombone, writing and teaching was surely enough for him.

Maurice Purtill
starring with
Glenn Miller
100% Slingerland
"Radio Kings"

PART 3
STORIES

Do You Know About Elmer's Tune? 32

A true story.

Bandleader Dick Jurgens played so often at the Aragon and Trianon Ballrooms that his outfit could have been considered a "house band." The Chicagoans were enthralled by Jurgens and his singers Eddy Howard, Harry Cool, and Buddy Moreno. He was so established there that he even used a room in the Aragon as a combination office and dressing room for the musicians.

Jurgens was in his office working away when he heard (daily) a noodling on the piano by an amateur who would sneak into the ballroom during his time off from his job. The job happened to be work in an undertaker's place of business just a couple of doors from the ballroom.

One day, Dick went out of his office and approached the fledgling pianist whose name was (and I guess is) Elmer Albrecht. It appeared as if Elmer could only noodle on one tune and it finally impressed Jurgens who told Elmer that it was a pretty catchy theme. Seemingly, Elmer did not have the capabilities to develop his idea into a fully blossomed piece of popular music. Jurgens suggested that the band's pianist and arranger, Lou Quadling, could round out the idea and arrange it for the band and that the band would play it for Elmer in the ballroom and even on the radio.

The next scene is that Glenn Miller heard a broadcast of the piece which was simply called "Elmer's Tune." Glenn phoned Dick and asked about the piece, implying that he would like to do the tune also. Jurgens told Miller that there were no lyrics, to which Miller replied that he really wouldn't be interested in that case. Jurgens then immediately contacted a clever lyricist named Sammy Gallop who asked how in the world he could write feasible lyrics to a selection merely entitled "Elmer's Tune"? When Gallop understood that Glenn Miller was interested, the lyrics were forthcoming in less than 24 hours.

The rest is sort of history. Miller turned the music over to arranger Jerry Gray and to the Modernaires and Ray Eberle. I don't truthfully know if the record "Elmer's Tune" was a million seller or not, but it was definitely a big hit, recorded in August of 1941.

Glenn, of course, collected performance royalties from the recording. I don't know if he also published it or not, which would have meant more royalties. The authors and composers doing well from Elmer's little ditty are Dick Jurgens, Sammy Gallop, and of course, Elmer Albrecht.

My only question is: with his bank account burgeoned by royalties from an extremely popular hit record, would Elmer go back to his job in the mortuary?

Christmas Spirit–Hawaiian Style 33

The Citizen, Del Mar Citizen, and La Costa
December 23, 1988

Some people think that the Christmas spirit must be a bit lacking in warm, lovely Hawaii. How could one embrace traditional attitudes so near the equator? Well, the Christmas spirit abounds in hula-land.

I was a teaching, soloing musician and I spent enough time on these particular islands to develop warm friendships.

One December, without notifying our Hawaiian friends, we visited Honolulu and planned a few surprise visits for Christmas Eve. At home on the mainland, my wife and I had wrapped numerous gifts for the children of our Hawaiian friends; some of these children did not expect many presents from Santa. We packed the gifts into massive cartons, attached our name and sent them to the hotel where we would be staying. Upon arriving in Honolulu on December 23rd, we had these gargantuan cartons hauled to our room where we unpacked and sorted them to be delivered the next evening. Then came the problem that I had never anticipated. A person should not try to rent a car in Honolulu on Christmas Eve without making the necessary arrangements in advance. We had no idea of the futility caused by such an oversight.

I walked from the hotel to a series of car rental offices and discovered that the earliest I could get a car was January 6. I was walking very dejectedly back toward the hotel when I passed by a small row of houses. I spotted a gentleman (I soon learned he was truly a gentle man), a very dark native type fellow (true Hawaiian style) languishing on his front stoop in a very relaxed manner (also true Hawaiian style). He was over six feet and closer to three hundred pounds than two hundred. I approached him and asked if he had any idea at all where I could rent a car. He agreed that on Christmas Eve, it would be tough and asked what my problem was. I proceeded to tell him my story in detail.

"Take my car," was his response, "absolutely no charge at all."

"But you don't even know me," I blurted.

"Where you gonna go, Brudda, it's an island."

Well, I borrowed his car, and even without reindeer, we were greeted with great enthusiasm at every visit. On the way back, we stopped at a gas station; the least we could do was to refill the gas tank. No luck. Our Santa had locked his tank and kept the key.

On returning the car, I related how we had tried to gas up his sleigh. He said, "I figured you would, that's why I kept the key."

All we could do was to thank him profusely and wish him the best life had to offer. This big hulk of a Hawaiian version of Santa Claus merely said, "Aloha and Merry Christmas."

The spirit of Christmas shines around the world.

You Don't Get Credit for an Empty Space 34

Printed in The Jazz Educator *in the 1980s*

I have always enjoyed articles concerned with the amusing responses that little children give to questions by adults. However, those of us who teach at college know that students seldom grow out of this delightful spontaneity even under the stress of examinations. These responses are from exams on the History of Jazz. The classes are huge, about 1,200 a quarter.

There are no technical aspects of a subject that today's college student cannot and will not absorb. These students are challengingly bright and even the non-music students will learn anything at all that they figure will be on a music test. Where the fun comes in is with those little non-technical questions that I consider to be no more than "zero-preventers." When you couple a student's aversion to leaving a space blank on an exam along with a good sense of humor, the bluffing becomes brilliant or absurd or hilarious. At least it is something I think should be shared with other teachers of jazz.

Question: What is the job of the music copyist?
Answers: He writes down the music that the real musicians play. He separates the instruments from the score. He separates the arrangements into scores. He makes sure everybody has the right part. He listens to the band play, then writes down their music. He is vital in stealing other performer's material. He hands out the music. Writes down what should have been played. Transforms an arrangement so that the public can hear it.

Question: Who was Ferdinand de Menthe?
Answers: Creme de Menthe's brother. Inventor of creme de Menthe. Chicago gangster married a girl named "Cream." Art Tatum. Scott Joplin. Fats Waller. Bix Beiderbecke. He was Ferdinand de Menthe? A Creole who played with Jelly Roll Morton. A Frenchman, I guess. He played Ragtime, also played piano. That's a good question. Can't remember everything. Good old what's-his-name. Just another pretty name. Very important, I guess.

Question: What is meant by "music from oral tradition"?
Answers: The music comes out of the mouth. The way music would sound if you spoke it. Music that has passed on. Music handed down from mouth to ear. Mouth to mouth singing.

Question: What were "race records"?
Answers: Records made in a hurry. Fast music. Musicians had to race to get it all recorded on a ten inch record. Name of a record company. Records that were played at higher RPM. Records sold prior to the 33⅓ RPM records. Records where Blacks played with Whites because no one could tell on a record. When black musicians made black records for the black public on the black market. Records sold at horse races. When one record company tries to get a tune on the market before the other record companies.

Question: What is an "ostinato bass"?
Answers: A tuba. A bass with an amplifier. Left handed piano playing in Boogie Woogie. An octave lower than the regular bass. I really don't know, but somehow it sounds nasty.

Question: What is the difference between a tuba and a bass violin?
Answers: One is bowed and one is blowed. The violin has more strings. The first is brass, the second is woodwind. One is wind and the other is string. The tuba has a larger bore. A tuba is bigger. Bass violin is bigger. The bass violin is harder to carry in a parade. Well, it's just hard to march with a bass.

Question: Name one Ragtime Band.
Answers: Alexander's Ragtime Band. The Disneyland Ragtime Band. None, it's piano music.

Question: What is a "fill-in"?
Answers: Somebody taking someone's place in a band for a night. The big band goes on a break and the little band plays. A spot in a number where someone plays in between the music. The music stops and a guy plays a solo. Instruments would play in between the measures. To add more players to the band. The fourth line of a three line blues. The writing on the album cover. What I'm doing right now.

Question: What does the phrase "top heavy" mean in regard to Swing bands?
Answers: Too many people playing rhythm over the melody. Refers to piling up of the rhythm section. Too many in the rhythm section, it loses momentum. Certain people in the band were overloading the notes. Too many instruments above the lead. Too much harmony, not enough melody. A

band with lots of really great players in it. Too many stars in the band. Groups who have top performers. Too many trumpets at the rear and top of the bandstand. Too much out front and not enough behind. An all girl band. Means you are playing every minute of the day.

Question: What is meant in your textbook by a "record ban"?
Answers: When you put a ban together just to make a record. A record that the public would not accept. What happens when a record is considered obscene. One tune on an album. Each selection on a record is a ban. Each song on a record is separated by silence, between the silences is the ban. The sections on a record between the pauses. The grooves on a record where the music is recorded. When record sales went way down. Juke box companies wanted three minute records, those longer were banned. The label it is put on. A contract with the record company. Deodorant for your albums.

Question: Give me another name (from your textbook) for Boogie Woogie.
Answers: Chapter Seven. Woogie-Boogie. Damned hard. You've got me.

Question: Who was Jack "Papa" Laine?
Answers: Mama Laine's husband. Frankie Laine's father. My grandfather. Famous polygamist. I give up.

Question: Who made the first instrumental jazz recordings?
Answers: F. Scott Fitzgerald. Ben Turpin. Jimmy the Greek. Columbia Records.

Question: What was the influence of the 33 one-third RPM records on improvisation?
Answers: Improvisation was slowed down. Could play faster. All the improvisation had to be planned. You could drop them on the floor and still have the improvisation.

Question: Name two methods of playing Boogie Woogie as far as the left hand is concerned.
Answers: Playing in C and playing in B flat. Playing chords and playing rhythm. Meade Lux Lewis Method and Jimmy Yancey Method.

Question: What was "Tin Pan Alley"?
Answers: Name of a Ragtime Band. Low class area that could only afford Boogie Woogie. Place where Dixieland was played. Where the clubs were in Kansas City. An area of jazz clubs in New York. The low rent district in New York City. Area leading from the back door of a brothel. The recording studios. Name of a tune. A composer and arranger. Where jazz musicians hang out. Musicians rehearsed in the back alley. Could play on streets leaving

tin pans out for collections. Refers to allies where jazz concerts were being performed underground in basement type rooms, other musicians would gather and listen outside. A type of dance. A juke box. A piece written for percussion instruments. A comic strip. Nickname for Mohammed Ali when he was in the hospital and needed a bed pan. A place where you got mugged with tin pans. Where Fritz, the Cat, hangs out. Don't tell me, it's right on the tip of my tongue.

Question: Who was Scott Joplin?
Answer: Janis Joplin's brother.

Question: What was Fletcher Henderson's importance in the Swing era?
Answer: He made Benny Goodman famous.

Question: Explain "walking bass."
Answer: The tuba in a parade.

Question: What was the Pendergast Machine?
Answer: The first juke box.

Question: Specify the differences between Early New Orleans Dixieland and Chicago Style Dixieland.
Answer: Several hundred miles.

Question: What form of jazz is said to have evolved from the three-guitar origin?
Answer: Jazz-Rock.

Question: When was the first instrumental jazz recorded (within three years)?
Answer: The answers have varied all the way from 1820 to 1971.

Question: What was the date of the first radio broadcast (within 5 years)?
Answers: The answers varied from 1888 to 1948.

Question: When did record companies begin producing 33 one-third RPM records (within 5 years)?
Answers: The answers varied from 1915 to 1969.

I am often amused at the phonetic spelling–Joe "King" Oliver sometimes ends up Joking Oliver. Bix Beiderbecke becomes Bick Spiderbeck, and "Birth of the Cool" becomes "Bertha the Cool."

I also like this answer to:

Question: Name three of the best known female Blues singers.

Answer: Bessie Smith, Ma Rainey, and Billie Strayhorn.

But one of my all time favorites has to be:

Question: What was the identifying feature of the Glenn Miller band?

Answer: He hired our professor!

35 Glenn Miller–A Soul Experience

A true story written on June 28, 1998 by Egil Oftedal.

From April 1940 to May 1945, my native Norway was occupied by the German Army. As a boy, I felt the bitterness of the situation not only as a personal emotion, but also as it was reflected from my parents. Sandnes, our town of about 4,000 inhabitants, had been occupied almost before we knew what was happening. No bombs were dropped. We were spared that devastation. But the enemy presence was a major disruption of our lives. My family fared better than many, but everyone felt the impact of foreign occupation.

The Gestapo came one day in 1942 and arrested our next door neighbor who had been warned. Later he was shot. When the Gestapo wagon was parked outside our home that day, my mother and I had been out. I'll never forget how my mother squeezed my hand. She thought the Gestapo was after my father.

I remember seeing soldiers who had been fighting the Russians going into stores and commandeering butter and chocolate, then cramming it into their mouths in the most gross manner. Almost all food was rationed, however, we always had potatoes. And we were lucky to live near the North Sea so we could usually get the fish we needed. In addition, the Fjord Country begins at the town of Sandnes. This made it easy for us to fish.

We were a musical family–I the least talented and the only one who didn't seriously take up an instrument or study music in some deeply academic way. I sang (until my voice changed, I took second to no one as a boy soprano) and I played the piano. That was it. To my father's great chagrin, I never would be a famous composer or conductor or arranger. That would be left to later generations, to other branches of the family. But I appreciated music and believed I had, still have, a good ear. Automatically I know, almost as a sixth sense, when I'm hearing something very right–or very wrong. In some ways that can be a curse since it keeps me from enjoying a lot of entertainment many people consider to be entirely satisfactory.

When the Germans came, I was part of a juvenile movement against them. We would smuggle raw fish to Polish and Russian military personnel incarcerated at the military camp the Germans had established in the middle of town. And we would do other things—things I wouldn't dare tell my parents about. Some survival instinct kept us from getting caught—except for one of my good friends, who always was blamed for everything. All this was our small part, our contribution to what we hoped would ultimately sabotage the entire German army. All of us were willing to do anything and everything and to take any risks to help bring that about.

We had been taught these people were bad, everything they did was bad and it would be bad to like anything about them. Imagine my youthful consternation, then, when one day in November 1944 I thought I had been corrupted by sounds from their Compound. I was standing outside a confiscated chapel the Germans had turned into a living billet for their soldiers, and from that awful place I heard something so beautiful it tore at my soul!

That day lives in my most vivid memory now as though it were yesterday. I was standing outside the Compound and I heard a radio broadcast. First, a man spoke in German, which I didn't understand. Then the music began, and it was so absolutely stirring, I felt each wonderful strain going through my body, touching the very fiber of my being, pulling at my heartstrings. How, I thought, could anything so beautiful come from a place so steeped in evil? I stood spellbound, afraid to move for fear of missing a single glorious note. When it was over, I quickly got hold of myself and ran away from there. It was frightening, almost as though I had heard the voice of Satan—and loved it! I could not dare to tell my father. For that matter, I could not share the experience with anyone. Truly, I felt like a traitor! This had to be a secret I would bury inside myself and pray no one else ever would know. (Actually, I wonder now if I would remember this today if I had not received some very special tapes in December 1991.)

While the Germans were there, we were under severe restrictions as to what we could do or not do, and getting permission for even a simple concert was a major project. My father and my uncle, however, succeeded in doing so, and their group, who played traditional music, invited another somewhat younger group of musicians to join them. This other group played swing and selections from American Big Bands. One of the restrictions imposed by the Germans was prohibiting use of any music titles that sounded like they could be American or English—so they changed the titles to Norwegian, hoping the Germans wouldn't figure it out.

While the concert was not an official competition, there was a certain rivalry between the two groups. My father, of course, considered his musicians and the traditional music they played to be unquestionably far superior. When he asked my opinion, it was very difficult for me not express what I really thought–that the swing style and the Big Band music was every bit as good, maybe even better! Of course, I never said that because he wouldn't have liked it. And anyway, I felt it was somehow disloyal not to think my father's music was better, so I hid my true feelings.

Ultimately, of course, allied troops marched into Norway and the Germans left. During the days of celebration–May 8 to May 17, 1945, we rejoiced in our freedom. Then life somehow rearranged itself back to a semblance of normalcy, though I really doubt whether people who have lived the dismay of military occupation can ever totally forget the indignity of it.

For me, that week was significant in another way. I heard the magnificent strains of soul-stirring music–and learned it was the sound of the Glenn Miller Orchestra! I must confess, from that moment forward my primary goal was to immigrate to America and meet this hero! That was the only thing I cared about. I finished school only because it was necessary, not because it was my life priority. At the time I had no idea Glenn Miller had gone down with a plane a few months earlier. That sad fact I learned in 1954 when I saw the movie *The Glenn Miller Story*. It was terribly disappointing to discover I would never have the pleasure of meeting and shaking the hand of this marvelous musician.

With that youthful dream put aside, I proceeded along a normal course through the usual stages of life: marriage, fatherhood, career, etc. Then another series of events began stacking up, putting me in line for several truly unique Miller experiences! After 28 years in banking and rising to vice-presidency, I finally retired. The stress had been getting to me and I really didn't want to push myself into a heart attack. My wife, Randi, and I sat in our living room talking after a New Year's Eve party as 1990 began, and she asked me, if I could do anything in the world I wanted to do, what would it be?

Without a moment's hesitation I answered, "I want to cruise with the Glenn Miller Orchestra," I told her. "How do you do this?" she asked. "First step, I have to become a cruise agent," I said. "Then do it," she responded. Within a week I had enrolled for special classes at a local college so I could learn all about the cruise business–with the goal of opening a cruise agency. Fan-To-Sea Cruise Club was incorporated in March of that year. We had the official ribbon-cutting ceremony aboard a cruise ship the next September–

with Chamber of Commerce Ambassadors, local beauty queens, and a large contingent of friends there to help celebrate.

Thus it was, I was in the cruise business, and soon went to my very first travel show in San Diego. There would be a special seminar presented by one of the cruise lines–but my attention would be diverted. I had arrived early and was seated at a table by myself, looking over the materials, when a striking looking white-bearded gentleman and a lady approached. No empty tables remained in the room and they asked if they might join me. I told them of course, and as they sat down, the man said to me, "I'm Paul Tanner." I looked up and with absolute assurance I answered him, "Yes, I know. You played trombone with the Glenn Miller Orchestra." Now that sounds reasonable enough. The thing is, I have no idea how I knew who he was. No doubt I had read or heard the name at some time, but I had no way of knowing what Dr. Paul Tanner looked like. Any pictures of him I might have seen would have been from his days with Glenn Miller–thus he would have been much younger. Yet I knew incontrovertibly, this gentleman was Paul Tanner who had played with the fabulous Glenn Miller! Perhaps this information was buried away in my psyche. That I don't know. But I had no conscious reason to have said what I did. Dr. Tanner was astounded at my comment. I guess he thought I was too young to know such a thing.

Why would Paul Tanner and his wife walk into my life at, of all places, a travel show? At that time Jan Tanner was a travel agent, but the chance of their ending up at my table was extremely remote. I told Dr. Tanner about my soul connection to Glenn Miller's music and my plan to specialize in Big Band Cruises, especially those featuring the Glenn Miller Orchestra.

Immediately after that I set up my first cruise group–through the Panama Canal with Today's Glenn Miller Orchestra! As it happened, a member of my group presented me with a series of 13 tapes that contained recordings I had not heard before, music by the Glenn Miller Air Force Orchestra. This was indeed a special treasure! I began playing them in order on my car stereo savoring every note and thoroughly enjoying any drive as I proceeded through the series.

One day in January 1992 I came to "Holiday for Strings"–and the feeling I had was so gripping I almost had to stop the car. I knew it was familiar to me, but I also knew it was quite impossible. Then the announcer explained: this selection was from recordings Glenn Miller made as propaganda to use against the Germans just as the Germans used Axis Sally against allied troops. I heard some words in German, and suddenly I knew where I had heard the music before. It was that day in 1944 when, as a nine-year old boy, I stood listening outside the German Compound. But because I believed it to be evil, I had put this outstanding music out of my conscious mind. Now I felt as though Glenn Miller had reached out to me from the grave to let me know it was all right to enjoy his music–and to lift the guilt that erased it from memory for so many years.

Of course, Paul Tanner and I became friends. When the Glenn Miller Orchestra plays on a cruise ship, he is my special guest celebrity.

36 A Talk with the Record Collectors

This essay is from a tape sent to me by a friend, Gene Funke, concerning a talk I gave to a convention of record collectors in Detroit about 1982 or so. I thought when I pulled the tape out of my collection that the talk was to be on how to catalogue your record collection or something along that order. When I played it, I found that it was on how to teach 75,000 students on the history of jazz. Then I got into a series of funny answers that students had given me on tests. Of course, I've included that in Chapter 34 called "You Don't Get Credit For an Empty Space." Then I did a short bit on cataloging records. But this was followed by many, many questions about the Glenn Miller Band. The audience was so receptive that the whole presentation ended up as an ego trip, I surely hope you get as much out of the written words.

Intro As a member of the host committee for 1982, we extend the most cordial welcome to all the members of the Association. We hope you'll really enjoy your stay here. It is our great privilege at this time to be able to introduce a man who I have long admired, Professor Paul Tanner from the University of California, L.A. He has taught a course in jazz for about 23 years, and has taught 75,000 students. So the title of his presentation will be "How In the World Do You Teach 75,000 Students About Jazz?" Professor Tanner.

PT I have some notes here, but don't worry about a thing, I won't read to you. Stammerers don't read, they can't get away with it. This is just to remind me to tell you some things. In the first place, what I was doing with the students, these were the general university students. I wasn't teaching people how to play jazz, I was teaching people about jazz, development and history of jazz. So I had a 9 o'clock class, a 10 o'clock class, and an 11 o'clock class. Because there were 528 seats in the auditorium, so I had 528 in the 9 o'clock, 528 in the 10 o'clock and 528 in the 11 o'clock. It gets tiresome, especially when it comes time to correct exams and things like that.

So there for a while, I was having 1,600 students every day, four days a week. That's a lot of people, you know. They would have more than 528, but the fire department wouldn't allow it, the students would keep trying to come in.

The course was elective, it wasn't required, so, it was a fun type course. You know, I'd stand up there and sing and dance. You tell them about Bix Beiderbecke, on and on; so, you sort of get into it yourself, so the students would get into it. So, it was a fun thing instead of a dry history course where they've got to remember which queen was married to which king and which prince was a bastard, you know, all that stuff. So, this was just a fun time.

So, plus the 528 people in each class, there was forgery. At UCLA, they have what they called a permission to enroll slip, and they take it to the computer and they're in. Well, the students found out they could sign my name on permission to enroll slips. And just in one class, I had 750 in the class. They were sitting in the aisles, all around the back of me, sitting on the stage. So I told them, "Cool it, we'll get through it all right, we'll make out." But there was one guy who wrote for the campus paper, they call it *The Bruin*. He was pretty salty because he couldn't get in there in time to get a seat. So he came to me and said, "I'm going to do an article on this and we'll take pictures and everything." I said, "Don't, you'll get a lot of people into trouble." So, he said, "No, this is something that should be written about in the campus paper." So, he wrote it, and they took pictures and everything. And this activated the fire department and it woke up the administration. So, then the fire department would stand at the doors and they would count the people coming in. When 528 were in, they locked the door. Then they would pipe me on down the hall to some other auditorium where the ones who were left over were sent. And if any of you have taught, you try eye control down the hall, that's a good trick. The funny part, this guy that wrote this article, he could no longer get there to get in the room. I told all the students about it, they thought that was beautiful, hang him up by his toes, or whatever, you know.

So, I really didn't mind the big classes. If you are talking to any group over 100 people, it doesn't matter. Over a hundred, there could be a thousand, it's the same thing. I don't know about you people who give lectures; I just can't talk to blank faces, I talk to this person, talk to that person, and everybody thinks you're talking to them. It didn't make any difference to me.

The only problem was the testing and that's always a hassle. So, I would give the exams; I would divide the classes up and take a quarter of them at a time, I would take them over to the auditorium that had 3,500 seats. There would be like two empty seats between each student, and an empty row between each one, and I had between four and six different exams going on, so there was nobody sitting near anybody who has the same exam. And then I got all these teaching assistants from the music department to come over, and they're walking up and down the aisles. And there was practically no cheating, you know.

Well, some of the students do better on objective things, so you have to ask some objective questions because some of them do much better on instant recall. And then, some of them do better on subjective, so you've got to give them a break too, where they have a little germ of an idea and they write you a paragraph, that's called B.S. So, I have to give them both a break. I should tell you that I corrected all the exams myself. Because there's nobody in the music department that would know. Even if I give them a check sheet, they go right straight down the check sheet and not give the student any kind of a break at all. So, I corrected them all myself, that was much easier than having to correct their corrections. I even tried a scantron machine, I couldn't use that either.

But I would ask them such things as I would ask them to write the blues. And I'm not talking about the chord symbols, I'm talking about the notes, in any key that I would say. OK, write me the 12 bar blues in the key of D, and they'd have to do it. The whole football team could write the blues. Sometimes I thought they could write the blues better than they could play football. But I could ask them to do technical things like that.

As far as handling the class is concerned, you have to have ground rules. So, in the first place, there would be no talking when I'm talking, because I tell them right off that I'm a stammerer and I can't talk when they talk. So the students would keep everybody quiet. If any one would start to mumble, they'd get on them in a hurry.

I would play a lot of music for them, play a lot of records, and I would tell them absolutely no talking when music is being played.

And the way to get away with that is to say, "'Cause this may be on the exam." Those are the magic words, you could do anything if you said that. I would have a record playing when they walked into class. It would either be a record of some older artist on a newer record, or a record of a new artist that I thought they should know about. So they would be listening as they came in. Then I'll stop the record, talk about it a while, then play some more of it. And those would show up on exams, so they had to be paying attention. And they would get credit for as much as they could tell me about it. If they could tell me the artist, what the artist played, a couple of tunes, the feel, the mood, how they liked it, why or why not, and so forth, and they'd get more credit, the more they could tell me about it.

When I told them I was going to leave, then they had a problem replacing me. They did the usual advertising, and had a whole gang of applications, but narrowed it down to five guys. So, then I said, "Now look, these classes have to flow, a continuity. I can't have somebody come in and just talk. You've got to hear these people. Some people are very glib and can talk to you across the lunch table, but you get them in front of a whole room full of people, and some of them come apart, all of a sudden, some of these glib guys freeze. You've got to hear these people talk in front of a whole room full of people." So, they said, "OK." So, I said, "Furthermore, some of these guys have got some real hot item that they are very hip on. So, you've got to be careful of that. And I do want continuity." So, I was to tell each guy what he was to talk about. Then on the midterm exam, I put each guy's name on the midterm with a little phrase to remind the students of each guy. And the students voted on the replacement. That's a rare thing, especially at a big college like that, students don't have anything to say at all about who gets hired, but they got to vote on this, which was a wild thing.

Well, Paul *(the introducer)* asked me to tell you a couple of things that happened to me in the class, he thought you might be interested in. At one time, there was a lot of protesting in the turbulent 60s, about the Vietnam War. One day, some guys came in with some bull horns and really coming on. I thought the students were going to throw them out, the students were going to get violent about the interruption. So, I told the guys with the bull horns, "Easy, if you've got something to say to these people, they're not cattle.

Come on up here to the microphone and say what you have to say." Well, they came up politely and gave their pitch about the protest and all. So, Bill Walton, the basketball player, asked if he could say something. So, Bill gave his pitch. And I told the students, "What you really want is a choice. Now if you think you can stop the War by one minute, then you've got to go out. You've got to go out there and protest if you think you can stop it by one minute. But in the meantime, I'm hired to teach here, and I'm going to go ahead with the class, and I'll do nothing that will hang you up come test time." Well, Bill was the only guy who left.

One day, I had a flasher come in the class. I'm standing up there in front of the auditorium, and you know, you can see something happening out of the corner of your eye, so you take a look. And here comes this lady, a fedora hat, dark glasses, and a trench coat. She walks out on the stage in front of the class, opens the coat, then closes it up, and walks off. The class said I turned purple. So, I told them that if anybody knows who that is, don't tell me, don't tell me anything. But there's one thing I can tell you, and that is that she's definitely a brunette, that's all I could tell them.

One day I was standing there explaining a Duke Ellington album, and I looked down there in the front row, and there's Herbie Hancock. I had never met him, so I walked off the stage and shook hands and asked him to come up and play something. So, he said, "Sure." He then came up and played two hours.

We didn't have a budget for people to come in and play, but people would call me on the phone and ask if they could come down. Stan Kenton would call and say, "I haven't been down to your classes for quite a while, when could I come down?" I'd say, "Any time, Stan." So he would come down, even though it was early in the morning for a guy to get up out of the sack. So, he'd come down and we'd both have microphones on and we'd have an open conversation and answer questions.

Johnny Guarnieri came out and sat at the piano and asked for requests. He was really too much, great player. He would ask for requests and what style they wanted it in. He'd play any request in anybody's style, but he played everything in five/four, five beats to the bar.

I've been serenaded by surprise on birthdays by 30 trombone players and once by the whole UCLA band. I've got to cut that out. Jon Hendricks called me once on the phone and brought his whole "Evolution of the Blues" show over. Super Sax came out and did a show plus a seminar about Charlie Parker.

One student asked me, "Professor Tanner, did they have groupies in your era?" I said, "Yes, your mom."

(At this point I'll skip a reiteration about the students giving me a day.)

(Also a reiteration about how to catalogue records.)

(Then came the questions.)

Question Doctor Tanner, is there any one area of collecting that you like the best, did you have any preferences?

PT I like anything at all as long as it's played well. If it's played poorly, I couldn't care less about it, no matter who played it.

Question I came in late, were you in the films the Glenn Miller Band made?

PT Yes, I was in them, I was three years old. I joined Glenn in the band that he kept, he had one band that he broke up, then he kept the next one, and I stayed with him until he broke it up. Oh yes, I was also in the Jimmy Stewart film.

Question Did the band, on Glenn's pictures, have to spend a lot of time to do a picture? Was it a matter of a few days or weeks?

PT It took six weeks to do each film as best I remember, that's besides any editing that was done after we left town. First, you do all the recording, except we recorded some things live on the set. Then you do the picture. They started at the beginning of the story and went straight on through so that they would have a flow. I understand that they don't do that all the time. It took us six weeks, but while we were working on that, we were also working on the Chesterfield programs. We asked not to be paid until after the picture was over. Then most of the guys headed straight for Detroit to buy a new car. All but me, I went to East Lansing to buy an Oldsmobile.

A talk about my home movies previously discussed in the interviews.

Question How long did you stay in the band?

PT Until September '42 when the band broke up.

(A reiteration about rehearsals.)

(A repeat of the problems of early records.)

(A repeat about 140 appearances in two weeks, substitutes at the Paramount.)

Question Paul, did Glenn ever mention that there was a guy from my hometown — ?

PT No, he never said anything about that.

Question There was Sterling Bose and Tweed Peterson. I think they helped to wreck the first Glenn Miller Band. Did he ever tell you any stories about them?

PT He didn't have to, we had our own.

(More questions, all pretty much covered in Part 2.)

PT It's really been an awful lot of fun.

A Tape from the Oklahoma School For the Blind

37

Oklahoma, 1960

"This is ...? back in ...? Oklahoma. We have just finished making a tape recording for Paul Tanner. This is an eight piece orchestra, all totally blind students of the Oklahoma School for the Blind. Four of the group this year are new students and never played in an orchestra before, and the four others have had one year or more experience."[1]

1 "I'm Getting Sentimental Over You"

(Tape of "I'm Getting Sentimental Over You" featuring, of course, the trombone.)

(The trombone did really well–plenty of applause.)

"Paul, this is the third tape we've made for you, and none too good because of the balance of the tape recording, but this was made in the chapel this morning, part of a regular assembly program. We hope you enjoy the tape."

("White Christmas"– again featuring the trombone–nice vibrato, feasible intonation.)[2]

2 "White Christmas"

"There are ninety-five students at the Oklahoma School for the Blind, and there are thirty-eight students playing musical instruments."

("Stardust"– this time the trombonist even gave his rendition of the famous Jack Jenny solo from the Artie Shaw record.)[3]

3 "Stardust"

"On listening to this, I can see that there is a lot to be desired on balance on the tape, but we just set up and recorded."[4]

4 "In My Solitude"

"Paul, the tape recording you sent was *very* enjoyable and we played it for many, many people. Wayne Arp has it as his property, and he's keeping it. He has used it over and over many times, we certainly appreciate it. Our boy, Wayne Arp, is a senior this year, the trombone player, and we don't know what his plans will be, but we'll try to make another tape before the end of the year.[5]

5 "Winter Wonderland"

When they first contacted me, this fellow, Wayne Arp, was a real introvert. He mainly crouched in a corner and was entirely without communication. Someone demonstrated a trombone to him, and he joined the human race as if it were a miracle. That is when I was contacted and asked for suggestions. I sent trombone exercises and a tape or so. What they are showing me in the tape is that this young recluse even became the leader and main soloist of the band. It was a long time ago, I never heard from them again after this tape. I often wonder about Wayne Arp; I can only wish him a good full life. I hope the trombone helped.

What Actually Happened To Glenn Miller 38

I have written about this question before; however, the latest and most conclusive response to this question has come fairly recently. The following documents will confirm my expressed beliefs. It concerns a generous gentleman named William Suitts, a dedicated Miller fan who resides near the area that raised Glenn. Instead of describing the correspondence, I think it is much more interesting if I simply show you the progression as I received it. This will put to rest the outrageous rumors that have spread about this so-called "mystery."

During a recent cruise, it was truly great fun to sit and chat with the many fans of the Glenn Miller Band. Gil Oftedal and his Fan-to-Sea Cruise Club gave me the opportunity to enjoy the really fine band under Larry O'Brien.

The questions varied greatly but the one that was the most persistent concerned Glenn Miller's disappearance. "What really happened to Glenn?" I decided that a short essay would be of help to many fans. There are so many rather bizarre directions that these thoughts have taken that I am reminded that so many of us seem to have an interest comparable to the tabloid newspapers in the grocery checkout lines. There is something about reading that some celebrity is involved in a situation we would consider far out of the ordinary for that person.

Concerning Glenn's disappearance, I have, of course, heard vivid stories of his being involved with a lady in Paris, being a basket case somewhere, hiding in Brazil, being a party to a narcotics ring, being stabbed by a jealous woman or a jealous husband, being murdered because he knew too much about someone else's clandestine dealings, about a nurse (sworn to secrecy) caring for him in some tent someplace, about a pilot who flew him everywhere so, of course, was privy to unusual information, that the plane never left England, and on and on. Most of these stories are told by sincere people who honestly believe in their versions.

Don Haynes was Glenn's personal manager before the war and executed that same job for Glenn in the service. Don's wife and my wife owned a bookstore together in the 1950s and 1960s. Don and I helped as much as we could, so we became even closer friends than before. My knowledge of Glenn's disappearance comes mostly from Don who tracked down every rumor to its very end in behalf of our mutual friend, Helen Miller.

I would like to relate quite simply that the most accepted and acceptable story on this subject has been brought to light on the following pages. The service band was, of course, in England and ready to fly to Paris to begin performing for the troops there. The problem was the weather. Glenn's impatience grew, he was not known as a patient man. Haynes told me that, in spite of the adverse flying conditions (and Glenn was not an enthusiastic flyer, especially in small planes), that Glenn decided to try to get a ride to Paris where he would set up the band's billeting and establish places to perform. Haynes was to wait until the weather cleared and then follow with the band. At Twinwood Farm on December 15, 1944, Don saw Glenn onto a plane with two others, Lt.Col. Norman F. Baessell and Flight Officer John R. S. Morgan. No other person was elected to be on this ill-fated plane. And any mention of this possibility is pure fallacy and from the imagination of the writer or speaker. The above actual facts have been proven although many people offer their "*versions* of proof" of what happened after that moment.

As I said, on to the most accepted and acceptable. The little plane carrying Glenn should never have taken off, the weather was bad, and the plane was without some feasible equipment. They flew into an area of the channel they should not have been in. In order to accomplish the flight, it had to be done in a hurried manner and a flight plan was not even registered. A group of bombers was returning from an aborted mission and it was necessary to dump their bombs in the channel before returning to a landing in England. The Miller plane was wrongly and unfortunately in the area where the bombs were to be dumped. There is no evidence that the bombs actually hit Glenn's plane, but the concussion from the water could have brought this small low-flying plane into the channel immediately. Haynes and the band showed up at Orly Airport in Paris and there was not a word of Glenn whatsoever.

For those who think Glenn was involved with some lady, they just have the wrong person, the wrong personality. Glenn was happily married to a lovely lady. In England, he showed trumpeter Zeke Zarchy and others the model of the house to be built in California where he was so looking forward to living. He had a newly adopted son whom he was eagerly looking forward to raising. He had a newly adopted daughter whom he hadn't even seen, but who totally thrilled him nevertheless. This was not a fellow to take off for Brazil or any place else with a new woman, absolutely not! Could he have been involved in narcotics or any other such money direction? Glenn was a rich man, he did not need the money. He was also protective of his image. What he wanted was what he had, to have a financially successful organization playing fine music. Would he have done anything at all to jeopardize Helen's well-being for the rest of her life? Absolutely not! What can possibly be the reasons for these outlandish insinuations, what is the object of all this? To sell book and articles?

What some people don't seem to realize is that by continuing their stories about Glenn's disappearance, they do a considerable disservice to a man who was one of America's heroes. He was not obligated to enter the service, his eyes and his age would have deterred a lesser man. Miller was absolutely a dedicated patriot. He gave up a country club style of living to take a piece of home to the service personnel taken from their homes and jobs to defend the country. These bizarre stories are detrimental to the memory of a fine man who gave us all so much pleasure. The good people who tell me these stories do believe them, they are not just imaging some tabloid tales They all feel that they have sources that are beyond reproach, and even though I talk with them quite conscientiously, a person convinced against his will is not convinced. However, I do hope that the following material brings any known facts and the logical unknown facts into a clearer light for them.

P.S. Incidentally, the English Channel must be *loaded* with airplanes.

Key to Glenn Miller mystery to be auctioned

By MARA D. BELLABY
Associated Press Writer

LONDON — A military logbook that sheds light on the mysterious disappearance of American bandleader Glenn Miller during World War II will be up for auction next week, offering a chance to own a clue to one of aviation's most captivating puzzles.

Miller, who created the 1940s big band sound, was en route to France to organize concerts for Allied troops when his plane disappeared over the English Channel on a foggy December day in 1944.

No trace has ever been found of the single-engine aircraft or its passengers.

Bad weather was the chief suspect until the flight log was produced, which suggests a more haunting — and now largely accepted — theory: Miller's plane may have been blasted out of the sky by bombs jettisoned by a Royal Air Force squadron returning from an aborted raid on Germany.

"There are many theories ... and we'll never know for sure what happened. But this is certainly an intriguing possibility," said Stephen Maycock, an aeronautical specialist with Sotheby's, which is auctioning the logbook Tuesday.

The book, which belonged to the late Royal Air Force navigator Fred Shaw, will be sold along with a letter from Britain's Ministry of Defense bolstering the theory and a bundle of newspaper clippings and other materials.

The items are expected to fetch $960 to $1,300.

"Glenn Miller is an extremely important character and this is a fascinating story that has captured people's imaginations," said Rachel Aked, a Sotheby's spokeswoman.

The trombonist's fans have spent decades trying to determine what happened to him on Dec. 15, 1944.

It wasn't until the mid-1980s that Shaw dug out his logbook after going to see the film "The Glenn Miller Story," which chronicles the life of the man who made enduring hits of such songs as "In the Mood" and "Moonlight Serenade"

In a single entry — "Ops' Siegen Canceled. Jettison Southern Area" — the logbook confirmed what Shaw suspected: Miller's plane disappeared on the same day Shaw's squadron aborted a bombing raid on Siegen, Germany, and let loose their 4,000-pound bombs over the English Channel.

The bombs, which had to be discarded before the bombers could safely land, exploded just above the water.

Shaw remembered seeing a small plane spiraling out of control after the bombs were dropped.

Fan buys clue to Glenn Miller disappearance

Purchases military logbook for $35,000

Associated Press

LONDON — An American fan of bandleader Glenn Miller paid $35,000 Tuesday for a military logbook that holds a clue to Miller's mysterious disappearance aboard an airplane during World War II.

"I've never done anything like this in my life," said William Suitts, a 76-year-old businessman from Boulder, Colo., who bid for the book by telephone to Sotheby's auction house.

"From the time I was about 18 years old, I've always been a great, great fan of his," Suitts said, adding that he served in the Army Air Corps during the World War II.

Glenn Miller led one of the most popular "swing" bands of the 1930s and '40s, which had huge hits with songs like "In The Mood," "Kalamazoo," and "Pennsylvania 6-5000." He was at the height of his fame when an airplane carrying him disappeared over the English Channel on a foggy December day in 1944.

No trace was ever found of the single-engine aircraft or its passengers.

One theory was that the plane went down due to bad weather, but a flight log belonging to the late Royal Air Force navigator Fred Shaw suggested Miller's plane may have been blown out of the sky by bombs jettisoned by a Royal Air Force squadron returning from an aborted raid on Germany.

Shaw found that the date the bombs were jettisoned was Dec. 14, the same day Miller's plane disappeared. He remembered seeing a small plane spiraling out of control as the bombs burst around it. In 1985, the Ministry of Defense wrote a letter to Shaw saying, "in retrospect we now lean towards this being the most likely solution to the mystery."

Suitts was drawn to the logbook by a series of coincidences.

In addition to being a lifelong Glenn Miller fan, he discovered when he moved to Boulder 40 years ago that it was where Miller had gone to college — at the University of Colorado. And Fort Morgan, Colo., where Suitts bought a piece of property, was where Miller went to high school.

When Suitts read that the logbook was going to be auctioned by Sotheby's, he decided he "just really would love to have it."

When he got to his office Tuesday and turned on the radio, he heard an announcement that June Allyson was going to be appearing at a Denver benefit — and she had co-starred in the movie "The Glenn Miller Story."

Then, thinking about making a bid, he went home.

"As I pulled into the driveway, the radio was playing Miller's 'Moonlight Serenade'" Suitts said in a telephone interview.

"It was fate," he concluded. "It was meant to be."

The winning bid was 20 times more than Sotheby's had expected.

Miller

William Suitts of Boulder phoned in the winning bid to Sotheby's auction in Birmingham, England, for a logbook that may hold clues to the disappearance of bandleader Glenn Miller in World War II.

Essdras M Suarez News Staff Photographer

In the mood for Glenn Miller treasure

Boulder fan, 75, top bidder on log that gives clues to bandleader's fatal flight

By Tillie Fong

News Staff Writer

BOULDER — William Suitts, a diehard Glenn Miller fan, was the top bidder for a military log said to hold a crucial clue to the bandleader's mysterious disappearance over the English Channel in World War II.

"I've never done anything this wild in my life," said Suitts, 75, the president and owner of Colorado Mortgage Co., who bought the book Tuesday by telephone bid to Sotheby's auction house in Birmingham, England.

"I didn't buy it for bragging rights. It was a purchase of love."

Suitts paid 19,000 pounds — just over $30,000 — for the log kept by Fred Shaw, a Royal Air Force navigator, and for a documentation letter from the British Air Ministry.

"It's just something that gives me a kind of closure that I have a piece of Glenn Miller that I can share with so many people, who loved Glenn Miller and fell in love dancing to his music," Suitts said Tuesday from his home in Boulder.

Anthony Harvey/Associated Press

The Royal Canadian Air Force logbook of navigator Fred Shaw mentions jettisoned bombs that may have hit Miller's plane.

Miller's band was of the most popular "swing" bands of the 1930s and '40s and had huge hits with songs including *In The Mood*, *Kalamazoo* and *Pennsylvania 6-5000*.

He was at the height of his fame wh[en] an airplane carrying him disappeared [on] a foggy December day in 1944. No tra[ce] was ever found of the single-engine ai[r]craft or its passengers.

One theory was that the plane we[nt] down in bad weather. But the flight l[og] belonging to Shaw raised questions. [It] suggested that Miller's plane might ha[ve] been blown out of the sky by bombs [a] Royal Air Force squadron jettisoned ov[er] the Channel while returning from [an] aborted raid on Germany.

The date the bombs were jettison[ed] was Dec. 14, the same day Miller's pla[ne] disappeared. Further, Shaw remember[ed] seeing a small plane spiraling out of co[n]trol as bombs burst around it.

In 1985, the Ministry of Defen[se] wrote a letter to Shaw saying, "in retr[o]spect we now lean towards this being t[he] most likely solution to the mystery."

But for Suitts, it's not so much t[he] mystery that enthralls him as the music[.]

"His music really filled a void in m[y] life," he said. "I did see (Frank) Sinat[ra]

See MILLER on 13

Wednesday, April 14, 1999

Glenn Miller fan wins the jackpot

MILLER from 4A

and Peggy Lee, but I was always closer to Glenn Miller than to the rest."

When he learned Saturday that the military log was up for auction, he leaped at the chance to bid.

"I felt it belonged in Colorado," he said. "Glenn Miller was raised in Fort Morgan, Colorado, and we have a place up there, too. He (attended) the University of Colorado, and they have a collection of his things. I just felt it was natural."

He called Sotheby's to find out how to bid on the item, and the action went from there.

"The radio was playing *Moonlight Serenade*, Glenn Miller's theme song," he said. "I felt that there was something going on, that I must have it. I had a great feeling when the bidding started."

The bidding began at 1,000 pounds, about $1,600. Suitts said he had planned to go only as high as $20,000, but suspected it might cost more. He was right.

The bidding was fast and rose in 200-pound increments. Within minutes, it had reached 10,000 pounds.

When the bids reached 19,000 pounds, Suitts was declared the winner. He didn't know exactly how much that was in U.S. dollars, but he was willing to pay the cost for the historic treasure.

Suitts said he doesn't know what he'll do with the log and the letter once he gets them.

However, he plans to take the items to Fort Morgan for the town's Glenn Miller celebrations on June 24-27.

"I would share it with anyone who would like to see it and hear the story," he said. "I'll make copies and send them to anybody who wants them."

In the meantime, he's going to call Sotheby's in England to find out how much he owes and where to send the money.

"They never asked me for a credit card or anything," he said.

"I've had Sam's Club treat me worse than this."

Glenn Miller box arrives

Winning bidder of logbook, other memorabilia to give talk at fest beginning today for fans of late band leader

By Tillie Fong

News Staff Writer

It took three weeks for a 10-inch square box from England to arrive at William Suitts' office.

But this was not an ordinary package.

Inside were pieces of Glenn Miller history, including a logbook kept by Royal Air Force navigator Fred Shaw that outlines the circumstances surrounding the band leader's death, and a letter from the British Air Ministry.

"I was very excited about it," said Suitts, owner and president of Colorado Mortgage Co. who had paid $32,864.78 for the items in April.

Sunday Suitts plans to talk about his treasures at the Glenn Miller Festival in Fort Morgan.

He will be part of a presentation given by Alan Cass, the curator of the Glenn Miller exhibit at the University of Colorado.

The logbook, a copy of the letter and several other pieces of memorabilia will be on display at the festival, which starts today and runs through Sunday.

Suitts also will have about 100 copies of the logbook to distribute to fans if they want it.

"That's the greatest thing about the whole thing — the sharing of it," said Suitts.

On April 13, Suitts, a die-hard Glenn Miller fan, made the top bid for the items to Sothesby's auction house in Birmingham, England.

The items are significant to Glenn Miller lore because the logbook holds a crucial clue to the bandleader's mysterious

See **MILLER** on **18A**

disappearance over the English Channel during World War II.

In the logbook, he suggested that Miller's plane might have been blown out of the sky by bombs a Royal Air Force squadron jettisoned over the Channel while returning from an aborted raid on Germany.

In 1985, the Ministry of Defense wrote a letter to Shaw, saying "in retrospect we now lean towards this being the most likely solution to the mystery."

Suitts said that when the box came, there was no listing of its contents.

The logbook was on top, but it took a little digging to find the ministry letter.

After emptying the box, he found that the second page of the letter was missing.

Despite the disappointing loss, however, Suitts said he was pleasantly surprised by what else he got.

For one thing, he inherited more than a dozen letters written by Shaw, including the ones in which he describes the events of the fateful day of the plane's disappearance, as well as his attempts to alert the media.

Suitts also has seven military medals Shaw received. They were stored in a tin cigarette box.

Photos of Shaw and his crew, as well as 20 newspaper articles from England and South Africa about Miller's disappearance also came in the package.

Since the news that Suitts had the logbook and the letter, he said he's received calls and letters from Glenn Miller fans around the world.

"It's been a real great ride," Suitts said.

"The fans are so sincere and so appreciative of this. So many people were so happy that it (the logbook) was in America and felt that's where it belonged — that it was part of history."

Steven R. Nickerson/News Staff Photographer

Colorado Mortgage Co. owner William Suitts, who was a radar navigator in Italy in World War II, sits among mementos relating to band legend Glenn Miller.

WILLIAM J. SUITTS
460 Paragon Drive
Boulder, CO 80303
Home - 303-494-7993 * Office - 303-499-5400

June, 1999

Dear Glenn Miller Fans:

I appreciate the interest that you have expressed in receiving a copy of the actual log page from the Fred Shaw's log book. He was the British Air Force Navigator on the British bomber that actually saw the single engine plane fall into the English Channel on December 15, 1944. The plane he saw was named the "Norseman" and it was built in Canada. Fred Shaw received his training as a Navigator in Canada and had flown in a Norseman so he recognized it at once. Major Glenn Miller was a passenger in a Norseman flying to Paris for a Christmas eve performance on that fateful day.

The bomber that Fred Shaw was on was returning from an aborted mission to Germany along with over a hundred other bombers. Not being allowed to land with a fused 4000 bomb on board, the planes were instructed to dump this large bomb together with over a 100,000 four pound incendiary bombs in a special area of the English Channel.

It has now been determined that if the plane Glenn Miller was on flew a direct course to Paris, it would have been over the same area of the Channel at the same time as Fred Shaw's bomber and others were dropping their bombs that were exploding with tremendous force.

I am also enclosing a copy of the letter from the British Government Ministry of Defence who, after much research, came to the conclusion that, "in retrospect we now lean towards this being the most likely solution to the 'mystery.'"

I have received correspondence and phone calls from Auckland, New Zealand, London, Paris, South Africa, as well as many of the States in these United States.

If I can be of further assistance, or if you wish to speak with me, I would be glad to hear from you.

Personal regards,

William J. Suitts

William J. Suitts

MINISTRY OF DEFENCE AHB5(RAF)

Lacon House Theobalds Road WC1X 8RY

Telephone (Direct Dialling) 01-430
(Switchboard) 01-430-5555

Mr F H Shaw
PO Box 6178
Johannesburg 2000
South Africa

Our reference
D/AHB(RAF)8/31

~~April~~ 1985
2 May 1985

Dear Mr Shaw

Thank you for your letter of 27 March 1985 in which you comment on various aspects of the loss of the late Major Glenn Miller on 15 December 1944. Your letter is most welcome in view of the conjecture surrounding this unhappy event.

For your own information, up until your story appeared in the South African press in 1984, the RAF had always regarded Miller's death as a strictly USAAF matter, as the result of some sort of flying accident, probably as a result of poor weather conditions. We have received letters at various times asking about it, some of which put forward theories, some feasible, some not so feasible. Up till 1984, the only RAF connection was that Miller's plane had taken off from the RAF airfield at Twinwood Farm, Bedfordshire, in weather conditions which could be described as "marginal" - or at least marginal for that type of aircraft (Norseman).

Your story, to a greater extent, changed this and we carried out an investigation earlier this year into the aborted Bomber Command operation of 15 December 1944. Because the operation was aborted, there is no "Raid Report" on BC records, as would have been customary with a completed operation. We did find reference to the intended course of the 3 Group force (see map enclosed) but that was all.

We could find no trace of the actual course flown, ie, after the operation was abandoned, and in many of the records of the 3 Group Squadrons, the only mention is that on 15 December the operations were aborted. (Some Squadrons do not even give this coverage).

Your letter, then, is most welcome, and in retrospect we now lean towards this being the most likely solution to the "mystery". It is certainly possible, and as we said in earlier letters, we have shown that Miller's aircraft was airborne at the same time that the 3 Group force was airborne. However, I should perhaps point out that, in spite of wide publicity in the British press, there has been, to our knowledge, no letters or stories appearing which would corroborate yours.

To come to points raised in your letter, we have not been able to trace in the voluminous BC records the lat/long co-ordinates of bomb jettison areas. A document showing these, either as co-ordinates or in map form, is not on our index, and we are unable to devote further time searching for a document which may not exist. We know that these jettison areas existed (Channel, Thames Estuary, North Sea etc) but that is all.

On the "Diver boxes" we can comment that by September 1944 the continental coast opposite our south coast and Straits of Dover was cleared of the enemy, except for small enclaves such as Calais. The Germans started launching V-1s from Holland, and air-launching these weapons from He 111s over the North Sea. To meet this threat the gun defences were moved from South East England to the East Coast in about September-October 1944. Again we have not been able to trace the precise lat/long co-ordinates of these "Diver" or AA gun areas.

To our knowledge, Miller's pilot did not file a flight plan, or at least, none has come to light in USAAF records, so any comment on this aspect would only be conjecture.

Finally you may like to know that the RAF's wartime records and papers are now kept at The Public Record Office at Kew. These papers include the Operation Record Books (War Diaries) of Bomber Command and its Groups and Squadrons. There is in Great Britain a widespread interest in Bomber Command and its activities, judging by the number of books published in recent years.

I hope you will find the above information of interest.

Yours sincerely

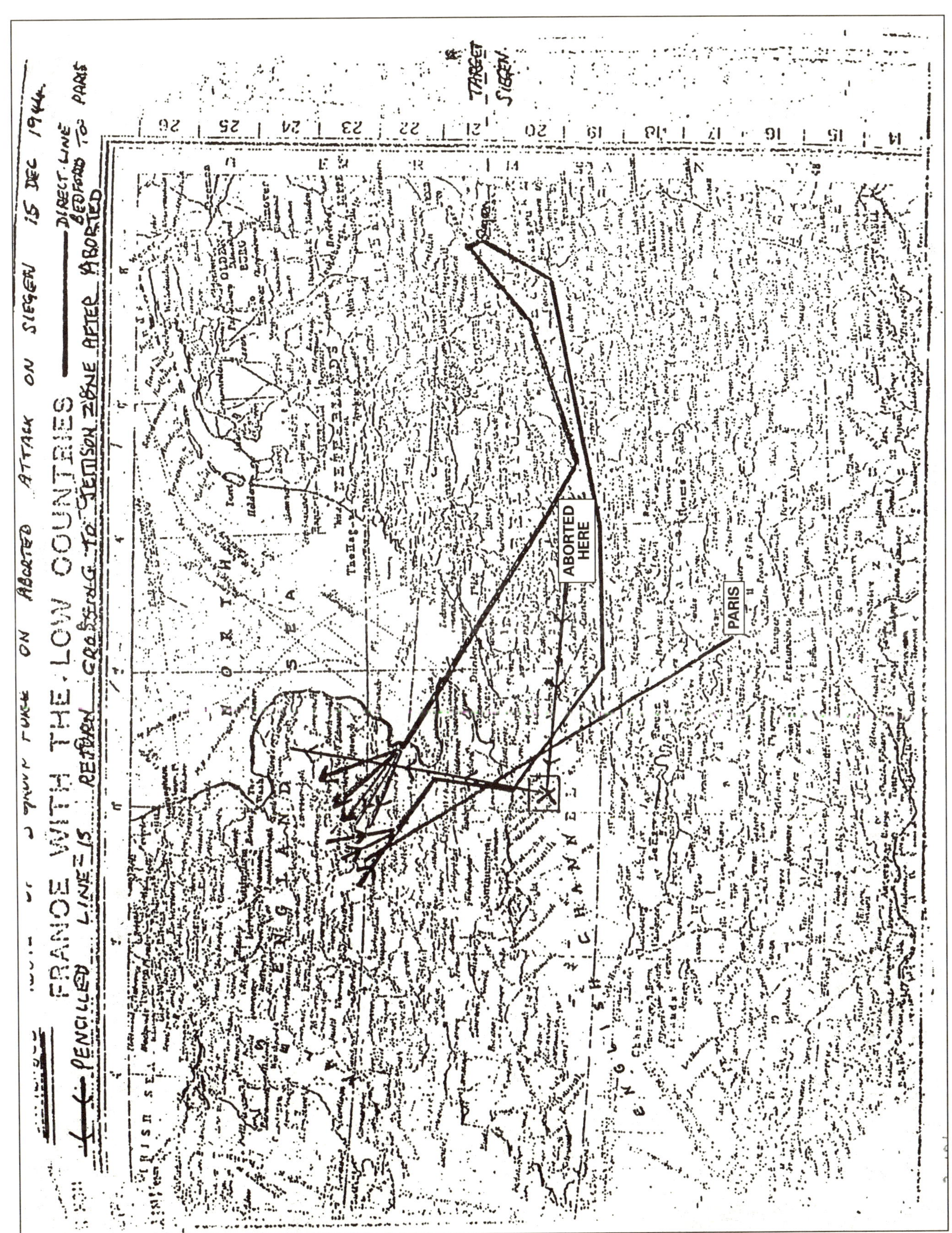

"Pencilled line is return crossing to jettison zone after aborted."

Date	Hour	Aircraft Type and No.	Pilot	Duty	Remarks (Including results of bombing, gunnery, exercises, etc.)	Flying Times Day	Flying Times Night
					Time Carried Forward:—	124·50	70·4
14·12·44	1500	N.F. 970 LANCASTER	F/O GREGORY	NAVIGATOR.	AIR TEST	1·15	3 34
15·12·44	1200	N.F. 973 LANCASTER	F/O GREGORY	NAVIGATOR	OPS. SIEGEN. CANCELLED. JETTISON SOUTHERN AREA	2·45	
17·12·44	1900	H.K. 652 LANCASTER	F/O GREGORY	NAVIGATOR	BULLSEYE, LONDON.		3·15
18·12·44	1500	H.K. 645 LANCASTER	F/O GREGORY	NAVIGATOR,	G.H., ELY, AV. ERROR 316 YDS.	1·40	
19·12·44	1130	N.G. 355 LANCASTER	F/O GREGORY	NAVIGATOR	OPS. TRIER, LANDED MANSTON ELEVATORS HOLED, LANDED F.I.D.O.	4·50	
23·12·44	1130	N.G. 355 LANCASTER	F/O GREGORY	NAVIGATOR	MANSTON – BASE	0·35	
24·12·44	1700	LANCASTER	F/O GREGORY	NAVIGATOR	OPS. BONNE-HANGELAR AIRFIELD (FIGHTER ATTACK OVER ▲)	–	5·25
28·12·44	1400	H.K. 652. LANCASTER	F/O GREGORY	NAVIGATOR	G.H. FRIDAY BRIDGE. G.H. U/S	1·05	
29·12·44	1200	H.K. 699 LANCASTER	F/O GREGORY	NAVIGATOR	OPS. KOBLENTZ FLAK HITS LANDED MANSTON (TANK HOLED)	4·55	
31·12·44	1430	H.K. 699 LANCASTER	F/O GREGORY	NAVIGATOR	MANSTON – BASE	0·35	
					Total Time...	142·30	79·2

15-12-44 is the highlighted entry in the navigator's log.